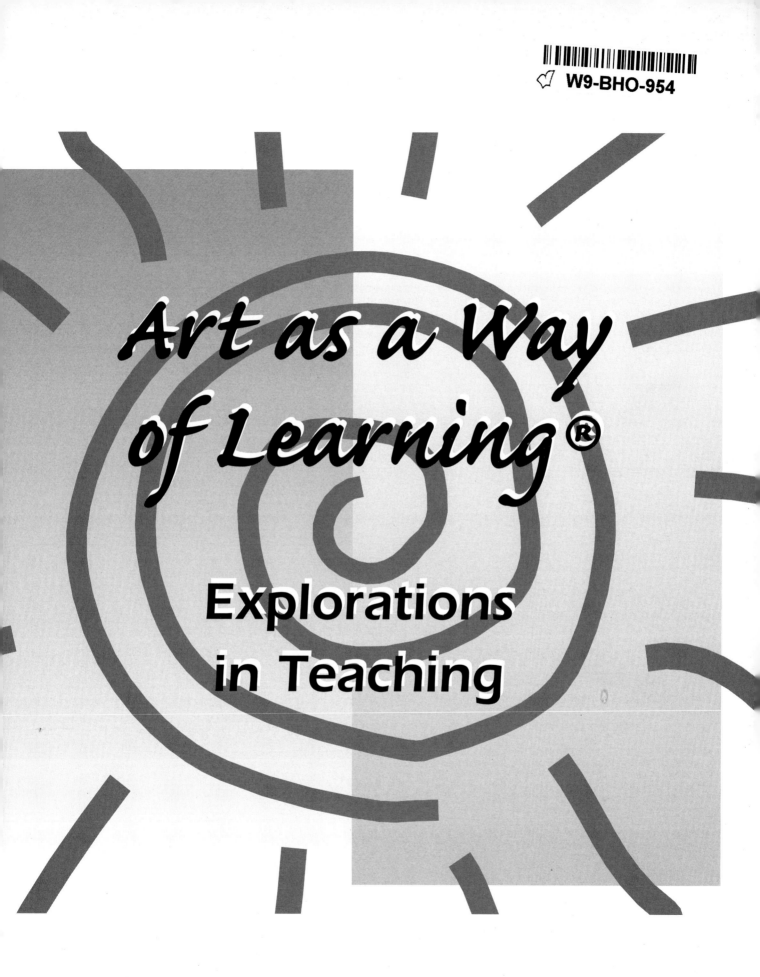

# Art as a Way of Learning®

## Explorations in Teaching

**ART AS A WAY OF LEARNING®**
Explorations in Teaching

by
Patricia Pinciotti, Ed.D.
with Diann Berry, Cheri Sterman, and Rebecca L. Gorton



Identified children's images courtesy of the Crayola® Dream-Makers® Program, Binney & Smith.

Art as a Way of Learning® was developed through a partnership between:

Binney & Smith Inc.
2035 Edgewood Ave.
Easton, PA 18042

and

Northampton Community College
3835 Green Pond Rd.
Bethlehem, PA 18017



Editor: Janet Brown McCracken, Subjects & Predicates Inc.

ISBN: 0-9672338-0-1
Library of Congress: TO COME

Printed in the United States of America

# Contents

Preface ..... vii
Acknowledgments ..... ix

**Art as a Way of Learning®** ..... 1
The Beginning... ..... 1
The Potential... ..... 3
For Your Professional Development ..... 3
For Children's Learning ..... 4

**Explorations in Teaching** ..... 6
Inquiring Minds at Work ..... 6
Why Are the Arts Languages? ..... 9
Ways Children Use the Arts ..... 11
When Art Leads Learning ..... 17
Children Are Intelligent, Creative Thinkers ..... 17
Children Are Actively Engaged ..... 18
Adults Guide Children's Learning ..... 21
The Arts at Center Stage ..... 26
A Challenging Journey... ..... 28

**Component One: Visual Literacy** ..... 33
**Module 1: Creative and Critical Thinking** ..... 34
The Cycle of Creative and Critical Thinking ..... 35
Explorations: Stages of the Thinking Cycle ..... 37
**Module 2: Elements and Principles of Visual Language** ..... 46
Formal Qualities of Artwork ..... 46
Explorations: Art Elements and Principles of Visual Organization ..... 47
**Module 3: Visual Artistry of Children** ..... 67
Development of Artistry in Childhood ..... 68
Explorations: Characteristics of Children's Artistry ..... 70
**Module 4: Visual Arts Curriculum Design** ..... 78
Understanding Curriculum ..... 78
Explorations: Curriculum Design ..... 81

**Component Two: Creative Collaboration** ..... 91
**Module 1: Discovering Your Art Partner** ..... 92
Finding a Collaborator ..... 92
Explorations: Stages of a Collaborative Relationship ..... 94
**Module 2: Ways Administrators Support Collaboration** ..... 100
**by Greg Naudascher**
Administrators Articulate the Vision ..... 100
Explorations: Administrators as Arts Advocates ..... 101
**Module 3: Collaboration in Action:**
**Planning for Arts-Integrated Learning** ..... 108
Sharing Planning and Teaching ..... 108
Explorations: Planning Frames to Integrate Art ..... 110
**Module 4: Developing Arts Advocates: Communicate and Network** 123
Building Momentum for the Arts ..... 123
Explorations: Generating New Support ..... 125

**Component Three: Aesthetic Environment** ............... 141
**Module 1: The Visual Learning Environment** ................ 142
Messages in Children's Surroundings ..................... 142
Explorations: Visual Thinking Connections ................. 143
**Module 2: Developing an Art Materials Center** ............... 152
Complementing and Extending Children's Learning ........... 152
Explorations: An Art Materials Center ..................... 154
**Module 3: Curriculum Connections: Imaginative Art Spaces** ..... 160
Finding Imaginative Spaces ............................ 160
Explorations: Transforming Learning Spaces ................ 161
**Module 4: Children's Art Explorations: Displays and Documentation** ........................... 170
Cherishing Children's Artistry ........................... 170
Explorations: Showcases for Learning .................... 173

**Component Four: Teaching Strategies** ................. 183
Art Is an Opportunity ................................ 184
Authentic Assessment ............................... 187
**Module 1: *Support:* Respond to Children's Ideas** ............. 189
The Dance of Learning ............................... 189
Explorations: Playful Nurturing .......................... 193
**Module 2: *Stimulate:* Increase Knowledge and Understanding** ... 202
Analyzing Art With Children ........................... 202
Explorations: Viewing and Responding to Art ............... 205
**Module 3: *Stretch:* Develop Imagination and Artistic Skills** ..... 214
Learning the Language Together ......................... 214
Explorations: Strategies for Artistic Learning ............... 217
**Module 4: *Spark!* Discover Personal Meaning** ............... 227
Scaffolding Artistic Thinking .......................... 228
Explorations: Wondering and Imagining .................. 231

**Appendices** ............................................ 235
I. Art as a Way of Learning® Five Guiding Principles .......... 236
II. Key Words ....................................... 239

**Index** ................................................ 243

# PREFACE

Welcome to *Art as a Way of Learning*®! *Art as a Way of Learning: Explorations in Teaching* is the guide to accompany the *Art as a Way of Learning* professional development inservice program for early childhood and elementary teachers and art specialists. This guide was developed as part of the *Art as a Way of Learning* partnership project between Binney & Smith Inc. and Northampton Community College. The mission of the project is to provide teachers with strategies to integrate visual art into the curriculum.

As you open and leaf through this book, you will find yourself embarking on an exciting professional journey. There are many paths that could have brought you to this point. How did you decide to learn more about integrating the arts into education?

- You may be a teacher or art specialist enrolled in the *Art as a Way of Learning* professional development program with the encouragement of your principal or program director.
- Perhaps you are an elementary principal or early childhood program administrator who saw the video that shows how *Art as a Way of Learning* is put into practice by real teachers and art specialists in real classrooms.
- Maybe you attended a workshop or seminar and heard educators exclaim how their creativity was reawakened as they applied these principles of teaching and learning.
- You might be an artist-in-residence seeking new ways to reach out to communities.
- Or it could be that you are using this book as a college text or are on a personal quest to learn more about how to integrate art into the curriculum.

However you came to *Art as a Way of Learning*, we are glad you are holding this unique publication in your hands. Unlike most books, we don't expect you to read this one from cover to cover. Instead, we imagine that you will want to sample each of the four components, much as happens in the *Art as a Way of Learning* workshops. Before long, we hope you will want to put the book down—so you can put the ideas you are constructing into practice.

Within these pages, you can discover new ways of teaching, build connections with your life experiences, develop valuable professional allies, respond to thought-provoking questions, accept some creative challenges, and reflect on your own learning and teaching. Prepare for a professional adventure!

# ACKNOWLEDGMENTS

From its very inception, *Art as a Way of Learning*® has been collaborative in the truest sense of the word. The classroom teachers and art specialists who comprised the Local Resource Team are recognized for their belief in the project and commitment to forging partnerships and exploring new ideas by implementing and assessing them. Cheri Sterman and Diann Berry, Binney & Smith Inc., were integral to the development of these teams. Members of the Local Resource Team who participated during the 3-year development period are:

Louise Cosgrove and Mary Richards, Salisbury School District

Dawn Dubbs and Sylvia Radvansky, Bethlehem School District

Jan Steigerwalt and Jane Oplinger, East Stroudsburg School District

Cindy Sames, Easton School District

Karen Klein and Kathy Roberti, Northampton Community College

Bonnie Pancoast, First Baptist Nursery School

Appreciation is also given to the following members who contributed: Beverly Snyder and Sandy Loss, Head Start of the Lehigh Valley; Mary Lambert and Shea Gary, Lehigh Valley Child Care; Marilyn Jacobs and Cathy Dornblaser, Bethlehem School District; Kathy Gruver and Katherine Alvaro, Allentown School District; Molly Gilley and Ray Hamilton, Palisades School District; Cindy Canfield, Betty Silfies, and Barbara Weinstein, Allentown School District.

Martha Posner and Leslie Fletcher, artists-in-residence to the Local Resource Team and Northampton Community College's Child Development Center (CDC) classroom, were our artistic guides who helped expand the team members' understanding of the visual arts and its role in developing children's higher-order thinking and creative expression. Gerald Rowan, art professor at Northampton Community College, offered ideas and insights which helped to get the project started. Roger Phillips, research consultant, provided the Local Resource Team members with a system for documenting their collaborative planning and classroom interactions.

Northampton Community College's Dean of Humanities and Social Sciences, Doreen Smith, facilitated the development phase of the project by providing direction and support to the staff. Dave Borofsky, former Dean of Community Education, gave the project life and moved it forward as a nationally recognized professional development program. His belief in the creative process and the authors provided a clear vision and kept our work on track. Paul Pierpoint, Dean of Community Education, has continued to support the many facets of *Art as a Way of Learning.*

This book—*Explorations in Teaching*—exists because of the expertise and creative energy of many individuals. I am especially indebted to my co-authors, who have been with the project from the very beginning and have nurtured, directed, inspired, and contributed more than they will ever know. I have learned a great deal from Becky Gorton, whose boundless energy and ability to find the essence has made my task, even at the dreariest moments, enjoyable. She has a sense of purpose, integrity, and wisdom that often takes us all aback. Her friendship, trust, and sense of humor I appreciate deeply.

Diann Berry, who has her hand on the pulse of arts education, has kept us true to this burgeoning field and the artist within us all. Her abundant knowledge and creative enthusiasm has spurred the entire project forward. The ability to see the whole as well as the parts is a gift Cheri Sterman shared generously along with her sagacious understanding of the child. Her questions always enlightened. In the spirit of collaboration I have learned much from each of you and am deeply grateful.

A special thank you to Greg Naudascher, former Principal of Resica Elementary School, who wrote the module on the administrator's role and has served as a model for us all. He demonstrates on a daily basis what true commitment and belief in the arts can accomplish. Thank you for the unique opportunity to work so closely with you and your staff. A special recognition also goes to Mary Richards and Louise Cosgrove, who contributed the levels of collaboration based on their own exciting journey.

The task of editing a collaborative manuscript is an immense challenge, and one which Janet Brown McCracken attacked head on with great aplomb. Her work was nothing short of brilliant, clarifying and connecting diverse strains of thought. She is a responsive, caring professional with a keen intellect to whom we owe a great deal.

Numerous others read and crafted various drafts, providing valuable insight and guidance. They include Leona Maxwell; Ron DeLong from Binney & Smith Inc.; Bruce and Freda Fishman; Mary Lisa Vertuca, Xavier University; Paula Kelberman, East Stroudsburg University; and Helane Rosenberg, Rutgers University. Margie Shotz, art educator from Central Bucks County, took on the task of gathering and organizing the wonderful photos found throughout the text. Much thanks. Binney & Smith Inc. summer interns, and classroom teachers Michele Balliet and Alison Saeger, assisted in compiling and checking resources.

Gratitude is also given to Binney & Smith Inc. and its belief in the power of the arts to transform teaching and learning in our schools. This vision served as a constant guide throughout the writing process. Rich Gurin's confidence and challenges made us all work hard and long with tremendous success. Kathleen Kankel and Gary Vorhees, Directors of Marketing, navigated us through uncharted waters. The photo contributions from Dream-Makers® are dazzling. Financial support from Binney & Smith Inc. has made the *Art as a Way of Learning*® professional development program possible.

A final thank you to all who have the resourcefulness and fortitude to create in collaboration, integrating the arts into the curriculum and enhancing children's lives—especially to all the *Art as a Way of Learning* trainers, teachers, art educators, and administrators who help tell our story.

*Patricia Pinciotti*

*September 1999*

*Art as a Way of Learning®*

# The Beginning . . .

*Art as a Way of Learning*® was launched in 1991 when Binney & Smith Inc. and Northampton Community College entered into a partnership to find ways to integrate the visual arts in early childhood, elementary, and teacher education curricula (Pinciotti & Gorton, 1998). Out of that partnership, a professional development program evolved. Designed by art educators, classroom teachers, and administrators, *Art as a Way of Learning* places the arts as central to teaching and learning.

National education reform movements (*The Goals 2000 Arts Education Partnership, 1995*) and research indicate that schools must reshape teaching and learning so that students can develop higher-order thinking skills and understanding. Attention to national standards, an awareness of the ways people learn, the cultural context of learning, and knowledge and skills for integrated teaching, authentic assessment, and use of technology are all essential ingredients for educational change (MENC, 1994).

Good teachers—of adults and children—are well aware that learning is most likely to occur when it is integrated and connected to a person's knowledge and background, not when it is doled out in isolation or in small disconnected segments. Authentic learning takes place as people interact with each other to answer questions that intrigue them, to construct and demonstrate what they know and are able to do. Learning creates understanding when individuals explore ideas deeply and represent their knowing in many forms. The arts provide a rich language for integrated, meaningful, engaging learning with both children and adults.

When teachers implement an arts-based curriculum, other educational reform concepts typically are addressed as well (*The Goals 2000 Arts Education Partnership, 1995*). Collaborative efforts by classroom teachers and art specialists create systemic change and a shared vision of an integrated curriculum. Collaboration extends into the community, businesses, and art agencies.

**Art fosters learning, creative and critical thinking, and self-expression—from early childhood through adulthood. Stronger preparation in the arts will enable our children to cooperate and compete with the other nations of the world.**

**– Richard Gurin,**
**CEO, Binney & Smith Inc.**

*Art is an expressive, cognitive process.*

*Art is a language through which all subjects can be learned.*

If our civilization is to continue to be both dynamic and nurturing, its success will ultimately depend on how well we develop the capacities of our children, not only to earn a living in a vastly complex world, but to live a life rich in meaning. This document affirms that a future worth having depends on being able to construct a vital relationship with the arts, and that doing so, as with any other subject, is a matter of discipline and study.

– *National Standards for Arts Education* (MENC, 1994, p. 5)

## What is creative and critical thinking?

The word *critical* has many meanings. One meaning, which *Art as a Way of Learning*® uses when referring to creative and critical thinking, refers to a decision-making process. In *Art as a Way of Learning*, the terms creative and critical thinking refer to the active process of generating, gathering, representing, analyzing, evaluating, and understanding new information in relation to prior knowledge. This thinking process involves imagination, creativity, genesis, analysis, reflection, synthesis, evaluation, and reasoning.

In other contexts, to be critical means to find fault with or to severely judge something. This is the role that art and music critics take on when they critique paintings or performances, for example. The concept of creative and critical thinking should not be confused with the judgmental role of an art or music critic, nor is it a process aimed at making adverse comments about or finding fault with the work or ideas of others.

Research by Gardner (1983a) and many others validates the importance of providing learners with multiple ways to construct knowledge, express ideas, and communicate. Differences in where and how individuals learn are supported and enhanced by a curriculum that is rich in opportunities to develop curiosity, success, originality, and satisfying relationships through artistic thinking and creating.

A **Local Resource Team** was assembled by the *Art as a Way of Learning* partners to develop and implement art integration techniques that would build on this professional knowledge base. Team members included classroom teachers and art specialists, art and education specialists from Binney & Smith Inc., early childhood and art faculty from Northampton Community College, educational researchers, and art consultants.

Through action research conducted in collaboration with art specialists, the Local Resource Team teachers came to recognize that children more completely understand concepts and retain knowledge when they use hands-on, engaging art explorations guided by an art specialist. As a result, the Local Resource Team reconceptualized art, defining it not as just an activity, but as an expressive, cognitive process.

The major premise of *Art as a Way of Learning*® is that with guided explorations, arts is a language through which all subjects can be learned. What this means, and the impact it can have on learning, will be explored throughout this book.

## The Potential . . .

*Art as a Way of Learning* holds great promise, not just as a stimulating experience for you as a teacher or administrator, but also as a way of thinking and teaching that improves children's learning. Consider the unlimited possibilities for furthering your professional growth and revitalizing children's everyday learning experiences.

### For Your Professional Development

Designed by teams of teachers, art specialists, and administrators, *Art as a Way of Learning* evolved into a dynamic, appealing professional development program for preservice and inservice educators. The program hinges on five guiding principles about children's learning:

- Art is a language
- Children use art
- Art leads learning
- Teachers guide learning
- Adults are learners and advocates

These principles, described at greater length in Appendix I, are drawn from educational research and best practice related to basic beliefs about art as a language, the artistry of children, the interactive learning process, and adult roles in facilitating the educational process.

The four professional development components of *Art as a Way of Learning*—Visual Literacy, Creative Collaboration, Aesthetic Environment, and Teaching Strategies—build upon these principles. All four components are detailed in separate chapters in this book.

Definitions of Key Words, meanings that were refined as the program progressed, are included in Appendix II for easy reference. We encourage you to check these words often to make sure you consider their full meanings as you think about the possibilities for teaching.

Educators, artists, and children's families who have become familiar with the guiding principles of *Art as a Way of Learning*® have come to embrace and incorporate its potential for enhancing child and adult knowledge and skills. Some ideas may be familiar and comfortable for you, while others may challenge your thinking or require a reassessment of some teaching practices. As your understandings deepen, and your learning experiences become more elaborate, you will build new collaborative relationships and refine your style of working with children. Whether you are a student, teacher, art specialist, or administrator, your creative energies will soar, and so will children's.

*Your creative energies will soar, and so will children's.*

## For Children's Learning

In addition to its role as a professional development program, *Art as a Way of Learning* offers an effective framework upon which to integrate the arts into early childhood and elementary education. Consistent with the *National Standards for Arts Education* (MENC, 1994) and educational reform ideas, the framework emphasizes these concepts:

- a shared vision to integrate art into the curriculum
- the collaborative nature of teaching
- the importance of strengthening classroom teachers' artistic literacy
- the development of visually rich learning environments
- specific teaching and assessment strategies that support multiple forms of communication and development of essential analytical skills

During hands-on workshops, participants use the arts to integrate their knowledge and reflect on current practice and the implications of educational research for teaching and administration. These experiences enable them to transform how curriculum is designed and implemented, as educators strive to make learning meaningful and engaging for all students.

When children produce and interpret visual art, they develop analytical thinking skills that support learning in academic domains. Their cognitive development blossoms as they sequence events, understand cause and effect, and make decisions. Their perceptual abilities—such as coordination, figure-ground orientation, fine-motor control—increase dramatically. They strengthen their abilities to communicate by developing their visual literacy; that is, they acquire another symbol system to represent their thoughts and feelings. Social skills are enhanced, too. They become more independent, express emotions in positive ways, delay gratification, resolve conflicts, and develop friendships as they work together. All this, and much more, occurs when children engage in *Art as a Way of Learning®*.

To increase the quantity and quality of children's learning, teachers, art specialists, and administrators, who are dedicated to this philosophy

- work in **collaborative teams**
- experience personal and professional growth that builds their own **art literacy**
- engage in **teaching strategies** that foster hands-on, arts-integrated experiences for children
- set up **aesthetic environments** and learning centers that support these activities

How do these principles translate into what happens in early childhood and elementary classrooms? Begin to explore some of the exciting possibilities by looking through the rest of this book.

## Bibliography


Gardner, H. (1982). *Art, mind, and brain.* New York: Basic Books.

Gardner, H. (1983a). *Frames of mind.* New York: Basic Books.

Gardner, H. (1983b). Artistic intelligences. *Art Education, 36,* 47-49.

Gardner, H. (1990). *Art education and human development.* Los Angeles: The Getty Center.

Gardner, H. (1991). *The unschooled mind: How children think and schools should teach.* New York: Basic Books.

Goals 2000 Arts Education Partnership, The. (1995). *The arts and education: Partners in achieving our national education goals.* Washington, DC: National Endowment for the Arts.

Lasky, L., & Mukerji-Bergeson, R. (1980). *Art: Basic for young children.* Washington, DC: National Association for the Education of Young Children.

Music Educators National Conference (MENC). (1994). *National standards for arts education.* Reston, VA: Author.

Pinciotti, P., & Gorton, R. (1998). Art as a Way of Learning®: A business and education partnership. In R.L. Irwin & A.M. Kindler (Eds.), *Beyond the school: Community and institutional partnerships in art education.* Reston, VA: National Art Education Association.

# Explorations in Teaching

*Art as a Way of Learning®* is an adventure in using the arts to construct new ways to think about teaching and learning. You start this journey by examining the value of the visual arts as they relate to the classroom curriculum. Along the way, you will develop a creative collaboration with an art partner with whom to share expertise and design engaging integrated curriculum.

**The arts are a vital resource for professional development; they renew creative energy and transform practices and programs.**

***– The Goals 2000 Arts Education Partnership*** **(1995, p. 9)**

Through collaboration with your partner—administrator, art specialist, classroom teacher, or artist-in-residence—the power of the arts will lead creative and critical thinking and understanding forward, both for yourself and for students. Your journey begins by visualizing the inquiring minds at work in Ms. Vista's classroom. Ms. Vista's class is a composite example of *Art as a Way of Learning* ideas generated by numerous classroom teachers and art specialists who have participated in this professional development program.

## Inquiring Minds at Work

Upon entering Ms. Vista's third grade room we see small groups of children constructing three-dimensional models of underground vehicles. Individuals refer to information about types and layers of rock in their visual journals and science text. The art teacher's chart on Paper Sculpture Techniques reminds them about his demonstration of various paper construction ideas. Conversations about vehicle speed, rock hardness, ways to connect rounded pieces, and what can be used to make a screw-like hood permeate the room.

Supplies are housed in an area marked by a sign reading Mechanical Minds At Work. Reproductions of machines from Leonardo daVinci's sketchbook grace the walls. Stories by Jules Verne, biographies on daVinci, Henry Ford, and Amelia Earhart, and *The Magic School Bus* collection, along with a wealth of books on vehicles, construction, and building, line a shelf. A transportation time line made from art postcards is being reviewed for great ideas, while a model of the earth's layers is creating a heated discussion at one table.

Ms. Vista believes that art is a way in which her third graders learn, construct, and communicate their understanding of the world. She collaborates regularly with the art teacher, Mr. Angelo, to design a curriculum rich with art explorations. These guided activities, which take place in either the art room or Ms. Vista's classroom, connect children's prior knowledge to a theme they are studying or an artistic question they are pursuing. This constructivist orientation views art as a language in which children create their own meaning through critical and creative thinking and individual creative expression.

What do you believe is happening in this classroom? Ms. Vista apparently has a deep respect for learners as individuals, their ideas, questions, and styles of working. She taps into children's interests and experiences while introducing new information and skills. Her students' elaborate underground vehicles reveal children's understandings and demonstrate their artistic competency. Multiple opportunities for children to use artistic language and visual thinking are evident. Ms. Vista and Mr. Angelo, the art teacher, who are collaborative partners, integrate learning experiences around concepts, themes, and aesthetic principles (see Figure E-3 and Component One, Module Two).

Ms. Vista's way of teaching—developed with the *Art as a Way of Learning*® framework—is based on knowledge about the potential of the arts as a language for thinking, communicating, and expressing knowledge. The arts are threads that unify learning across curricular domains—language arts, mathematics, science, and social studies. Children's emerging artistic literacy enables them to critically and creatively analyze situations, construct knowledge, and communicate ideas visually.

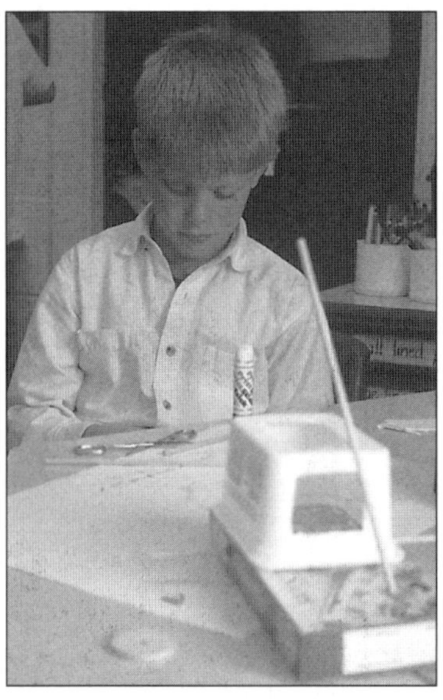

*Figure E-1.* A student constructing an underground vehicle. Photographs on this page courtesy of Whitecoate Primary School, Leeds, England.

*Figure E-2.* The arts are threads that unify learning across curricular domains—language arts, mathematics, science, and social studies.

The art specialist, Mr. Angelo, and I always begin our discussion of a new theme or topic in a rather playful way. Over a cup of tea during our planning time we bring to the table the curriculum content each of us is working on, what we need to cover, and what the children particularly like about this topic. After we have shared this, the fun begins and we write every idea down no matter how silly or far out. Mr. Angelo usually draws the ideas as I write them down.

For example, we were about to begin work on the earth, its layers, and the forces which shape its topography (volcanoes, earthquakes). Mr. Angelo felt the students could use further drawing work with an emphasis on textures, perspective, and shadows. We decided that a good generative theme that would capture the imagination of the students (and ours) would be "Underground" and this became our brainstorming starting place, letting our ideas just flow out in any order and with any connections.

We then shifted our focus to the actual content we knew the children responded to and the district curriculum guidelines for science and visual art. From here, a list of guided explorations developed which would integrate our work and make learning rich, creative, and meaningful. We presented the ideas to the children the next day and they made suggestions for the classroom learning center. We're on the road to the underground!

– Ms. Vista

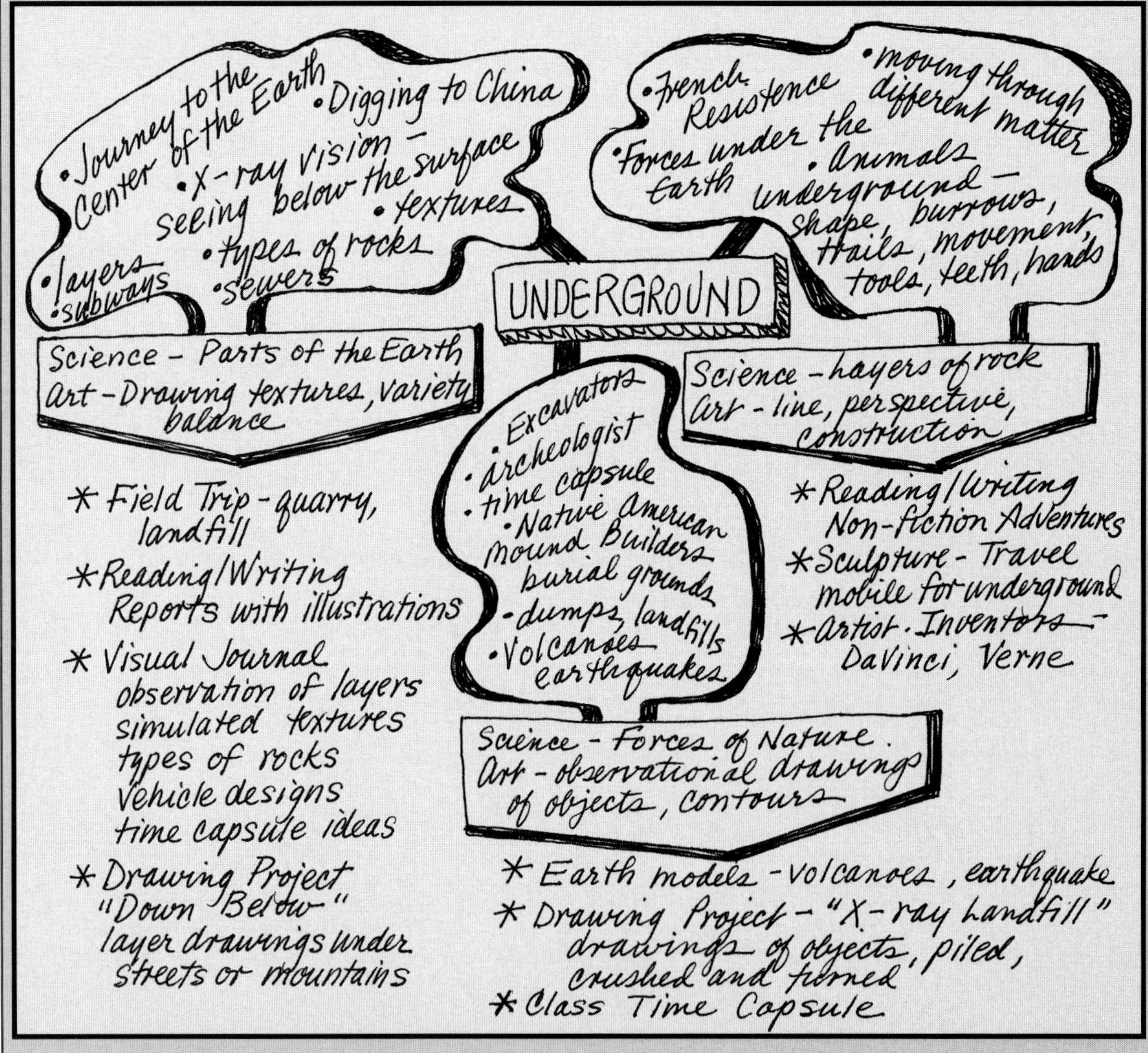


*Figure E-3.* Collaborative mind map on the topic of the earth, created by partners Ms. Vista and Mr. Angelo.

## Why Are the Arts Languages?

A language, or symbol system, is a tool through which humans can better understand each other. Language enables us to identify what we know and then to use this knowledge to communicate. Natural language systems include

- *verbal*—listening, speaking, reading, and writing
- *gestural or kinesthetic*—creating, performing, and responding in drama, movement, and dance
- *musical*—creating, performing, and responding to rhythm, melody, and tone
- *mathematical*—dealing with numbers, patterns, and operations
- *visual or graphic*—creating and responding in drawing, painting, and sculpting

Each language has unique structural aspects. The structural aspects of verbal language include knowledge of sentence elements (grammar) and how to combine them into sequences that conform to the language's rules (syntax). We combine these elements into written and spoken works of art such as books, plays, and poetry.

The structural aspects of visual language include the elements (line, shape, color, texture, and form) and principles (unity, variety, balance, proportion, repetition, emphasis, and movement) of visual organization and reasoning. These elements and principles are combined into paintings, sculpture, or other visual works of art.

The more we use a language, the greater our ability to access its power and apply its nuances. Anyone who is learning to play a musical instrument, for example, knows the value of daily practice. This ability to use various symbol systems to construct and communicate is part of our human sense (Donaldson, 1978).

No symbol system is inherently artistic or nonartistic (Gardner, 1983). The functional aspect of language allows us to use its elements to communicate, think, and resolve questions. We use the verbal system when we write a grocery list or read a great novel. Similarly, we use visual language to figure out a wiring diagram or interpret a sculpture. If we limit education only to the functional uses of any language, we risk losing the unique power of that language to inspire the critical and creative thinking that leads knowledge forward.

**The world is out there, but descriptions of the world are not—the world does not speak. Only we do.**

**—Richard Rorty**

*The arts, as languages, empower children to construct, communicate, and express understanding and meaning.*

**If the teacher does not concern herself with helping children learn what is important in the arts, there is little reason for children to believe that the arts have something worth learning.**

**– Elliot Eisner**

**Using a language aesthetically requires creative and critical thinking**

- gathering information with perceptual sensitivity
- connecting knowledge to personal experiences
- thoughtful manipulation of media and images
- representing ideas in different ways
- analysis from various perspectives
- reflection, questioning, and uncertainty
- synthesis to generate novel combinations
- continuous evaluation and feedback
- understanding and personal meaning

Fortunately, all symbol systems have an aesthetic potential in which we can imagine new artistic possibilities, express strong feelings, evoke subtle meanings, and creatively combine structural aspects of the language (Gardner, 1990). Our aesthetic use of language is more dynamic, nonlinear, and is governed by principles of beauty, culture, and personal meaning.

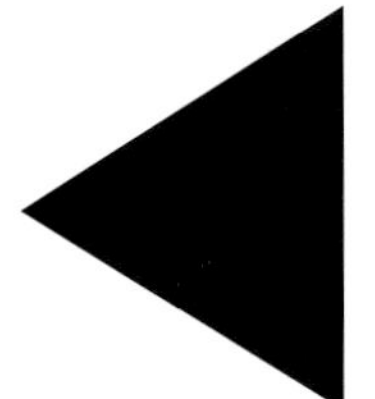

**Guiding Principle 1—Art Is a Language**
The arts are symbol systems organized by elements and principles which provide a medium for communicating information, posing and solving artistic problems, and expressing feelings.

**No one can claim to be truly educated who lacks basic knowledge and skills in the arts.**

**– National Standards for Arts Education (MENC, 1994, p. 5)**

When we use language for artistic ends, we call attention to the symbol system's unique form, which in turn allows us to discover something new about ourselves and the world. Each symbol system's unique form involves structural content and reasoning processes that actively engage us in knowing differently. "A multiplicity of symbol systems is required to provide a more complete picture and a more comprehensive education" notes Fowler (1994, p. 5). Consider the different kinds of understandings, knowledge, and emotions conveyed in

- a historical description of George Washington's crossing of the Delaware on Christmas Eve
- Washington's letter to Martha about the crossing
- the painting of the event by Leutze, or Larry Rivers' abstract representation

The aesthetic aspect of any language allows us to explore the qualities and depth of an experience and transcend its reality to make connections to our own lives.

The aesthetic use of a language is deeply rooted in what we know and feel about that knowing. Aesthetic forms of communication are thus tied directly to personal experiences and cultural contexts. Aesthetic creations depict the fullness of humanity and our potential to create change, develop new understandings, and transform perspectives. Personal, expressive use of language demands critical and creative thinking and results in self-discovery and new knowledge.

*Figure E-4.* Personal, expressive use of language demands analytical and creative thinking and results in self-discovery and new knowledge. ***Ocean Paradise***, Edith Gregson, age 9, tempera paint and markers. Courtesy Crayola® Dream-Makers® Program.

## Ways Children Use the Arts

Young children demonstrate a natural, spontaneous ability to use and develop competency in the various symbol systems of their culture. The arts (dance, drama, music, and visual arts) are languages which enable children to construct and communicate their knowledge, skills, dispositions, and feelings both functionally and aesthetically.

Children's abilities to feel competent and creative span all of their languages, and they quite readily share ideas and feelings through various artistic forms beginning at a young age. Their singing, dancing, dramas, and paintings demonstrate an unabashed enthusiasm for artistic communication.

Each symbol system involves a developmental progression that facilitates mastery of the language. Our goal as educators is to nurture children's intense interest in language systems so that they develop a powerful repertoire of skills with which to commu-

**For both teacher and child, the arts offer an expanded notion of classroom discourse that is not solely grounded in linear, objective language and thinking, but rather recognizes the full range of human potential for expression and understanding** (Gallas, 1991, p. 42).

nicate. The outcome is learning—both in the artistic language and the language of the content area.

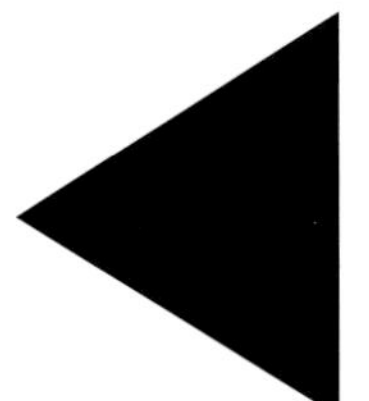

**Guiding Principle 2—Children Use Art**
The arts are a natural language which must be nurtured and developed so children remain creative and literate in multiple symbol systems.

*The aesthetic aspect of any language allows us to make connections to our own lives.*

Childrcn rclish the opportunity to represent ideas in multiple forms. Their questions give us insight into the visual and technical dilemmas they encounter as they grapple with various artistic media. Interactions with adults or more capable peers who act as guides can lead children to deeper understanding and greater artistic expression (Vygotsky, 1978; Berk & Winsler, 1995). When teachers respect each child's unique contributions, children are encouraged to construct meaningful knowledge through art. A visit to another school setting demonstrates some of the ways that children can use the arts.

> Our goal was to integrate poetry and portraiture into a performance piece. This grew out of an exhibition at the Newark Museum, "A World of Their Own," that dealt with American Folk Art, both historic and contemporary. We envisioned a half-year project for our middle school students that would combine both the written arts and visual arts into a sort of Spoon River Anthology of a deaf community.
>
> These children come here from many different school districts and we wanted to encourage friendships and unique kinds of sharing of families, feelings, hopes, and dreams. In art we used the interview information that they had gleaned from each other to draw portraits that captured not only their smile or sad eyes but a bit of their life. The drama teacher worked on the poems which connected to the portraits as well as the presentation of the performance piece.
>
> The final presentation, "A Deaf Anthology of Folk Art: Portraits and Poetry," was a moving experience for us all—teachers, parents, and our students.
>
> – Denise Mastroieni, art educator;<br>Kathy Tilley, drama teacher/librarian;<br>Lake Drive School for Deaf and<br>Hard of Hearing Children,<br>Mountain Lakes, New Jersey

## Radha Warty
### by June Ho Pak

I am a girl with short hair
I don't have brother and sister
I am aaallooonnneee with my parents
I like to play tennis

I lived in a hot place in India, but now I
live in a good place in West Orange
Many trees
many animals
and few schools
My house has ooonnneee family

When I was eight years old
I
leave
India
for
United States
When I was little girl..........I push my friend
then my teacher was mad at me
I was in big trouble

I was new kid in 1987
I was nervous in school
I understand English in school

My memory of little kids 5 years ago
My memory is being nice to my friends

I want to be an artist
I want to teach the person to draw the picture

I am fine........some family sign, some family speech
I want to become like hearing kids
When I go to movies, I can hear a little

I like my friends they have fun
some friends come over to my house

I can hear with hearing aides
but I can hear when my friends use voice
I have television with closed caption

When I was baby
I became sick
my mom drove me to doctor
Doctor poked my ears
Tomorrow I am deaf
I feel fine. I feel okay
I teach a boy to sign

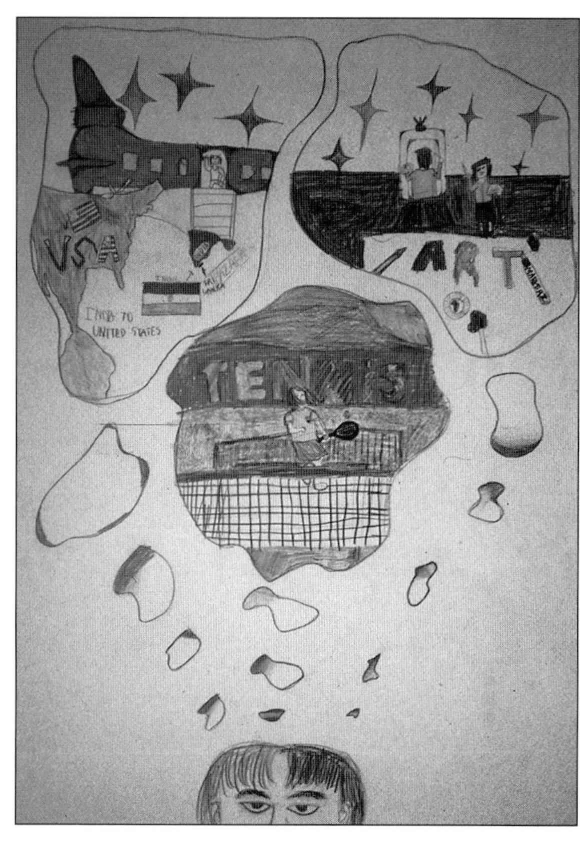


*Figure E-5.* June Ho Pak's portrait of and poem about Radha Warty. Lake Drive School for Deaf and Hard of Hearing Children, Mountain Lakes, New Jersey.

Figure E-6. Stephen MacDonald's portrait of and poem about David Guardino. Lake Drive School for Deaf and Hard of Hearing Children, Mountain Lakes, New Jersey.

## David Guardino
### by Stephen MacDonald

I am Boy........who went to 3 hard of hearing
schools
I live in Pine Brook
h Me.......
a I want to be
v famous actor
e and to be very very very RICH!!!!
Hamster
and
fish
Born in
Long Island
Grandpa..........born in Italy
I don't like bats
am scared about BATS
I love pizza
i
z
z
a is so good!

I will be happy and laughing
I am going to a deaf school to have FUNNNNN!

heard
my mom bomb in house
FIRE
next door
call 911
In school I
feel like a boy
in prison working
and working hard
..........to
finish
my
papers and I am ..........
free again.
I
wish to be a mean
football player

being deaf means to me by being
very silent or quiet being a kid
means exciting and playful

Feel like
I a deaf kid loving to
play basketball I will feel
happy TODAY
and find a lot of
surprises

Gardner (1982) refers to young children's "first draft" knowledge of the arts, which includes the knowledge, skills, and processes involved in artistic reasoning and meaning making. As children become increasingly competent with the structural aspects of artistic language, they are more able to use visual thinking for aesthetic ends. Every artistic creation is embedded in the child's realm of experience, demonstrates the child's natural aesthetic judgments, and communicates understandings and feelings.

**Art is a way that we tell stories about ourselves to ourselves and others.**

**– Daniel Walsh (1993, p. 20)**

Children who set out to represent an experience in a visual language are likely to encounter challenges when they use art materials to communicate, as evidenced by Nicole's experiences.

Nicole, a competent reader and drawer at age 6, is becoming a soccer player. She poses a problem for herself by announcing, "I will draw Jesse (her younger brother) doing every sport I know!" Through her drawings she solves both visual and personal challenges. Questions such as "How can I make the soccer ball look like it's moving?" and "How do you make hands on a baseball bat?" or "What do the lines look like on a tennis net?" demonstrate her ability to think visually and ask for technical assistance.

She also asked questions about who can score in soccer, names of positions, and what you should be doing if the ball is not near you. Her seven drawings (Figures E-7 through 13), done over a 2-week period, depict her brother in various sports poses, but careful observation also demonstrates her emerging competency in physical activity and ability to represent her experiences visually.

*Figures E-7 through 13.* Drawings done by 6-year-old Nicole, depicting her brother in various sports poses. Notice the continuous addition of visual conventions to depict movement and perspective of the athelete.

*E-7*

*E-8*

*Children's questions give insight into the visual and technical dilemmas they encounter.*

E-9

E-10

E-11

E-12

E-13

## When Art Leads Learning

When children use art as a language, their learning becomes integrated and meaningful. Through art, children are provided with opportunities, skills, and tools to become literate in both the structural content and reasoning processes of the language. This competence enables them to use art both functionally and aesthetically.

In classrooms that use the *Art as a Way of Learning*® framework, teachers and art specialists employ a constructive, integrated approach to learning. This guide and the related professional development workshops are designed to help you learn how to create an environment that empowers children to construct, communicate, and express understanding and meaning through the arts.

**Guiding Principle 3—Art Leads Learning**
The arts provide a medium for creative and critical thinking.

### Children Are Intelligent, Creative Thinkers

Adults are well aware that children ask important, interesting questions that rarely have simple answers. Their questions, which may address multiple layers of knowledge and complicated topics, often include aspects of physical movement, rich perceptual qualities, and affective connotations. These questions are the real curriculum.

Children and teachers alike have much to gain when we explore children's pressing questions. Higher-order, creative thinking is essential. As Katz and Chard point out, "Sustained interaction requires content that is relevant, vivid, engaging, significant, and meaningful to the participants" (1989, p. 43).

You can use any language or art form to explore children's questions or their interests. This process, of posing and solving intriguing questions through artistic forms, is exactly how artists think and work. The challenge for you as a teacher is to move toward the aesthetic content in the question or idea and explore possible solutions. Here is how a sophisticated topic was approached in one *Art as a Way of Learning* classroom.

*Figure E-14.* Four- and 5-year-old children at Northampton Community College Child Development Center working on presidential commission sculpture. Notice drawings on wall behind them that are being used for reference.

It's February, the month of presidents, but can this topic make sense to a group of 4 and 5 year olds in a child care center on a community college campus? The early childhood teacher and the visiting artist-in-residence asked the children. "We have a president at this college. Do any of you know him?" A look of surprise and animated interaction indicated the project's potential.

The children made an appointment and visited the president's office with visual journals in hand. They drew him, asked him many important questions (mostly about what he did all day), measured him, photocopied his hands, and drew the things on his desk. He was astonished by their curiosity and depth of interest.

Back in the classroom, the presidential sculpture commission commenced. An area was set up for sculpture work which included the children's drawings as visual references. Reproductions of sculptures and presidents hung on the wall side by side. Children engaged in a great deal of problem solving about the president's pose and activity. Technical questions included how to make the sculpture stick together.

The final sculpture, a seated, papier-mâché figure of the president with a red phone (because that's what he did most, make important phone calls), stands four feet high (Figure E-14). It represents a truly fitting presidential project.

– Karen Klein, Northampton Community College
Child Development Center,
and Martha Posner, artist-in-residence,
Bethlehem, Pennsylvania

*Learning engages children in thinking and doing with others.*

## Children Are Actively Engaged

Children's natural ability to use symbol systems to construct knowledge and skills does not happen in a vacuum. The dynamic relationship between learning and development relies heavily on good teaching and engaging children actively in thinking and doing with others (Berk & Winsler, 1995). Learning within the culture (at home, school, in play yards, and from people, nature, books, and technology) moves children's development forward. Some interactions, however, are more powerful than others.

Children's natural dispositions toward curiosity and sensory learning lead directly into art explorations. Moreover, artistic learning requires coordination of mind and body, eye and hand. Children become visually literate by exploring the content of the elements of visual organization—line, shape, color, texture, form, and the principles which coordinate them into a composition—in multiple experiences.

At the same time, children develop skills and tools to communicate effectively and specific ways of reasoning such as visual thinking, image making, and problem solving. The visual arts provide a physical medium in which children manipulate, alter, and receive immediate visual and kinesthetic feedback. This collaborative project, involving an art specialist, classroom teachers, and media specialist, is a rich example of children's learning through social and physical interaction.

**These classrooms look and sound different. [They are] alive with problem-solving, peer critiquing, and aesthetically enriched.**

**– Kathy Van Rijn,**
**school board member,**
**Mountain Lakes, New Jersey**

Pairs of first graders and fourth graders are huddled around computers. Both classes are studying about animals in science and the use of computer technology in art at different levels. Marie, the art teacher, has just finished a lesson on how to use the computer paint program, focusing on shapes, color, texture, and movement in animals and their habitats. Children also looked at realistic and abstract animals in art.

Sharing their knowledge of hypertext, the fourth graders are assisting the younger students to create a card with an animal drawing. The older children ask questions about the color, shapes, and texture. "How fuzzy is Snowball's fur?" or about the science content, "Where do snakes live? How will you show me that?" The younger students ask for technical assistance in using computers to draw or add animal sounds to their pictures.

The result is a hypertext presentation about animals and their habitats. Among the records documenting the project are photos of children at work, fourth graders explaining the animal habitats and technological processes, the art reproductions that were studied, notes on animal sounds, and the realistic and abstract drawings created by the first graders.

– Marie Cattaffo and Anne Brown,
Wildwood School, Mountain Lakes, New Jersey

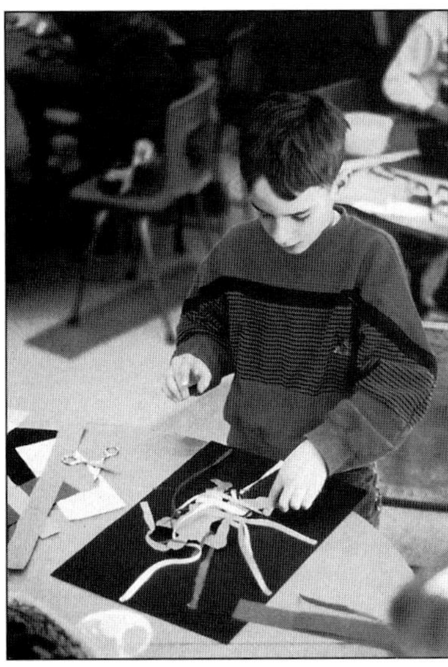

*Figure E-15.* The visual arts provide a physical medium in which children manipulate, alter, and receive immediate visual and kinesthetic feedback. Third grade movement sculpture, Cindy Canfield, art teacher, Hiram Dodd Elementary School, Allentown, Pennsylvania.

**Genuine understanding is most likely to emerge, and be apparent to others, if people possess a number of ways of representing knowledge of a concept or skill and can move readily back and forth among these forms of knowing.**

**– Howard Gardner (1991, p. 13)**

### Characteristics of *Art as a Way of Learning*® Classrooms

- The arts play an integral role in utilizing visual thinking as children draw and record findings; express feelings and ideas in sketchbooks; and demonstrate concepts, skills, and understanding through integrated projects and artistic problem-solving.
- Teachers are responsive to children's interests and learning styles.
- Classrooms are alive with curiosity, questioning, reflecting, interacting, creating, and knowing in a variety of forms and different contexts.
- Time, space, and materials are used in unique ways to design aesthetic environments that validate and extend learning.
- Children, teachers, and art specialists are actively engaged in a process of learning which demonstrates knowledge, skills, feelings, and dispositions about the topic being studied (Katz & Chard, 1989).
- The focus is on learning, rather than teaching, and learning is integrated (Brooks & Brooks, 1993).
- Themes with related, ongoing projects connect learning across the curriculum and throughout the school day.
- Teachers and art specialists create learning centers, designate areas of the classroom, or design whole spaces within the school where projects can take place over time and learning can be displayed and documented.
- Children discover and construct meaning with others about any big topic or interesting theme.
- Adults and children alike communicate the sheer joy of learning.

Making meaning involves critical and creative thinking, the gathering, representing, analyzing, evaluating, understanding of new information in relation to prior knowledge, and creative representation. Teaching strategies which stimulate, stretch, support, and spark artistic learning create a coherent web of knowing. One goal of the *Art as a Way of Learning* approach is for us as teachers to value and nurture a sense of wonder. A single drawing, or a neatly completed worksheet, or a model made as a culminating activity, does not allow learners to grapple with the multidimensionality of any idea, topic, or feeling.

## Adults Guide Children's Learning

Teachers and art specialists support knowledge, skills, dispositions, and feelings to assure that children actively engage in learning. This concept of learning, in which children's capacities are matched with teaching strategies and curriculum content in ways that help children construct knowledge, is also called scaffolding. *Art as a Way of Learning*® includes strategies that enable teachers to scaffold children's learning.

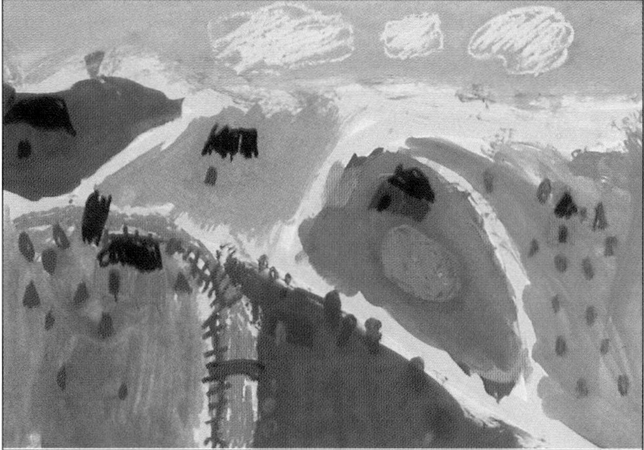

*Figure E-16.* Teachers are responsive to individual learner's feelings and interests. Untitled, Melissa Murphy, age 6, tempera paint.

Inherent in this type of teaching is an attitude that is responsive to individual learner's feelings and interests and that supports critical and creative thinking and nonlinear problem solving. Knowledge and skills related to the visual arts are necessary to stimulate and stretch student thinking, creative activity, and response/reflection skills. Opportunities to pose questions and represent unique solutions in multiple forms spark connections between students and among disciplines.

You are probably already aware that an intriguing work of art or bit of knowledge can focus a group's visual attention. Experience has led you to understand the importance of sensitivity to how children see something, what they know about it, and how they feel about it. You have observed mutual respect develop as individuals in a group see a range of ways to think and feel about the same thing. You know that the best teachers seek and extend children's interests, points of view, or interpretations.

In your teaching, you probably use the process of attending together frequently: as a vehicle to introduce new vocabulary, convey information, or demonstrate skills. Your use of responsive teaching strategies enables you to scaffold children's learning. In this book, you will learn more about how to

**The Four Ss Educators Use to Scaffold Children's Learning with *Art as a Way of Learning*®**

- **Support**—responding to children's ideas, feelings, interests, and creative and critical thinking skills
- **Stimulate**—increasing knowledge and understanding, inspiring visual reasoning
- **Stretch**—developing children's artistic imagination and skills in their ability to reflect, respond, and create
- **Spark!**—enabling children to discover meaning by building connections among themselves and their ability to see relationships among various knowledge disciplines

support children's learning by modeling—art techniques, ways to look at a work of art, and visual thinking processes—much as these teachers did not only for the children in their classes, but also for another teacher.

***Art as a Way of Learning*® is not a curriculum, but a way of teaching that is both artistic and child-focused.**

**– Dawn Dubbs, classroom teacher, Bethlehem School District, Pennsylvania**

Karen and Jean are novice first grade teachers with strong visual arts backgrounds. They collaborate easily with the art specialist, using her as a resource and colleague in planning curricula.

While working on a farm unit which included pastoral landscapes, the concept of the horizon line was raised. Both teachers, each in her own way, addressed this topic. The children went outside; observed carefully; sketched what they saw; referred to landscapes painted by Corot, Benton, and Homer; and discussed the visual and scientific relationship between the sky and earth. Through artistic problem solving, the children demonstrated their understanding visually and cognitively in their landscape paintings.

Carol, a colleague and veteran teacher who had been resistant to assessing children's artistic endeavors, marveled at these paintings and the fact that they were missing the strip of blue sky that had graced her first graders drawings for 20 years. Jean and Karen shared the thinking and creative solutions the children pursued. Carol tried similar strategies in her classroom. She was thrilled with what the children learned, but was more excited about her new insights into the visual art teaching, learning, and assessing process.

Art, defined and explored as a language, activates a constructive approach to teaching and learning. Student curiosity is nurtured and individual interests and perceptual strengths are appreciated. In *Art as a Way of Learning*® classrooms children are seen as competent and with emerging abilities to demonstrate what and how they know.

Research reveals three different belief systems about art education in the schools, which view art as self-expression, entertainment, or as a language for learning (Stake, Bresler, & Mabry, 1991; Bresler, 1992; 1993). A comparison of these three models, based on Bresler's work, may give you a better sense of how the approach taken in *Art as a Way of Learning* differs from the first two more traditional perspectives (Table E-1).

*Table E-1.*

**Comparison of three orientations toward art in the schools**

| Art as self-expression | Art as entertainment | Art as a Way of Learning® |
|---|---|---|
| Art seen as self-expression. Whatever children do is fine, good, precious, or cute. | Art seen as entertainment. Products may be used for displays or bulletin boards, and works all look the same. | Art seen as language. Communication and self-discovery are related to the structural aspects of art, artistic reasoning, and personal meaning making. |
| Romantic notion. All children are creative artists. They just need encouragement and materials. | Ideal notion. There is a correct form for art. Children need to learn skills and follow directions. | Cognitive notion. All children can learn to use art to communicate and construct ideas, images, feelings, and meaning. |
| Knowledge of art comes from within the child. Children are free to make anything they want. | Knowledge of art comes from the environment. Children are instructed to "make it look like this." | Knowledge of art comes from interaction between child and physical and social environment. Children build on their experiences, impressions, and understandings. |
| Teachers (classroom or art) do not intervene in children's creations. They provide a positive climate, time, and interesting materials for art making. | Teachers provide the model, pattern, or step-by-step directions for all children to follow. They teach specific skills. Activity is product-oriented. | Teachers (classroom or art) are guides. They provide engaging opportunities to learn and use the language of art both functionally and aesthetically. Classroom teachers and art specialists collaborate to rethink curriculum and design guided explorations for children. Teachers are responsive to children's thinking and scaffold learning accordingly. |
| Every child's work is different. Children demonstrate use of materials, level (or lack) of skills, and exhibit wide variations in abilities. Children develop knowledge of materials rather than art processes, artists, society, or analytical thinking skills. Children may not connect their art activities to other learning or curriculum content. Art is used for relaxation, fun, and to decrease pressure of academic schooling. | Every child's work looks the same. Children demonstrate ability to learn skills (cut, paste), follow directions, conform to expectations, and think linearly. Knowledge of skills does not include divergent art processes. Children develop belief in correct forms, one way art should look through use of patterns and pre-made materials. Art projects often connect directly to curriculum content (shamrock people in March). | Every child's work depicts an individual interpretation using the structural knowledge of visual language and creative thinking to produce a meaningful solution or response to an artistic problem. Children demonstrate original thinking, understanding, and personal meaning. Children integrate, connect, and transfer learning among curriculum disciplines. |

*Mutual respect develops as individuals see a range of ways to think and feel about the same thing.*

## Impact on teaching of an arts-integrated curriculum

A research study by Bray and Pinciotti (1997) examined the impact of an arts-integrated curriculum on elementary teachers' beliefs, concerns, and classroom teaching. This study demonstrated a systemic shift as teachers embraced and implemented this model of teaching and learning.

Teachers were involved in professional development on how to use *Art as a Way of Learning®*. They collaborated actively with grade-level teachers, art specialists, and artists-in-residence within the school setting.

Seven dimensions were identified in the Framework for Artistic Concerns. Teachers indicated an initial movement from concerns about a common language, purpose, and direction (*essential* level) to an awareness of their strengths and weaknesses artistically and an assessment of their personal knowledge and skills (*comfort* level).

As they continued to learn and work together, teachers began to demonstrate an openness and to seek advice from art specialists (*trust* level) and value the interactive aspects of the collaborative process (*expansive* level) as ideas began to flow freely between them. Interest and enthusiasm for the project grew.

In the next set of levels, teachers expressed and demonstrated a paradigm shift from concern about teaching to concern about individual learners. At the *impact* level, children's unique ways of learning as well as their cultural and creative perspectives are both recognized and appreciated. The curriculum became more responsive and constructive (*transformational* level) as art integration became meaningful and not just additive. A number of teachers indicated the *potential* level, where their concerns demonstrated knowledge and skill as they exhibited a range of possible choices; generative topics that flowed from collaboration with the art specialist, grade-level team members, and the students themselves; and a dynamic understanding of arts integration and the unique role the art specialist plays in the process.

This research validates the professional growth process that is needed for arts integration to occur throughout a school and the systemic change that arts integration brings about in both the teachers and the curriculum.

Children's learning—quantity and quality—can be systematically captured with a variety of research tools and assessment strategies, one of which is observation. By watching children as they learn, paying attention, and seeing them in new ways, teachers as researchers are able to describe, explain, decide on, and document student products and problem-solving processes (Armstrong, 1994). This allows you to consistently make wise decisions about children and curriculum. Skills to enhance your observational abilities, reflectivity, and documentation procedures are essential to establish your credibility and enable you to objectively evaluate your program and student success.

## Guiding Principle 4— Teachers Guide Learning

The arts provide a central thread to guide and integrate learning across all curricular domains.

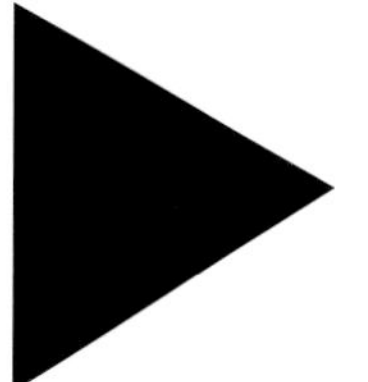

*Figures E-17 and 18.* The most important component of observation is the documentation of student products and problem-solving processes. Jesse, age 5, painting outdoors, is reflecting the colors and movements of a fall day.

## The Arts at Center Stage

> Now the classroom teachers view me as a resource ... a partner who has expertise that can help them.
>
> – Louise Cosgrove, art educator, Salisbury School District, Pennsylvania

The first step in becoming an *Art as a Way of Learning*® educator—something we anticipate you are eager to do—is to examine your beliefs about art as a language. The next step is to develop your knowledge and skills related to the structure, function, and aesthetic use of the visual language. We hope you can do this through collaboration with an art partner—a teacher, art specialist, librarian, artist-in-residence, or administrator. Collaboration provides the ideal social context for partners to respect individual expertise, learn from each other, and understand the process in children.

*Art as a Way of Learning* capitalizes on the unique thinking that occurs during collaboration. You and your partner will share curiosity about the arts, connect curriculum, and consult with each other about children's developmental needs and interests. Together, you will build a rewarding relationship in which you reawaken your creative selves and explore new avenues for artistic expression. Administrators, who are key partners, are expected to facilitate collaboration and advocate arts integration. This approach to teaching and learning is personally satisfying and professionally energizing.

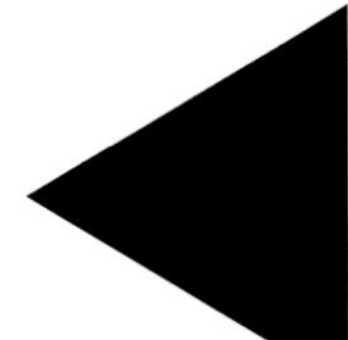

### Guiding Principle 5—Adults Are Learners and Advocates

The arts, when central to a school, create a dynamic collaborative environment for teaching and learning.

> This professional development program is dramatically changing the way the staff is approaching teaching, learning, and assessment. Visual communication is recognized and strengthened as an essential language.
>
> – Greg Naudascher, Principal, Resica Elementary School, East Stroudsburg, Pennsylvania

In *Art as a Way of Learning*, assessment occurs regularly as partners and students record and evaluate the process, product, and understandings gained from various explorations. Formal and informal assessment practices add insight into learning as it occurs, not just at the end. Authentic assessment focuses on quality of learning, not quantity of teaching. How do you create an authentic developmental picture of each child's learning and understanding? Some common techniques that are described in the course of this book include observation and narrative reporting, process portfolios, checklists, rubrics, and work samples (Armstrong, 1994; Brooks & Brooks, 1993; Perrone, 1991).

Bob, a fourth grade teacher, has taught for 5 years. His school is using an arts-based curriculum and he is slowly making changes. He is concerned about a girl in his lowest-level math class because he is not quite sure how to help her learn.

One day, standing in the hall outside his room, he looks at topographical maps made by students in another fourth grade social studies class. These maps, done in collaboration with the art specialist, include impressive textures and shapes. He becomes engrossed in the detail and subtleties of one particular map. He thinks, "This is amazingly realistic, I can almost feel the movement!" when he realizes the map was done by his failing math student.

Bob went directly to the principal's office and recounted with great excitement his three new understandings: 1) This girl is smart. 2) I'm not teaching her the way she learns. 3) This art thing really works! Bob is discovering the impact and benefits of *Art as a Way of Learning*®.

You will soon find that *Art as a Way of Learning*® extends beyond your school walls into the community. Families and community arts resource people will rally in support of your efforts. Adults may ask for opportunities to learn more about the arts, volunteers will be eager to participate, collaborative grants are more likely to ensue, and within your community you will realize a deeper understanding of what good learning and teaching is all about. The arts provide the creative spark for the development of a supportive environment where learning through the arts takes center stage!

*Figure E-19.* Art specialists can expand the context for artistic learning by connecting it in a meaningful way within the overall curriculum. Third grader painting, Cindy Canfield, art teacher, Hiram Dodd Elementary School, Allentown, Pennsylvania.

**Guiding Principles of Art as a Way of Learning**

1. Art is a language
2. Children use art
3. Art leads learning
4. Teachers guide learning
5. Adults are learners and advocates

*Art as a Way of Learning extends into the community.*

## A Challenging Journey. . .

Your *Art as a Way of Learning*® journey will be an exciting adventure with sequential stops and random discoveries. You will begin to set your own course when you answer the Guiding Questions that follow this section. Your gear includes this text, a willingness to learn, and a sense of adventure. You will take trips into four distinct yet complementary territories that we refer to as Program Components:

- ***Visual Literacy***
- ***Creative Collaboration***
- ***Aesthetic Environment***
- ***Teaching Strategies***

Each component consists of a set of four Modules with information and questions to guide your explorations into new ways of thinking. You will examine the way you teach, assess, and think about art, children's learning, and the curriculum. Also included are challenges to direct your actions and reflections to review where you have been. The four components together create a systemic way to restructure education and place the arts as central to that process.

**I now think art! Art is the unifying element in my curriculum planning. The art experience, whether open-ended or project related, helps to unite the class environment and curriculum. While I have always included art activities as part of the curriculum, I have re-evaluated the motivating reason for and frequency of the experience.**

**– Bonnie Pancoast,**
**classroom teacher,**
**First Baptist Nursery School**

### Guiding Questions

Questions to guide your thinking, learning, and actions are found throughout the *Art as a Way of Learning* professional development program. These questions frame challenges you will encounter along the way and foreshadow changes that will occur in your school, classrooms, and within yourself. Each partner—classroom teacher, art specialist, and administrator—is asked to take these questions seriously. Your thoughtful answers plot the map for your individual journey.

#### Questions for classroom teachers

- How are art experiences included in your teaching now?
- How is learning—in math, science, language arts, or social studies—similar to or different from lessons by an art specialist or artist-in-residence? In what ways do you communicate with art specialists about the curriculum?
- How comfortable are you with your skills related to an art

form or media?
- What do you know or learn when you look at students' artwork?
- How do you enhance the aesthetics of your teaching environment?

### Questions for art specialists and artists-in-residence

- How do you connect to each teacher's classroom curriculum? In what ways are you a resource to teachers?
- How is learning in an art lesson similar to or different from classroom experiences in math, science, language arts, or social studies?
- In what ways do you use the National Standards for Arts Education, state frameworks, or district curriculum guides in your teaching and assessment?
- What is your responsibility for the overall aesthetic appearance of the building?
- How do you advocate for the arts with your school's administrator, families, teachers, and students?

### Questions for education administrators

- How are the arts discussed or referred to in school documents or publications?
- Where do you see enthusiastic, engaging, exciting learning occurring in your school?
- What collaborative planning opportunities do you provide for in the schedule?
- How do you acknowledge student and staff creative efforts?
- What is the visual message in your building about learning and the role of the arts?
- What is your comfort level in explaining the benefits of integrated learning to staff, children's families, other administrators, and the community?

**Belief check**—Reflect on a children's art experience that resulted in an art product. Write about the lesson and/or look at examples of artwork done by students. Answer the following questions to determine your current beliefs. What is the nature of art? What was the purpose of this art? What was learned? What did you do to facilitate learning? How are the students' works similar or different? What would the students say they did and learned? If asked why they did this activity, what

*Figure E-20.* Basic K-W-L chart.

| What do I KNOW or can do? | What do I WONDER about? | What have I LEARNED? |
|---|---|---|
| | | |

would they say?

**Performance check**—Review the Guiding Questions. Answer them thoughtfully. Fill out the K-W-L chart (Figure E-20) to assess what you already know about using art as a way of learning, and what questions you may have at this point. Also record any new learning that you have experienced already.

**Feeling check**—Exploring new ideas and uncharted territory can conjure up a variety of feelings, both positive and negative. Monitoring how you feel often gives insight into the learning process, because learning cannot happen without feeling. Create a representation of your feelings through a collage, drawing, painting, or sculpture embellished with words, color, and lines.

**Child check**—You and your partner select the same child to observe over a short period of time. Keep notes about how and what the child learns. What types of questions are asked? How does he or she use visual thinking and representation? With whom does the child interact and use as experts? What kinds of information does this child need before beginning to work? What does the child do if she or he gets stuck? Do other children come to this child for information, ideas, technical skills, or feelings? Discover the many ways to see children by comparing your observations.

## Bibliography


Armstrong, T. (1994). *Multiple intelligence in the classroom.* Alexandria, VA: Association for Supervision and Curriculum Development.

Berk, L.D., & Winsler, A. (1995). *Scaffolding children's learning.* Washington, DC: National Association for the Education of Young Children.

Bray, J., & Pinciotti, P. (1997). Success in education: Creating a community of learners through the arts. *Arts and Learning Research, 13*(1), 79-92.

Bresler, L. (1992). Visual art in primary grades: A portrait and analysis. *Early Childhood Research Quarterly, 7*, 397-414.

Bresler, L. (1993). Three orientations of arts in the primary grades: Implications for curriculum reform. *Arts Education Policy Review, 94*(6), 29-34.

Brooks, J.G., & Brooks, M.G. (1993). *The case for constructivist classrooms.* Alexandria, VA: Association for Supervision and Curriculum Development.

Donaldson, M. (1978). *Children's minds.* New York: Norton.

Eisner, E. (1972). *Educating artistic vision.* New York: Macmillan.

Fowler, C. (1994). Strong arts, strong schools. *Educational Leadership, 2*(5), 4-9.

Gallas, K. (1991). Arts as epistemology: Enabling children to know what they know. *Harvard Educational Review,* 61(1), 40-50.

Gardner, H. (1982). *Art, mind, and brain.* New York: Basic Books.

Gardner, H. (1983a). *Frames of mind.* New York: Basic Books.

Gardner, H. (1983b). Artistic intelligences. *Art Education, 36*, 47-49.

Gardner, H. (1990). *Art education and human development.* Los Angeles: The Getty Education Institute for the Arts.

Gardner, H. (1991). *The unschooled mind: How children think and schools should teach.* New York: Basic Books.

Goals 2000 Arts Education Partnership, The. (1995). *The arts and education: Partners in achieving our national education goals.* Washington, DC: National Endowment for the Arts.

Katz. L., & Chard, S. (1989). *Engaging children's minds: The project approach.* Norwood, NJ: Ablex.

Music Educators National Conference (MENC). (1994). *National standards for arts education.* Reston, VA: Author.

Perrone, V. (Ed.). (1991). *Expanding student assessment.* Alexandria, VA: Association for Supervision and Curriculum Development.

Stake, R., Bresler, L., & Mabry, L. (1991). *Customs and cherishings: The arts in elementary schools.* Urbana, IL: Council of Research in Music Education.

Thompson, C.M. (1995). Transforming curriculum in the visual arts. In S. Bredekamp & T. Rosegrant (Eds.), *Reaching potentials: Transforming early childhood curriculum and assessment. Vol. 2* (pp. 81-98). Washington, DC: National Association for the Education of Young Children.

Vygotsky, L.S. (1978). *Mind in society.* Cambridge: Harvard University Press.

Walsh, D. (1993). Art as socially constructed narrative: Implications for early childhood education. *Arts Education Policy Review, 94*(6), 18-22.

COMPONENT ONE

# Visual Literacy

MODULES

- Creative and Critical Thinking
- Elements and Principles of Visual Language
- Visual Artistry of Children
- Visual Arts Curriculum

# MODULE 1
# CREATIVE AND CRITICAL THINKING

**Imagination is more important than knowledge.**

**– Albert Einstein**

Ms. Vista's classroom, which we visited in the Explorations in Teaching section earlier, illustrates how children perceive and demonstrate their understanding through arts-integrated learning and their constructions of underground vehicles. This guided exploration required experimentation and manipulation of sculpture materials and imaginative ideas. As the vehicles took shape, students evaluated their ideas, rejecting some and refining others, all the while testing them against the scientific and artistic criteria established at the onset of the project.

*Figure 1-1.* Layers of the earth are depicted with texture, color, line, and shapes. Breeanna Calvin, age 9, modeling compound/foil, markers, tissue (detail). Courtesy Crayola® Dream-Makers® Program.

Children in every culture engage in this process of thinking visually and solving artistic questions within their realms of experiences. Learning occurs when children use their prior knowledge, are given more information, are encouraged to develop further skills, and use imaginative thinking. They use art as a language to connect their experiences and create meaning.

*Art as a Way of Learning*® engages children in meaningful projects that stimulate **creative and critical thinking**. The act of thinking both creatively and critically is necessary for mindful learning and deep understanding (Gardner & Perkins, 1989; Langer, 1997). Critical thinking "involves grasping the deeper meaning of problems, keeping an open mind about different approaches and perspectives, and thinking reflectively rather than accepting statements and carrying out procedures without significant understanding and evaluation" (Santrock, 1995, p. 391).

As children carry out their original artistic work, with the guidance of teachers and art specialists, they connect their learning to what they already know and to other areas of study.

## The Cycle of Creative and Critical Thinking

Shapes are part of the kindergarten curriculum and the art standards. The art teacher and I wanted to activate learning by making everyday connections to the children's world and stretch their artistic knowledge and skills by introducing them to abstract art and patterns.

We began by looking for shapes in our classroom, our clothing, and in both realistic and abstract works of art (**perception**). The activity that really captured young children's imagination was the quantity and variety of shapes found throughout their houses, in the furnishings and patterns on walls, floors, fabrics. Our list seemed endless. The idea of building and designing a "House of Shapes" began to emerge as a way to integrate their learning in language arts, math, and art.

In the classroom, children explored what could be in each room and the shapes, objects, or patterns they would find. In art class, they sketched designs, learned how to build miniature cardboard furniture, and decorated walls and floors with shapes (**construction**). They had to measure, cut, fold, secure, paint all the furnishings, and use printing, collage, and painting techniques to embellish the rooms. In every room, variety and design using shapes were important. The amount of children's thinking, visual problem solving, reflecting, and evaluating – individually and together – was amazing (**performance**). The librarian asked to make our Shape House a permanent display. The children were delighted.

– Robin Graff, kindergarten teacher,
Resica Elementary School,
East Stroudsburg, Pennsylvania

*Figure 1-2.* "Our house is in great shape." Kindergarten house project using guided exploration to activate critical and creative thinking about shapes. Robin Graff, kindergarten teacher, Resica Elementary School, East Stroudsburg, Pennsylvania.

Original visual thinking, which is illustrated so well by these kindergarten children's Shape House, involves heightened perception, intelligent imaginative construction, and reflective thought in the creation of the artistic product. For children to apply independent, aesthetic thought to different contexts, they must know something about the language's structure and skills. Through the collaborative efforts of the art specialist and the classroom teacher, children were mindfully engaged in a continuous cycle of learning. This sparked the children's imagination and generated understanding and an unforgettable, meaningful product.

*Figure 1-3.* Geometric shapes abound in cubist work, much to children's delight. ***Cubist Still Life***, 1974. Roy Lichtenstein, born 1923, American. Oil and magna on canvas. © Board of Trustees, National Gallery of Art, Washington, D.C. Gift of Lila Acheson Wallace.

The *Art as a Way of Learning*® framework looks at both the internal and external processes involved in creative and critical thinking. The processes found in three dynamic and interconnected aspects—**perception, construction,** and **performance**—form a cycle which delineates learning in any symbol system and in any cultural context (Figure 1-4). At each point there are different types of problem-solving strategies that incorporate and extend visual thinking. This cyclic framework is based on research including that of Gardner and Perkins' ideas of teaching for understanding (1989), Rosenberg's study of imagination in action (1987), the policy perspectives in the *Visual Arts Education Reform Handbook* (NAEA, 1995), and the learning cycle in Bredekamp and Rosegrant (1995).

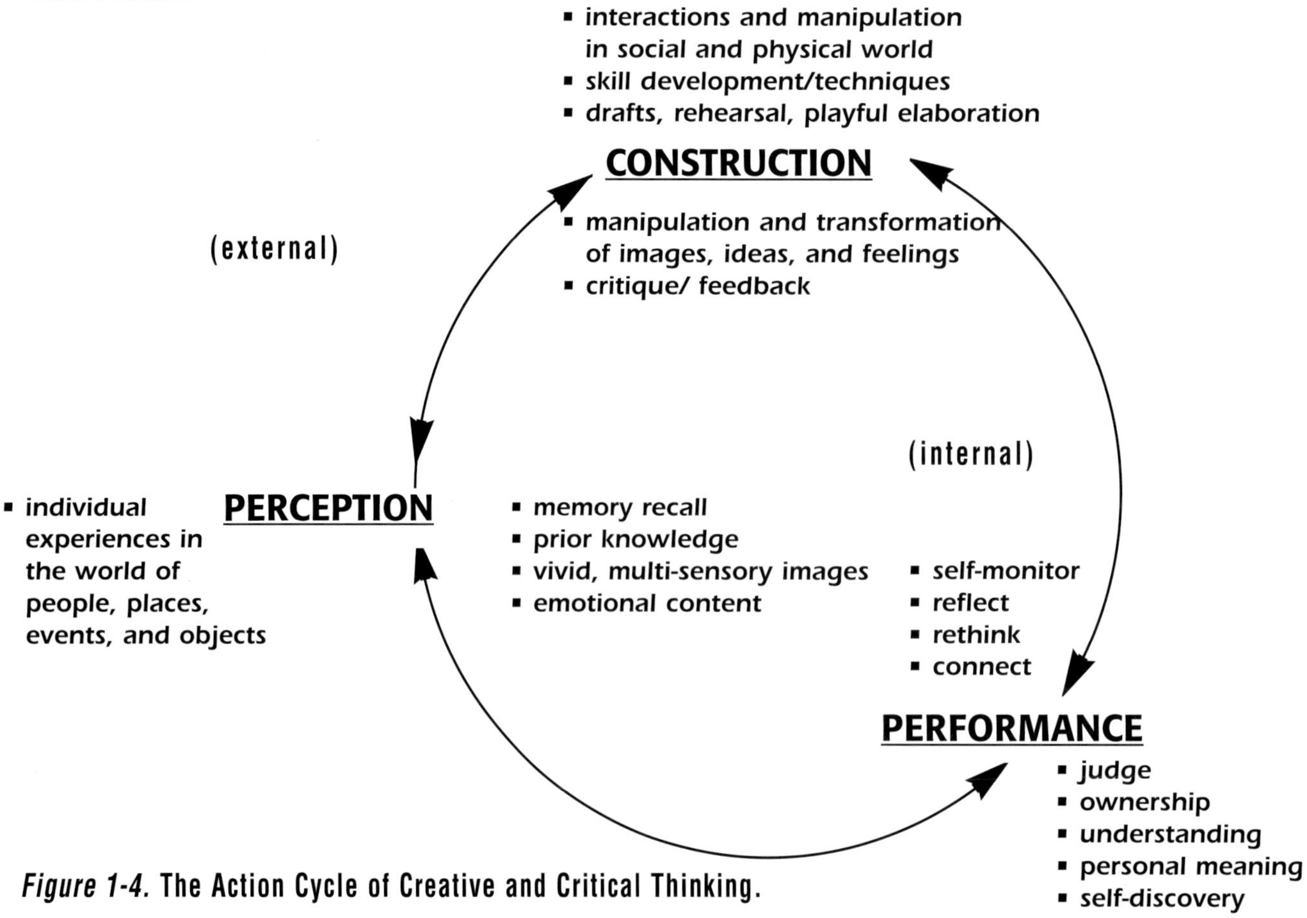

- interactions and manipulation in social and physical world
- skill development/techniques
- drafts, rehearsal, playful elaboration

**CONSTRUCTION**

- manipulation and transformation of images, ideas, and feelings
- critique/ feedback

(external)

(internal)

- individual experiences in the world of people, places, events, and objects

**PERCEPTION**

- memory recall
- prior knowledge
- vivid, multi-sensory images
- emotional content

- self-monitor
- reflect
- rethink
- connect

**PERFORMANCE**

- judge
- ownership
- understanding
- personal meaning
- self-discovery

***Figure 1-4.*** **The Action Cycle of Creative and Critical Thinking.**

Through arts-integrated explorations, children naturally engage in using the thinking cycle. This cycle leads to independent creative work and the aesthetic use of a language. As teachers, we observe children's imaginations in action when they demonstrate understanding through what we call performance.

> Wherever art takes a motif from actuality—a flowering branch, a bit of landscape, a historic event or a personal memory, any model or theme from life—it transforms it into a piece of imagination, and imbues its image with artistic vitality. The result is an impregnation of ordinary reality with the significance of created form.
>
> – Susanne Langer (1997)

## Guiding Questions

We encourage you and your collaborative **art partner** to use these questions to reflect upon your own thinking processes and the culture in which they developed. Observe children involved in perception, construction, and performance. Create opportunities for students to discuss how they make meaning with the visual language.

- How would you describe your critical and creative thinking processes? What perceptual aspects of your experiences do you recall vividly? What strategies do you use to recall them? How do you mull over ideas, feelings, and images, internally and externally? How do you select the best ideas for your final product? What do you learn from the process? From the final product?
- What perceptual aspects of prior knowledge do your students vividly remember? What additional experiences do you need to provide to increase their image storehouses? What strategies do you already use to help them recall, work with, and select images, ideas, and feelings with which to create?
- How do different artists in various cultures express the same images of family, nature, the sea, sadness, and other topics? What aspect of their understanding did they choose to express? How did the artist work with the medium or the image?

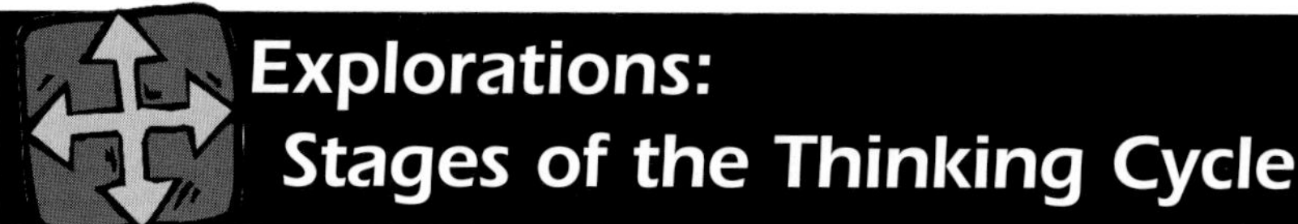

## Explorations: Stages of the Thinking Cycle

Young children have a natural capacity to think creatively, as indicated by the transformation of their classroom into a space laboratory. They are curious and internally motivated to master cultural symbols through their experiences. Learning is far more likely to transfer into children's creative work when we encourage their individual capacities to create in different contexts. As children's learning strengthens, their knowing, critical and creative thinking, and feeling are deeper and fuller.

*Inspire children's imaginations!*

*Figure 1-5.* ***Aliens sculptures.*** Armature, plaster gauze, and tempera. Jane Oplinger's art class, Resica Elementary School, East Stroudsburg, Pennsylvania. Photo by Jane Oplinger.

Jane Oplinger, the art specialist, and I began by sharing our knowledge about the curriculum theme which was space, and what she thought we could do artistically. We spent a good bit of time brainstorming and explaining to each other content knowledge and artistic knowledge, and the skills related to both.

After we decided on a number of explorations, I had to create an environment for the children to connect their prior knowledge and to experience space as fully as possible (since none of us had ever been there!). We both began gathering resources and I created a space corner in my classroom with books, games, art references, and other materials.

Art knowledge and skills began entering the classroom and knowledge about space was used in the art class. The children transformed our room into a working space laboratory with their space mobile, alien creatures (Figure 1-5), glow-in-the-dark constellations on ceiling tiles, project cubes, and Planet Portfolios.

Our collaboration allowed for full exploration of the topic. The arts were fully integrated in the assessment of students' understanding (Figure 1-6). The space unit was a huge success. We are planning a space musical for next year.

– Jan Steigerwalt, third grade teacher,
Resica Elementary School,
East Stroudsburg, Pennsylvania

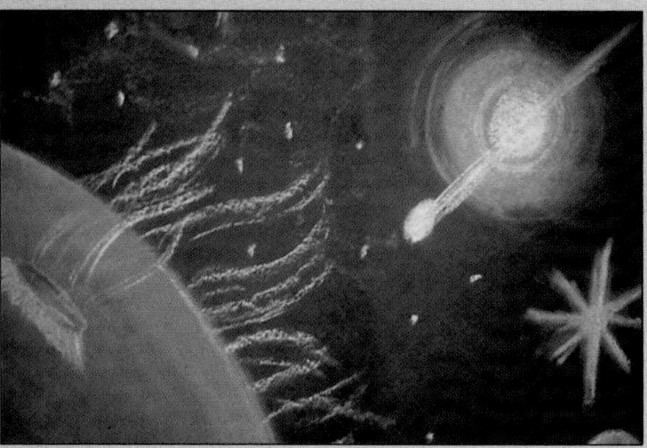

*Figure 1-6.* The arts were fully integrated in the assessment of students' understanding. Chalk drawings demonstrating ability to perceive planets in space, relative size, and depth. Resica Elementary School, East Stroudsburg, Pennsylvania. Photo by Jane Oplinger.

The processes involved in making meaningful use of the visual language are evident in the *Art as a Way of Learning*® creative and critical thinking cycle depicted in Figure 1-4.

- **Perception processes** involve sensitivity to the world around us and strategies used to recall personal memory images rich in sensory information and affective content.
- **Construction processes** facilitate the exploration, development, and playful elaboration of ideas, images, and feelings using the structural content of the visual art language.
- **Performance processes** develop the ability to rethink, analyze, monitor, and ultimately evaluate, own, and transfer understanding through artistic endeavors.

These processes are at the core of independent creative work and involve children in aesthetic use of the artistic language.

Our goal during arts-integrated explorations is for children to develop these critical and creative thinking processes and nurture their conscious use of them. When we enhance children's creative processes, we increase their potential to understand and transfer their learning. Each process allows them to access deeper personal meaning and to express aesthetic content in the final product. The ability to use a full range of thinking processes increases their connections between thinking and feeling, and develops metacognitive strategies for posing and solving **visual problems**.

*Young children have a natural capacity to think creatively.*

Looking closely at the cycle, we see that each stage—perception, construction, and performance—has *internal* processes which occur within mind and body, and *external* processes in which we consciously and unconsciously engage. The dynamic interaction between these processes, as demonstrated by the third grade astronomers, provides us with the opportunity to elaborate, refine, and embed learning in personal meaning making.

The oscillation between internal and external processes results in **metacognition**, or awareness of one's own thinking (Berk, 1996). Metacognition about self, task, or others can occur at each phase of the cycle (Rosenberg, 1987). This process demonstrates the power of the cycle to facilitate the transfer of learning.

**Capturing the ephemeral changes of light and atmosphere ... are the very essence of painting. Perhaps my originality boils down to being a hypersensitive receptor.**

**– Claude Monet**



## Perception

Perception is the ability to experience the world fully, building a rich sensory storehouse of images and feelings that can be recalled vividly for visual thinking and problem solving. The external processes involve perceptual sensitivity to our experiences, which are closely tied to our social and cultural environment and individual perceptual strengths. Each of us attends to different sensory or perceptual aspects. Some of us are more aware of visual or auditory aspects; others may be more sensitive to the kinesthetic. These perceptual filters explain our uniqueness and diverse ways in which we recall and communicate understanding.

*Children search their environment for artistic images.*

Individual perceptual strengths and interests focus attention on different artistic aspects of the visual language as well. Some children are more sensitive to color or shapes, movements or patterns, so each child's knowledge contains unique information and feelings. Artistic elements carry different meaning in various cultures. For example, the mainstream culture in the United States perceives dark purple as passion, while in India, saffron yellow carries that connotation. We wear black at a funeral to convey grief; Japanese mourners wear white. Cultural environments play a key role in shaping individual perceptions. Within each culture some experiences, attributes, and skills are highly valued, while others receive less attention.

External experiences create internal images. Remembering our experiences constitutes the internal processes of perception. Our multi-sensory images may be vivid and carry emotional content. Recall a ride you took on a roller coaster. Notice what you perceive, the physical sensations, and your feelings. The ability to remember prior experiences, real or imagined, in vivid detail facilitates each new stage of thinking. A vast storehouse of images and feelings enriches the process for construction of knowledge. Metacognition results as children consciously search their environment for artistic material and demonstrate a confidence in knowing that they know.

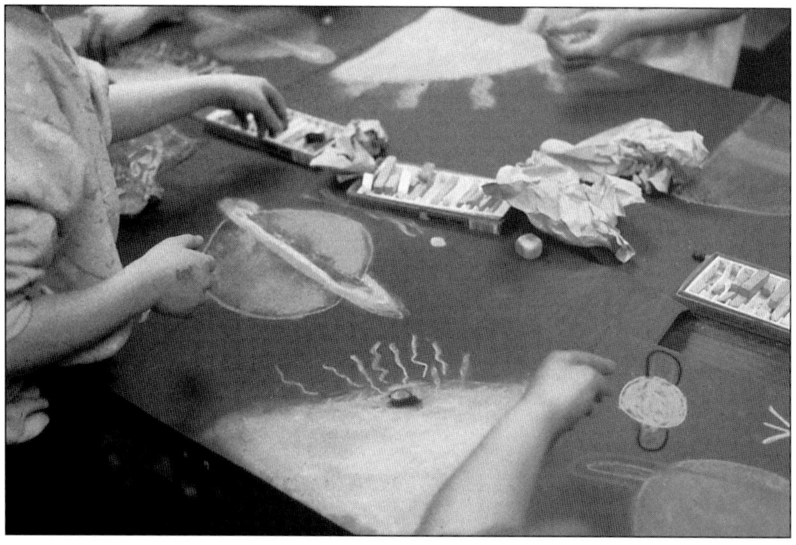

*Figure 1-7.* Critical and creative thinking through construction warrants ample time, space, opportunity, and interaction with others. These students are making their own unique interpretations in chalk. Resica Elementary School, East Stroudsburg, Pennsylvania. Photo by Jane Oplinger.

## Construction

Construction is the active exploration of possibilities. It requires flexible thinking, playful elaboration, and serious work. Structural knowledge, technical skills, and the imaginative content for art making are developed and refined. During construction, children use the language of art in both external and internal processes.

Children use the structural language of art in the *external processes* of construction. Through multiple drafts and rehearsals, they become able to use their knowledge and skills of the language both functionally and aesthetically. As children become more competent with materials, they discern each medium's physical properties through visual and kinesthetic feedback. They challenge themselves to use materials in a variety of ways to construct meaning. In arts-integrated explorations, therefore, we emphasize skills, techniques, a playful attitude, elaboration, embellishment, and individual interpretation.

*Emphasize skills, techniques, a playful attitude, elaboration, embellishment, and individual expression.*

In the *internal processes* of construction, children use visual thinking to identify and solve artistic questions. Numerous problem-solving strategies strengthen flexibility and the ability to manipulate and transform images, ideas, and feelings. The metacognitive process of compressed mental rehearsal, the ability to perform an action in our mind's eye in anticipation of its possible consequences, requires feedback and self-assessment.

Construction generates innovation and elaborate imaginative images infused with personal experiences. Critical and creative thinking through construction warrants ample time, space, opportunity, and interaction with others (Figure 1-7).

## Performance

In the thinking cycle, perception and construction should result in performance, which is the artistic product or visual representation. Understanding, imagination, and personal meaning are evident at this phase. Performance requires evaluation, a constant in all creative work. Using *internal processes*, children make decisions as they select and reject images, techniques, and ideas. They analyze and synthesize their choices while making original connections between performance and product.

*External processes* allow children to consider the artistic product. Their performance demonstrates both understanding and the thinking process of putting artistic imagination into action. With their creations, children can authentically assess how well they have mastered the aesthetic use of the language and developed personal meaning.

Children monitor their actions and imagination while they work, and develop metacognitive skills as they do so. As children become aware of the connections their experiences have to new knowledge and future planning, they grow in self-discovery. The critical and creative thinking processes involved in each stage—perception, construction, and performance—together create a dynamic system through which we help children to develop their visual thinking, encourage their aesthetic use of visual language, and facilitate the transfer of learning. In doing so, the classroom used as an example here was transformed into a space laboratory, with children's sights set on the stars.

**We especially need imagination in sciences. It is not all mathematics, nor all logic, but it is somewhat beauty and poetry. Use your eyes. Watch the rising and setting of the sun from morning to morning, from night to night. Let nature be your blackboard. Spread your triangle upon land and sky. We see most when we are most determined to see.**

**– Maria Mitchell,**
**America's first female astronomer**

## Challenges

As you teach using the *Art as a Way of Learning*® approach, children continue to develop a storehouse of personal memories to inspire their creative work. These are some things you can do to expand children's *perceptions*:

- Provide inviting perceptual experiences for children to look at, touch, smell, hear, taste, and encourage them to describe their responses to different stimuli.
- Create word spills and language experience charts where children tell what they know or remember about an event.
- Encourage children to make observation drawings, sketches, and expressive representations of objects, people, places, and experiences in a sketchbook.
- Ask children to write about their perceptions in a visual journal.
- Draw attention to the personal, cultural, affective component of images.
- Web a theme, topic, or idea individually or as a group.

*Construction generates creative images for art making.*

Through *construction*, children use artistic language aesthetically. Your own playful explorations with art media will enhance your teaching skills.

- Take guided imagery adventures.
- Develop skills and techniques.
- Explore media and materials fully.
- Create drafts or idea folders and charts.
- Elaborate and embellish thoughts.
- Create imaginative images based on personal experiences.

You most likely will aim your *performance* outcomes toward developing children's abilities to select, analyze, and craft an original artistic product. Children discover something about themselves while they:

- Work the same image from different perspectives or contexts.
- Engage in a series of works about a topic or theme.
- Use art to express feelings and moods.
- Use another artist's work as the inspiration for original work.
- Work in pairs, then work alone.
- Reflect together about their best work, sources of ideas, and strategies.
- Discuss personal meaning and individual interpretations.

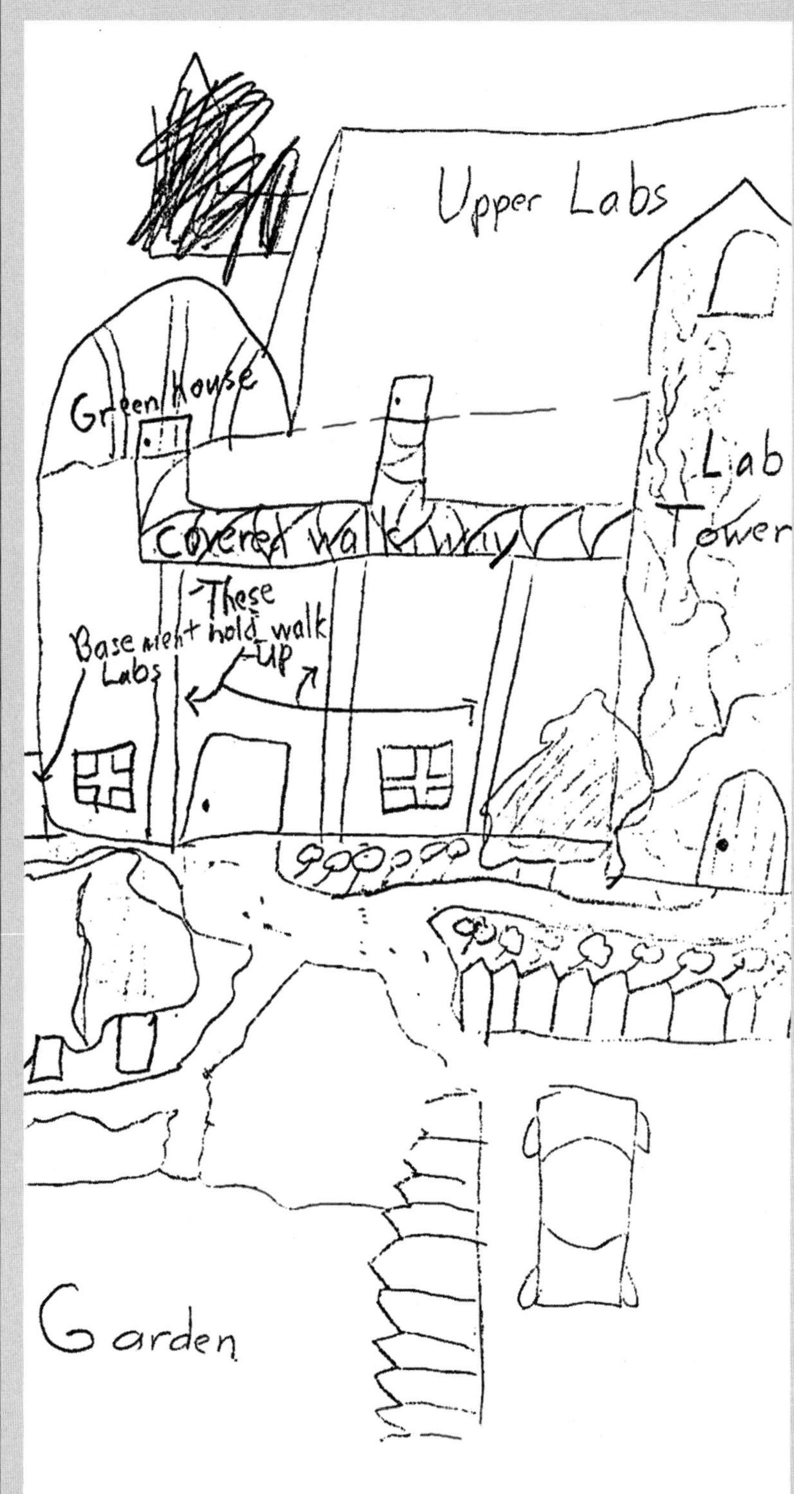


Figure 1-8. Page of Sean McFarland's sketchbook for fourth grade math unit on geometry. Hereford Elementary School, Pennsylvania.

I wanted to include more visual thinking in my fourth grade class, particularly to meet the needs of my students who have spatial and kinesthetic intelligence. The art teacher suggested we revisit drawing. I introduced the idea of visual journals at the start of the school year. We intertwined geometry, a unit often left to the end of the school year, with observational drawing. This has formed the basis for observing, recording, drafting, recalling, and reflecting on so much this year. I cannot think of beginning the year any other way.

– Bruce Fishman, fourth grade teacher, Hereford Elementary School, Pennsylvania

## Visual Journal

Visual journals, which are similar to verbal journals, aid development of **visual literacy**. In a sketch journal, children record their perceptions and draft a visual representation of their ideas, feelings, and movements (see Figures 1-8, 9, and 10). The sketch journal is the jumping-off point for interactive dialogue among adults and children. Frequency in using these journals is the key to visual thinking and documentation of creative thoughts. Picasso has 175 sketchbooks!

Artists use a sketch journal to remember the composition of shapes, details in texture or line, representation of light or colors, essence of movement or value, and to represent ideas visually. Children's journals will help develop their perceptual awareness and build connections between their ideas and images with artistic production (Thompson, 1995a; Robinson, 1996).

*Figure 1-10.* Children develop a storehouse of personal memories to inspire their creative work. Preschool sketchbook. Northampton Community College Child Development Center, Bethlehem, Pennsylvania.

**Suggestions for visual journals:**

- Date every sketch entry.
- Encourage children not to erase any ideas, just move to another page.
- Sketch at least three times a week.
- Encourage the use of symbols or words to describe feelings or ideas.
- Refer back to journals as a source of visual ideas.
- Include responses to works of art, displays, or finished products.
- Put completed sketch journals into the process section of each child's portfolio.

*Figure 1-9.* Sample page of drawings from the visual journals of Edward Casagrande, sculptor, Earth Orchestra, Cincinnati, Ohio, who "draws every day, because I'm afraid I'll forget." These sketches inspired his "Manhattan Angels" series of ornate garden sculptures.

*Figure 1-11.* Through construction, children demonstrate what they know and value about their world. Preschool sketchbook. Northampton Community College Child Development Center, Bethlehem, Pennsylvania.

## Reflections

Begin your reflections by watching for the dynamic thinking process at work with children. As you read the vignettes woven throughout this text, think about the cycle, how children engage in the process, and are guided by teachers and art specialists. How do you introduce and nurture this critical and creative thinking cycle—perception, construction, performance—with children? Ask children to articulate their thinking process in words or pictures. What do children's visual journals tell about their visual thinking?

Look at the *Art as a Way of Learning*® teaching strategies for ways to enhance and extend the cycle. Reflect on your classroom planning as evidence of your own creative work and cultural perspective. Keep a daily visual journal. Describe an imagination-in-action scenario for yourself. How do you tap into children's prior knowledge, interests, memories, and imagery storehouse? How often do children have time to playfully construct with ideas or media?

# MODULE 2
# ELEMENTS AND PRINCIPLES OF VISUAL LANGUAGE

When the artist is alive in any person, whatever his kind of work may be, he becomes an inventive, searching, daring, self-expressing creature. He becomes interesting to other people. He disturbs, upsets, enlightens, and he opens ways for a better understanding.

– Robert Henri (1923)

There is a "crucial difference between making art and merely doing something with materials" (Zurmuehlen, 1990, p. 1). The goal in *Art as a Way of Learning*® is to know and be able to use the structural aspects of the language to express imagination and communicate something meaningful. This module explores the basics of visual language. The more you understand about visual language, the better able you will be to inspire and engage students in the critical and creative thinking cycle.

If you are like most teachers, art specialists, and administrators, collaboration will lead to the most important benefits of your participation in *Art as a Way of Learning*. Your joint learning experiences will enhance your knowledge about effective teaching practices, as well as your creative and critical thinking, and ability to use the arts in a meaningful way.

Before using this approach, many classroom teachers and administrators feel ill-prepared to incorporate the visual arts language in the curriculum. Perhaps you are uncertain about what artists know and their skills, and may be even less sure of your own expressive qualities and elusive imagination. Many adults have limited exposure to artistic techniques and materials, so you may not yet be comfortable with various media. Have you ever finger painted? Or played with clay? Or worked with a brayer? Now is the time to take the plunge!

Rest assured that through collaboration, your visual literacy will increase along with your confidence. If you are a professional with a background in art, you can use that understanding as a starting place.

Art production involves aspects of *form* and *content* that should be addressed with students throughout the learning process. *Content is what one wants to say; and form is how one says it.* The elements and principles of design are the perceptual tools shaping the visual forms of artistic expression.

(Kindler, 1995, p.10)

## Formal Qualities of Artwork

Every work of art is organized by using art elements and principles of visual organization. The **elements** of art include line, shape, form, color, and texture. **Principles of visual organization** include unity; variety; balance; repetition, rhythm, and pattern; emphasis; proportion; and movement. The principles of visual organization are also known as the principles of design. Each element and principle is described more fully in this module.

Art elements and the principles of visual organization are known as the formal **qualities of artwork**. These formal qualities, along with the expressive, technical, and historical-cultural contexts of art, form the visual language through which meaning is conveyed.

Artists emphasize and combine these elements and principles with one another to create a composition. You and your art partner will use these elements and principles nearly every time you share artistic knowledge with children. They are the "basics of visual communication the same way spelling, punctuation, and grammar are considered the basics of linguistic communication" (Kindler, 1995, p. 10). However, "instruction in the elements and principles of design should be a natural part of learning to communicate ideas, rather than a separate set of skills learned out of context" (Kindler, p. 10).

Children often respond strongly to these elements, and have a proclivity to use one or more in their artwork. This knowledge enables children to learn more about themselves, their own work, and the works of others. When children use these elements to meet meaningful, authentic artistic challenges, learning can be exciting and full of discovery.

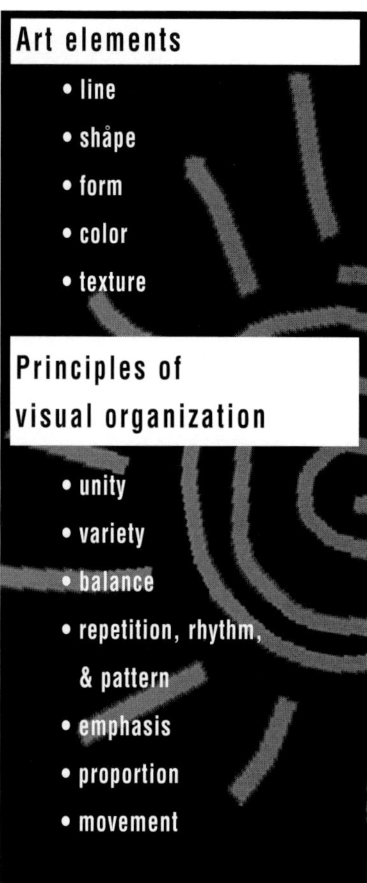




## Guiding Questions

These questions are designed to help you and your art partner consider how people use the elements and principles of visual organization to create and respond to art.

- Of which elements and principles are you most aware? Which do you use in your artwork? Your home? Classroom? Dress?
- What cultural or personal experiences provide visual context for your perceptions?
- How can you help children become more sensitive to the elements and principles they use regularly?
- How will you provide time for children to respond to those qualities in their own and others' work?

*Use artistic elements and principles every time you share artistic knowledge.*

## Explorations: Art Elements and Principles of Visual Organization

Together with the principles of visual organization, the art elements constitute the basic structural language of visual art. These basic explanations are just a beginning. Check with your art partner and books on the topic for further ideas and information.

## LINE—straight, horizontal, vertical, diagonal, curving, smooth, broken, fuzzy, blurred, spiraling, zigzag, outline, energetic, delicate, strong

*Line* is a mark or stroke long in proportion to its breadth, made with a pen, marker, pencil, crayon, or tool on a surface. Line can be used to express many ideas and feelings as well as lead our eyes through a work of art. Among many things, lines can be:

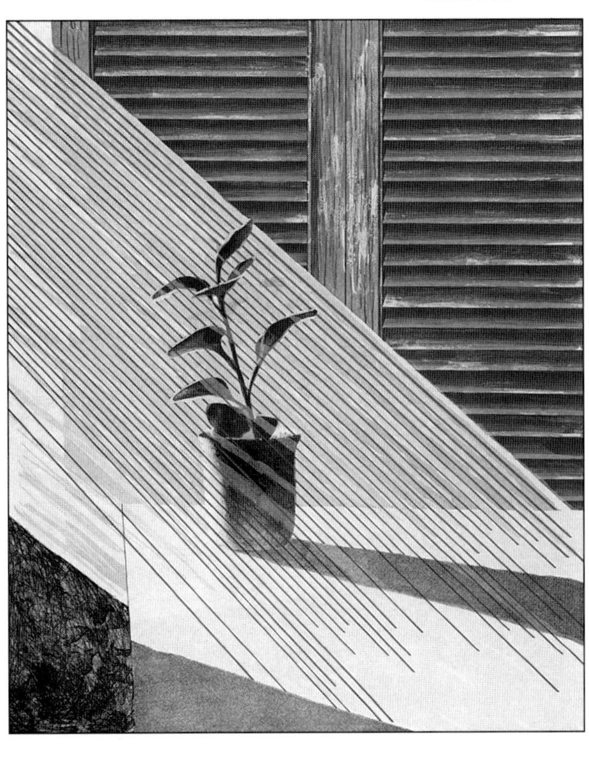

*Figure 1-12.* ***Sun***, 1973. David Hockney, born 1937, British. Color lithograph. © Board of Trustees, National Gallery of Art, Washington, D.C. Gift of Woodward Foundation.

- connections between two particular points, starting and ending at particular locations in space
- static (motionless) or dynamic (active)—they an point in a particular direction or designate a relationship
- ways to illustrate rhythm or movement such as running or hopping
- edges and contours for surfaces and structures
- a way to create an illusion of depth
- used to create texture

Compare and contrast the many different uses of line as expressed by many different artists in a variety of media (Figures 1-12 through 1-18).

Line is a valuable tool for creating and responding to works of art, especially from a kinetic perspective. Connected lines can be made with jump ropes, necklaces, beads, blocks, toy animals, trucks, markers, and with tools such as a stick in soil or sand or a brush with water. Children can walk in a line, steady themselves on a line like a balance beam, or follow a line in their own work or in someone else's.

*Figure 1-13.* ***Washo Bowl.*** Baskets of Northern California, late 19th century. Collection of R. DeLong, C. McAnall.

Here is a brief collection of ways to explore lines with groups of children.

***Looking for lines.*** Children could cut out examples of different kinds of lines from magazines or catalogues, and categorize them according to types of lines. Children might select which lines they like best and create a line collage with letters of their name.

*Figure 1-14.* ***Acoma polychrome water jar*** with banded designs on neck and body, Acoma, New Mexico, ca. 1970. Collection of R. Delong, C. McAnall.

***Moving lines.*** Create lines for children to walk on—sticky tiles, masking tape, rubber blocks, balance beams, crepe paper. Make sure the surface is not slippery. Children could meander within lines as in a maze, or trace their fingers on a line. Finger painting is a natural extension of this activity. Use descriptive kinesthetic language as children move and create lines, texture, patterns, and shapes.

***Talking lines.*** Line can sometimes be funny. Let children create sound effects to describe lines. This stimulates auditory images of objects in the environment and increases sensitivity to the environment. Or start with sound effects and make lines to match.

***On line.*** Think of many different ways to line up. How many different ways can a line of people move? Draw these lines on long paper.

*Figure 1-15.* ***Self-Portrait,*** ca. 1902. Pablo Picasso, 1881-1973, Spanish. Black crayon with color washes. © Board of Trustees, National Gallery of Art, Washington, D.C. Ailsa Mellon Bruce Collection.

***Dancing lines.*** Children draw lines on large sheets of paper (a roll would work wonderfully) to music. Vary the music and have them change colors. Use music from different countries to enhance their listening and movement.

***Nature lines.*** Create monoprints using finger paints on cookie trays, with lines inspired from the rhythms of nature: waves, wind, falling leaves, animal trails, a shooting star, or something else that captures their imaginations. Recordings of environmental sounds, available at nature stores, can inspire ideas.

*Figure 1-16.* ***Glitter Sun.*** Devin Ward, age 11. Glitter crayons, Overwriters™ and Changeables™ markers. Courtesy Crayola® Dream-Makers® Program.

*Use music from different countries to enhance listening and movement.*

*Figure 1-17.* ***Ships on a Shelf.*** Zac Tait, age 11. Pencil.

*Figure 1-18.* ***The Garden.*** Jessica Lillard, age 11. Tempera and oil pastel. Courtesy Crayola® Dream-Makers® Program.

We find ourselves looking more at the line as well as shape of things: the landscape, the horizon line, the swirling patterns of snow. We also squint, or move to see things from different perspectives and notice the different meandering on line when we move. Karen (the teacher) demonstrated some ways in which we make lines when we paint: wavy, straight, dotted. The children produced pictures using these types of lines in different ways. Shaina's picture (3 years) was all about movement and experimentation. Rebecca's picture (4 years) was more representational and told a story.

– Kathy Roberti, director,
Northampton Community College
Child Development Center,
Bethlehem, Pennsylvania

## SHAPE—angular, rounded, free-form, small, large, repeated, irregular, heavy, geometric, expressive, positive, negative, silhouette, symbolic

*Shape* is the term used to describe the quality of a distinct flat object, any two-dimensional surface, or enclosed space which is surrounded by an edge or an outline of specific form or figure. It may also refer to the outline of a three-dimensional object—its **silhouette**. Shape also possesses **area**, which is a functional relationship between width and height. Shape is an interesting element to study in relation to math (geometric solids and planes), science (geometric and organic shapes), and in the environment (such as buildings, transportation).

Shapes may appear to be **symmetrical**, with mirror images on either side of a central axis, or **asymmetrical**, with dissimilar shapes and images on either side of a central axis. Shapes of liv-

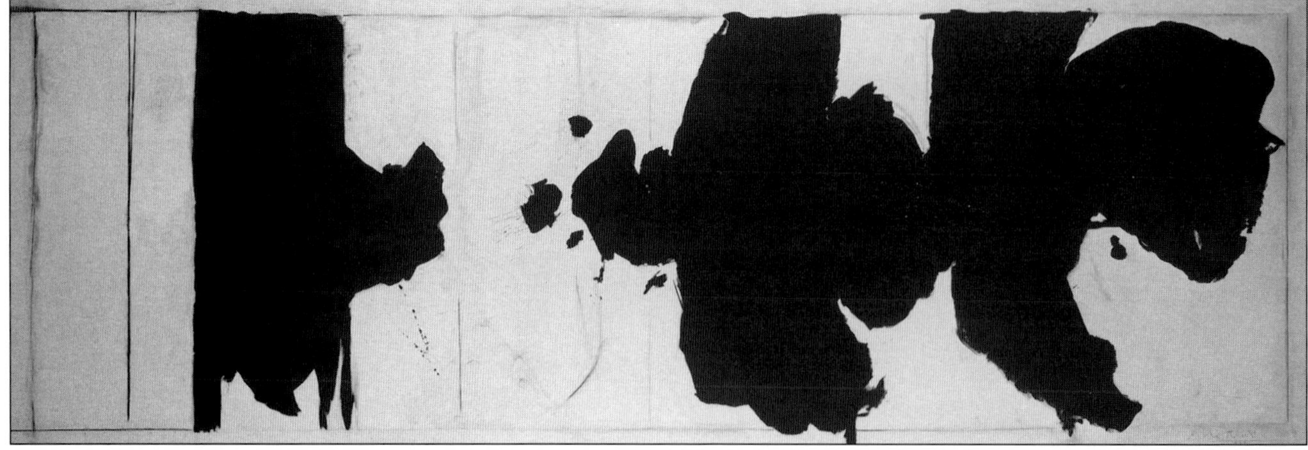

*Figure 1-19.* ***Reconciliation Elegy,*** 1978. Robert Motherwell, 1915-1991, American. Acrylic on canvas. © Board of Trustees, National Gallery of Art, Washington, D.C. Gift of Collector's Committee.

ing organisms can appear to be very complex; **irregular, free-flowing** shapes are a superb starting place to integrate the arts in the curriculum. Children are fascinated with how shapes are connected and joined together. Discovering part-to-whole relationships can become a valuable visual tool. What shapes can you identify in Figures 1-19 through 1-25? How are these shapes connected and combined in creative ways?

Shapes connect to many curriculum areas, especially science and math. Discover the power that shapes have in children's understanding of nature and their ability to making meaning.

*Figure 1-20.* ***Still Life***, 1918. Pablo Picasso, 1881-1973, Spanish. Canvas. © Board of Trustees, National Gallery of Art, Washington, D.C. Chester Dale Collection.

***Looking and seeing.*** Observational drawing and discussion about the drawing process create opportunities to explore shapes and how they connect. Children who are not visual learners may need help to see these relationships.

***Nature.*** The relation between shapes found in nature and human-made shapes is fascinating. Older primary children can begin to discover concepts of design as they compare natural shapes with the geometric shapes of architecture, sculptures, furniture, and other everyday objects.

***Technology.*** Many computer drawing programs rely on shapes to create designs and realistic pictures. Shapes can be made by using different drawing tools which allow an infinite number of shapes and combinations.

***Outlines.*** Children draw outlines of objects in their classroom, homes, and even themselves. Find shapes in the outline. This also could be done on mural paper,

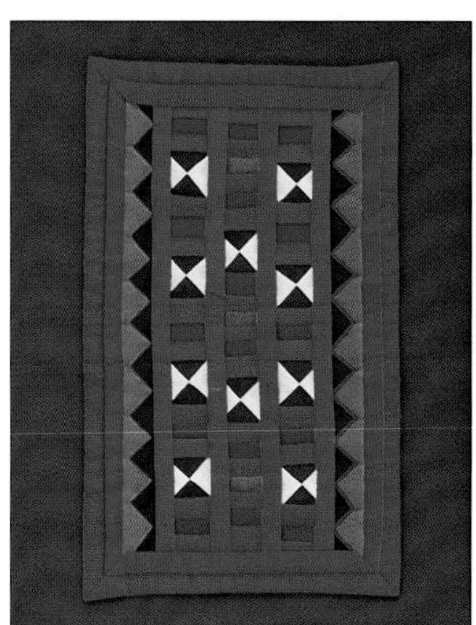

*Figure 1-21.* ***Woven Navajo rug***. Ganado, Arizona, ca. 1960. Collection of R. Delong, C. McAnall.

*Figure 1-22.* ***Neon Shapes.*** Rocky Pinciotti. Photo by Joan Glase.

**Shapes jump out at me.**

**– Georgia O'Keeffe**

*Figure 1-23.* ***Rainbow Bird.*** Trevor Hyatt, age 9. Collage (mola design). Courtesy Crayola® Dream-Makers® Program.

overlapping objects or bodies and coloring in the overlapping shapes.

***Connections.*** When children begin to draw more complex objects (i.e., sculptures or buildings) they need to see that they can overlap and connect simple shapes to create more elaborate shapes. Explorations that help children understand how to join shapes give them endless possibilities. Let the imagination soar!

***Moving objects.*** Use a desk or a table for this moving drawing. Select a number of objects that would be found on or in a desk (notebook, pencil, box of crayons, tissues, erasers, books). Draw the outline of the objects, then move each object the same amount of inches and direction (such as three inches to the left); draw again on top of the other drawing. Continue moving objects and drawing until the page is filled with moving objects.

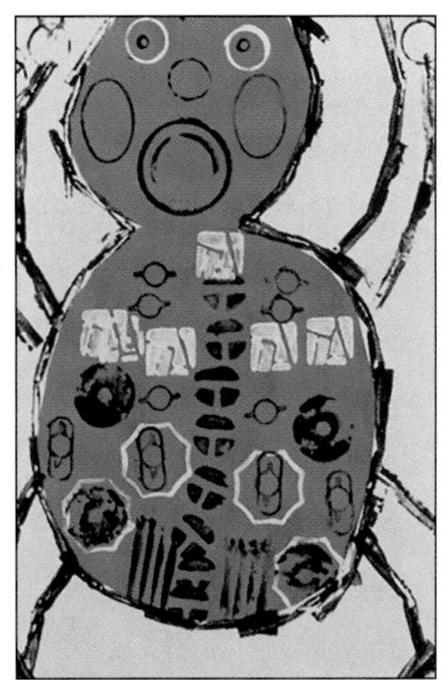

*Figure 1-24.* ***Spider.*** Mark Shearer, age 7. Tempera paints, gadget print on collage. Courtesy Crayola® Dream-Makers® Program.

> We visited the Campus Gallery to view still-life drawings which were very much about shape, form, and line. At group time I presented the Montessori geometric solids as a way to discuss two- and three-dimensional shapes. We also referred to a still life by Picasso and pointed out the shapes we saw. We continually revisit drawing, showing children how to see the shapes that make up the whole of an object. It is important for adults to believe that if you look at shapes and how they are connected you can represent anything.
>
> – Karen Klein, teacher, Northampton Community College Child Development Center, Bethlehem, Pennsylvania

*Let the imagination soar!*

*Figure 1-25.* ***Night Desert Scene.*** Rachel Kuck, age 12. Collage materials: construction paper, Overwriter™ markers, glue prints, Styrofoam™ prints. Courtesy Crayola® Dream-Makers® Program.

## FORM—three-dimensional, additive, subtractive, positive and negative space, abstract, symmetrical, in space, surface, scale, movement, contour

*Form* in art has to do with objects that have three dimensions—length, width, and depth. Forms have presence because they take up space and enclose space. You must move around the object or pick it up to discover how it looks from all sides. Sculpture, architecture, and various craft products, such as ceramics, are the artworks most representative of form. Because they have three-dimensional form, you must share space with them to truly understand what the artist is trying to communicate.

Sculpture is about transformations, changing one thing into something else. This can happen in a number of subtle or dramatic ways. **Subtracting** or removing selective parts of an object can reveal a new and imaginative form. Many artists talk about revealing the form inside a piece of stone or wood when they work in this way. Some plan ahead by drawing sketches, while others let the idea come to them as they chip away. These forms may be realistic and true to nature, or idealistic as in Michaelangelo's *David.* They may be abstract, with some reference to realistic form, or nonrepresentational, without reference to realism.

In **additive processes**, the artist builds up a form by adding pieces of clay, soft wax, and other forms. Another technique to create forms is **modeling**, using soft, flexible substances and then adding detail and texture to the piece. These fragile forms must be fired or preserved in some solid substance or they will deteriorate. Sometimes the final form is cast in metal when it is finished.

Two more modern ways to create forms are either by **construction** or **selection.**

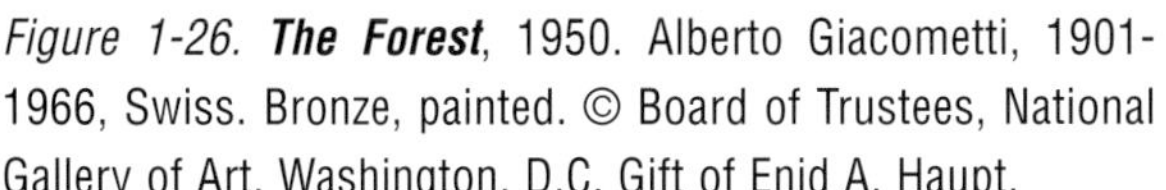

*Figure 1-26.* ***The Forest***, 1950. Alberto Giacometti, 1901-1966, Swiss. Bronze, painted. © Board of Trustees, National Gallery of Art, Washington, D.C. Gift of Enid A. Haupt.

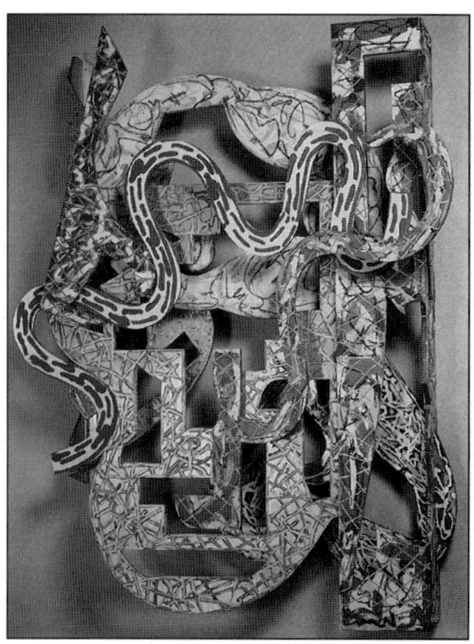

*Figure 1-27.* ***Jarama II***, 1982. Frank Stella, born 1936, American. Mixed media on etched magnesium. © Board of Trustees, National Gallery of Art, Washington, D.C. Gift of Lila Acheson Wallace.

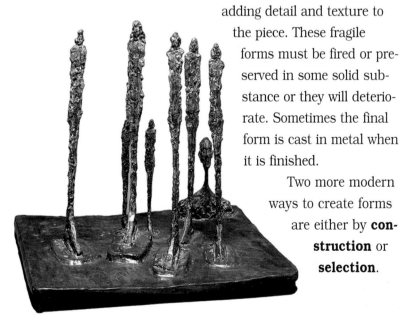

*Figure 1-28.* Masks from different cultures.

*Figure 1-29.* ***Korean folk art*** created with handmade paper.

Construction is also an additive process where the form is pieced together. Forms are often assembled with everyday materials such as wood, metal, cardboard, plastic, string, and scraps of just about anything! Sculptures created by a selection process take construction a step further by actually choosing ready-made objects and juxtaposing them in relation to other objects to create a new form. These types of sculptures often challenge us to view familiar objects in a new light.

Working with three-dimensional forms requires specific techniques to join pieces. Also, skill and safety are major considerations when working with sharp or heavy tools. Ask your art partner for technical demonstrations.

*Figure 1-30.* ***Sculpture****.* Emily Koval. Natural materials, plastercraft, and tempera. Courtesy Crayola® Dream-Makers® Program.

Sculpture and architecture communicate through three-dimensional form and the way that form changes the surrounding space. Children may actually have a better understanding of forms in space because of their size, agility, and interest in moving over, under, and through various forms. Whether the form is common, an animal, tree, or geometric solid, or original, it still has properties which can be considered. The general properties of form include its outer shape or **contour**; use of **interior space**; the relationship of form to **gravity** and **movement**; and its **scale**, **surface**, **volume**, and **context**. Note how these different properties contribute to the forms in Figures 1-26 through 31.

Be especially observant of children's ability to explore form because some of them are particularly sensitive to the physical properties of materials and have a rather astute understanding of forms, weight, and movement in space. Here are a few ideas regarding form to incorporate into children's experiences.

*Children are particularly sensitive to the physical properties of materials.*

*Figure 1-31.* Preschool sculpture.

***Blocks and building.*** Blocks and other building materials provide the perfect tools for discovering forms and their interrelatedness. Provide opportunities for representing a two-dimensional drawing or collage in three-dimensional form.

***Found objects.*** Collect large safe parts of toys, household objects, pieces of machines, games, and other items. Let children find new relationships and objects by transforming pieces of items into a new creation. Naming these works is always fun.

***Recycled art.*** With an emphasis on recycling, suggest artistic problems relevant to science, social studies, and math. Children can invent new products or images by constructing with recycled materials. Many contemporary artists are exploring this form of sculpture.

***Bigger than life.*** Creating a class or grade sculpture is an event worth remembering! Children select an image that is dear to them (e.g., sneakers, pizza, television) and design a way to create the image on a grand scale, bigger than life. With old sneakers from every fourth grader, a giant sneaker can be designed, or a fabric-stuffed pizza can become a comfy seat in the reading corner.

***The magic of modeling.*** Using a soft, flexible modeling compound, children explore positive and negative space as well as create surface texture. Very young children can cut with plastic utensils.

***I am a rock.*** Begin with a fist-size lump of self-hardening clay. Use pieces of clay to connect small everyday objects and materials to create a form. String, twigs, bamboo skewers, and wire can add interest to the clay. Paint the completed form with white glue for permanence.

*Forms are often assembled with everyday materials.*



**COLOR—warm, cool, glowing, soft, monochromatic, light, dark, clashing, intense, dull, happy, sad, primary, complementary, dark, opaque, transparent**

*Color* is the quality of an object or substance with respect to light reflected by the object. It is a vital element in design. Young children respond easily to a variety of colors, have favorite colors, and talk about the feeling of colors. The study of color can be very complicated, because a huge range of colors exists. Also, light and dark throughout the day change our perception of color.

*Figure 1-32.* ***California Dream House***, 1977. Joan Snyder. Oil, acrylic, fabric, wallpaper, paper maché on canvas. Photo ©Zindman/Fremont.

The expressive potential of color is personal, and can create a wide range of emotions and responses. Different ages, cultures, philosophies, and sexes perceive and value colors in different ways. Appreciating each child's sense of color demonstrates how we value children as individuals. What responses do you have to the use of color by the various artists who created Figures 1-32 through 37? What might children's impressions be?

A basic color wheel (Figure 1-33) shows the relationships between various colors. This color wheel is based on pigments rather than optical light, so if you mix all the colors together you will get a brownish-black, not the white that mixing the colors of light would produce. The spectrum for pigment-based colors is **subtractive**; therefore the more pigments you combine, the less white light is reflected back into your eyes. If you combine all the pigment colors, little or no light at all is reflected, and you see black, or an absence of light. There are three basic types of colors:

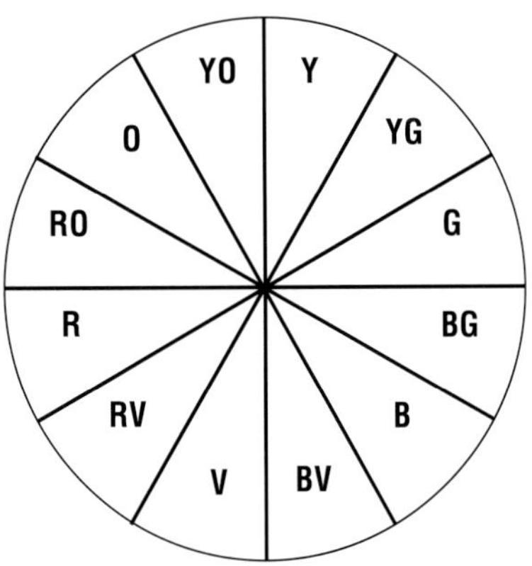


*Figure 1-33.* A basic color wheel.

- Colors which cannot be derived from other colors are called **primary** colors (red, yellow, blue).
- Colors produced from mixing any two primary colors are called **secondary** colors.
- Colors produced from a mixture of a primary and a secondary color are called **intermediate** colors.

Complementary colors (Figure 1-35) are the ones which appear directly opposite each other on the color wheel—red and green, blue and orange, yellow and violet. Mixing a color with its complement results in grayed tones or grays, depending on the color proportions. When brought near a swatch of one of the two colors, these neutral grays will appear to change toward the complement of this color. That is just one reason why color is so interesting and compelling to study, and for artists to use to change mood and challenge viewers.

*Figure 1-34.* ***The big fish and his new friend***. Kristyn Snyder, age 6. Watercolor crayon, construction paper, marker. Courtesy Crayola® DreamMakers® Program.

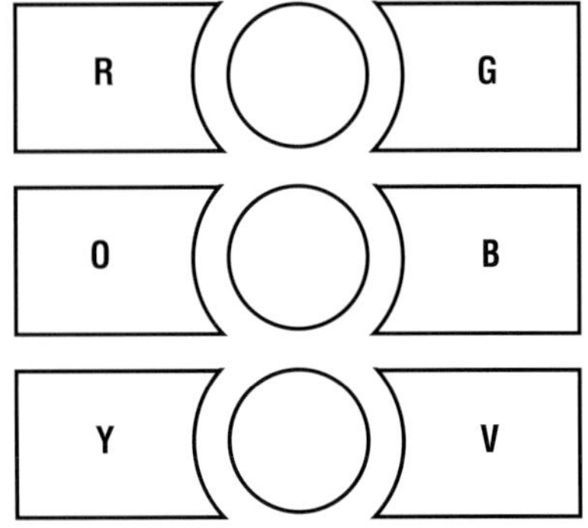


*Figure 1-35.* Complementary color chart.

*Figure 1-36.* Japanese scroll paintings. Fourth grade. Watercolor. Resica Elementary School, East Stroudsburg, Pennsylvania.

Use the language of color to enhance children's knowledge, increase vocabulary, and express feelings. Consider the aesthetic environment as you fill rooms or exhibit areas with color. Create a display about artwork with colors that evoke moods, such as works or referents of works from Mexico, South America, Asia, India, Thailand, and China. These are but a few ways to bring color to life in a school.

*Bring color to life in your school.*

***Color match game.*** Using color tablets, colored paper, or spools of thread, have children look about the room for a color match. Begin with primary colors and add secondary and intermediate colors. Include tints (white with small amounts of color added) and shades (a color darkened by the addition of black or its complement) to extend color learning about value (the lightness or darkness of a color). Value also can be used to create the illusion of form by shading to show sharp or gradual changes in form.

***Feeling colors.*** Create a color wheel of feelings. Refer to the qualities of colors such as intense (bright) colors, dull colors, transparent (thin, see-through colors), and opaque colors (dense, solid colors). Children write feeling words for each color. Colors can also describe relationships, such as harmonious colors (those that blend with one another) and discordant colors (those that clash or oppose each other). Note that feelings about color may be culturally influenced.

*Figure 1-37.* ***Sunny Day***. Beth Harrison, age 8. Tempera paint. Courtesy Crayola® Dream-Makers® Program.

**When I choose a color it is not because of any scientific theory. It comes from observation, from feeling, from the innermost nature of the experience in question.**

**– Henri Matisse**

***Transition games.*** Use colors to ease transitions between activities ("If you are wearing red, you may wash your hands for lunch") or as a game to identify colors ("Blue stand up, yellow sit down"). Expand the color language of older children by using more specific color words (magenta, ebony, cerise).

***Moving colors.*** Discuss the temperature and movement quality of colors. Some colors are warm, active, and advancing while others can be cool, quiet, and receding. This helps explain why fire engines and stop signs are red.

***Light and dark.*** Explore tints and shades of a color by using paint strips (from paint stores) that have a range of either tints or shades. Create a hue from a color wheel of paints and then add white or black to replicate the paint strip. With the newly-made colors paint a **monochromatic** (variations on one color) picture using themes from nature, such as seascapes and sunsets.

***Rose is a rose, is a rose.*** Children could create a collage of one color and discover all the different kinds of reds or other colors there are related to objects, plants, or animals. They might also paint around collage pieces in various hues, tints, and shades to match their discoveries and extend their color knowledge.

*Figure 1-38.* ***Earth Passages #3***. Thom Crawford. Photo by Ed Echstein.

*Different ages, cultures, philosophies, and sexes perceive and value colors in different ways.*

*Figure 1-39.* ***Earth Passages #9***. Thom Crawford. Photo by Ed Echstein.

> We have encouraged children to use color as a starting point if they desire to talk about their work. Color has proven to be a great motivation for language about artwork. We continue to enhance their knowledge and experiences with color by providing many color explorations and opportunities from mixing color, discovering color, identifying and naming, matching, feeling, and tasting colors!
>
> – Karen Klein, teacher, Northampton Community College Child Development Center, Bethlehem, Pennsylvania

## TEXTURE—rough, smooth, slick, bumpy, fuzzy, flat, soft, tactile, visual, shiny, gooey, spikey, grainy

*Texture* is the tactile quality of the surface or a representative of that surface. All surfaces have some type of texture. A surface that seems smooth when compared to another surface will seem rough when compared with a third. Young children may have very strong responses and sensitivities to texture. Look for texture words to describe clothing, food, and the environment.

*Figure 1-40.* ***Fanny/Fingerpainting,*** 1985. Chuck Close, born 1940, American. Oil on canvas. © Board of Trustees, National Gallery of Art, Washington, D.C. Gift of Lila Acheson Wallace.

A patterned surface can sometimes look textured even though it is smooth to the touch, because there are two different types of texture. The way a surface feels to the touch—such as rough or smooth, hard or soft—is considered **tactile texture**. An effect created by pattern or contrast between light and dark areas on a flat surface is called **visual texture**. Visual texture looks textured but is smooth to the touch. Repeated lines, shapes, and colors can create visual texture. How do you think the textures were created in Figures 1-40 through 46? Consider how children might create textures using similar materials.

Provide artistic opportunities for children to explore both tactile and visual textures, so they will know the difference and discover how they could use both in their art making.

*Figure 1-41.* ***Children Leaving School,*** c. 1895. Pierre Bounard, 1967-1947, French. Cardboard on wood. © Board of Trustees, National Gallery of Art, Washington, D.C. Ailsa Mellon Bruce Collection.

*Young children may have very strong responses to texture. Explore both tactile and visual textures.*

Visual Literacy

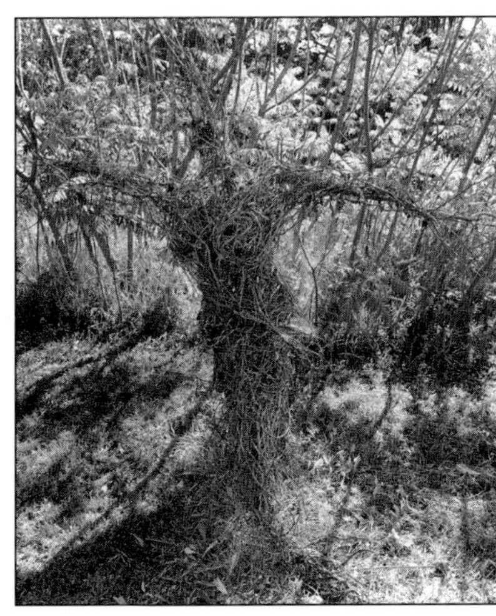

*Figure 1-42.* ***Waking the Wood.*** Martha Posner. Sculpture. Larry Fink, photo ©1994.

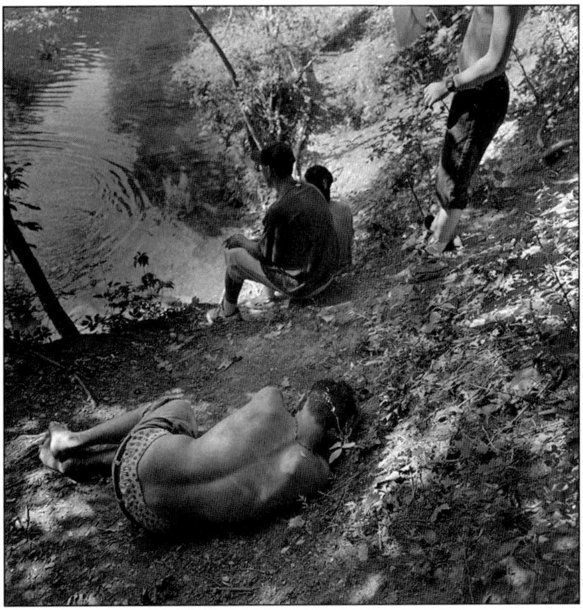

*Figure 1-43.* Larry Fink. Photo ©1994.

### *Touching textures—"Please touch"*

- Collages: prepare them with textured fabric on cardboard or in boxes into which children crawl.
- Impressions in clay: Create impression tiles with a variety of objects, making two of each texture, then children use them as a matching game.
- Collect different textures: for example, tennis balls, golf balls, basketball, baseball, string ball.
- Collographs: Have your art partner show you how to create a printing plate of low-relief textured materials or use masking tape or white glue to make textured designs on cardboard. Allow glue to dry. Pull a textured print when dry, using methods your art partner suggests.
- Add glitter or sand to wet paint for a painting, print, or collage.
- Draw with crayons on sandpaper. Adults can transfer the drawing to paper by placing it face down on paper and ironing the back with a warm iron, creating a highly textured dotted effect.
- Have children hunt for different textures outside or around the house (kitchens are great for this) using a crayon-rubbing technique. Place paper over an object (or a part of it) and rub lightly over the object with an unlabeled crayon to create a rubbing.

### *Looking textures —"Please look"*

- Picture collage: Find textures in magazines and create a collage.
- Pencil textures: Discover what a pencil can create in the way of visual texture by repeating short snappy lines, dots and bubbles, zigzags and curves.
- Look at two- and three-dimensional works of art and discover the subtle textures. Use descriptive language.
- Look at a collographic print and imagine the collage that made it.
- Use textured tiles to print with, and then match the picture of a texture to the texture itself.
- Create papers with visual texture for collage by sponging, marbling, bubble painting, and moving forks or other tools around in wet paint.
- Create a landscape texture collage from different rubbings.
- Design a quilt made from fabric crayon rubbings. Follow directions on the fabric crayon box.

*Figure 1-44.* ***The Open Window.*** Amber Martinez, age 9. Tempera and oil pastels.

Texture also evokes a strong response from children, the tactile sense being one that develops at a very early age. Texture, like color, is quite capable of producing an emotional reaction, such as comfort, excitement, or discomfort. Having experienced this, children are much better prepared to respond to texture that is visually presented. Clay rubbings and collographs are wonderful materials for discovering texture.

– Karen Klein, teacher, Northampton Community College Child Development Center, Bethlehem, Pennsylvania

*Figure 1-45.* ***Dream Chaser***. Coleman McNider, age 9. Watercolor and tempera. Courtesy Crayola® Dream-Makers® Program.



## Principles of Visual Organization

The relationship between the art elements and the principles of visual organization have been compared to a recipe (Herberholz & Herberholz, 1994, p. 77). The elements constitute the basic ingredients (flour, salt, oil), and the principles tell us how much (1 cup, 1/4 tsp.), in which form (sifted, crushed), combined in what order, and what to do to facilitate the process before it is done (bake at 350°, use a Bundt® pan). The principles are the basic guidelines for planning, using, and controlling the elements: How much color? What type of lines? Order or sequence of shapes? Amount of texture? Kind of form? Artists thoughtfully use art elements and principles to evoke particular responses from viewers.

Some artists, just like cooks, conscientiously follow specific rules set by the culture, an art style, or their own formula for artistic success. Other artists rely on instinct or feeling to achieve a desired effect. The principles allow people to pose and solve artistic problems and make value judgments about art. They provide insight into artistic learning, cultural norms, and individual style.

Children need to know and use various principles in their art explorations and in their interpretation and response to works of art. The ability to respond and create works of art using the principles is an important part of perception, construction, and performance. They are essential ingredients to communicate meaning and demonstrate understanding in an aesthetic manner.

The principles of art include: balance; emphasis; movement; rhythm, repetition, and pattern; proportion; unity; and variety, and include the characteristics listed here.

*The principles evoke an effect on the viewer, who therefore can respond to works of art because of how the artist used the elements.*

*Figure 1-46.* ***World scenery seen from a bike***. Enoch Chang, age 11. Tempera, crayon, watercolor, marker. Courtesy Crayola® Dream-Makers® Program.

## Definitions of Principles of Visual Organization

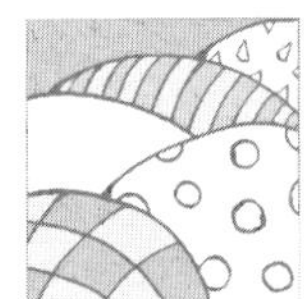

### UNITY

Harmony among artistic elements such that the viewer of a work of art senses its completeness. Techniques to achieve harmony include clustering, overlapping, opposing (see variety), and interlocking shapes.

### VARIETY

Varying art elements in a composition to create interest. For example, a composition featuring large and small triangles exhibits variety of size (or scale). A composition featuring rough and slick textures exhibits variety of texture.

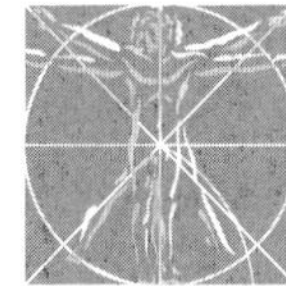

### BALANCE

Distribution of visual weights in a work of art which arrives at an equilibrium of the art elements. Balance can be formal (symmetric, radial), with identical forms/images/colors placed equidistant from a central axis; or informal (asymmetric), having dissimilar, unequal parts that balance in the eyes of the beholder.

### RHYTHMREPETITIONPATTERN REPETITIONPATTERNRHYTHM PATTERNRHYTHMREPETITION

Arrangement or grouping of the elements of works of art so the parts appear to have an ordered or planned relationship. The effect can be regular or irregular.

### EMPHASIS

Use of an artistic device to draw attention or give importance to one or more focal points. Subject matter, increased detail, light, contrast, visual pointers, and converging lines are commonly used to emphasize portions of a work of art.

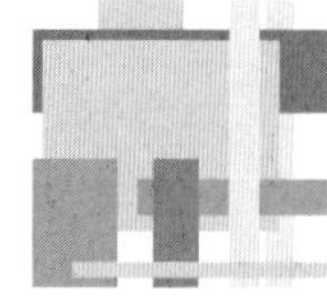

### PROPORTION

The relationship of one part to another and of each part to the whole in terms of size, mass or volume, weight, linear dimension, and color. Proportion may be realistic, exaggerated, or distorted.

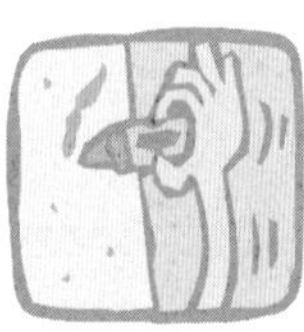

### MOVEMENT

An effect or representation of motion. Movement can be perceived (e.g., an illusion created by patterns) or real (e.g., a mobile) in a work of art.

With your art partner, talk about these principles and their relation to the elements. Look at samples of children's work and art reproductions to discover the harmony, variations, and subtleties they create. Consider the intention and meaning the artist is communicating by choosing to use the elements and principles in a particular way, either consciously or unconsciously.

Observe how your art partner uses words to describe works, asks questions to elicit responses to works of art, and comments on students' work. Encourage children to use the principles when they discuss their work and that of others. Art critics make this their life's work! Using the structural aspect of the language to describe, analyze, interpret, and judge works of art is discuss-ed more fully in the chapter on Teaching Strategies (Module 2).

*Encourage children to use the principles when they discuss their work and that of others.*

Accept the challenge of becoming visually literate. Observe the elements and principles in the world around you. Visit museums and galleries, mindful of these aspects. View your school, classroom, and displays from this perspective. Become aware of your own artistic sensitivities and those of your students. Engage in aesthetic dialogue, judging works of art based on artistic merit and aesthetic use of the structural language.

## Challenges

The artistic challenges found in the structural language of the visual arts relate directly to how well we look, see, touch, and feel. As you scaffold children's learning, they will become increasingly sensitive to the visual aspects of everything around them.

The questions suggested by Engel (1995) are built around these ideas, and as such offer a good starting point for engaging in conversations with children about artwork, either their own or that of another artist (Table 1-1). They also lend themselves well for guiding discussion about the qualities of any other objects that appeal to children. Think, for example, how they might be used to focus a discussion about a children's book, an aquarium filled with fish, or a diorama of a local farmer's market.

Table 1-1. **Descriptive Characteristics in Considering a Child's Artwork.**

| What is it made of? In what context? | What can the observer see? | What does it represent? |
|---|---|---|
| Materials/context, such as:<br>size<br>tools<br>medium<br>techniques<br>at home<br>on a school trip<br>in class | Basic elements [such as]:<br>lines/angles<br>shapes<br>colors/values | Character of communication, such as:<br>design<br>story<br>scene<br>symbol |
| **How is it organized?** | **What is it about?** | **Where does the idea come from?** |
| Aspects of organization/ meaning, such as:<br>perspective<br>composition<br>action<br>point of view<br>completion<br>symmetry<br>overlapping | Function/intent, such as:<br>providing information<br>explaining/investigating<br>expressing feelings<br>entertaining/amusing<br>narrating/recalling<br>experimenting<br>exploring ideas | Sources/origin, such as:<br>imagination<br>observation<br>literature<br>imitation<br>TV<br>conversation<br>assignments<br>"messing about" |

***Note:*** From *Considering Children's Art: Why and How to Value Their Works* (p. 32), by B.S. Engel, 1995, Washington, DC: National Association for the Education of Young Children. Copyright © 1995 by NAEYC. Reprinted with permission.

*Scaffold children's learning so they become sensitive to the visual aspects of everything around them.*

Here are some other ways in which you, and your students, can become more in tune with the artistic elements embedded in your surroundings.

***Take stock***—What is in your visual closet? Look at what you wear and have around your house. Determine which visual aspects are necessary for you to be comfortable. Which do you most respond to and from which do you shy away? Develop a list of reasons for your response by using the art elements to describe your reflections. Does this coincide with the use of elements in your artwork? How can you challenge yourself to experiment and explore other visual aspects of your surroundings?

***Find relevant art works and artists***—Artists consciously and unconsciously explore elements, themes, ideas, concepts, and feelings in their art. Which artists or works of art can be used as examples to highlight an element, principle, or combination of elements and principles of visual organization? Which visual aspects does each artist consistently use? How do these choices enhance the meaning of the artwork?

***Keep a perceptual diary***—Encourage children to find things they respond to in magazines, photos, or objects which attract them. Paste them in their sketch book or begin a perceptual diary, then collect real items to which they respond. Share these regularly. Be conscious of your insights about the children as they share the visual aspects to which they are most sensitive.

**Upon viewing a Jackson Pollock action painting for the first time, a 4-year-old with strong visual and kinesthetic sensitivities remarked with amazement, hands outstretched and absolutely frozen in front of the painting, "I think I've been here before."**

*Figure 1-47.* ***Number 1, (Lavendar Mist),*** 1950. Jackson Pollock, born 1912, American. Oil, enamel, and aluminum on canvas. © Board of Trustees, National Gallery of Art, Washington, D.C. Ailsa Mellon Bruce Fund.

## Reflections

Ask yourself these questions as you ponder the elements and principles of visual language.

- What impact have your experiences made on your visual awareness and sensitivities?
- How can you increase your ability to use and become more aware of the elements and principles of visual organization? How can you share this with students?
- How do you recognize children's ability to demonstrate visual organization?

# MODULE 3
# VISUAL ARTISTRY OF CHILDREN

Because the visual arts are a language, it is imperative that we develop children's visual language abilities. Just as with verbal language learning, there should be visual opportunities:

- to gain experience and become skillful with media and the underlying elements and principles of visual organization
- to interact with adults or other children who can extend and elaborate visual thinking and assist in technical issues
- to experience historical and cultural references which stimulate and extend the context for meaning making
- to use visual language for meaningful communication, insightful interpretation, critical thinking, and creative expression

Teachers and art specialists guide children to become active learners of their culture's visual language. Artistic explorations begin with what children know—they are rooted in their culture and prior knowledge—and then open new doors:

- **technically,** in the skillful use of materials and technique
- **informationally,** in the acquisition of new knowledge, and
- **personally,** in the identification and elaboration of visual thinking and feeling

**The Four Ss Educators Use to Scaffold Children's Learning with *Art as a Way of Learning*®**

- **Support**—responding to children's ideas, feelings, interests, and creative and critical thinking skills
- **Stimulate**—increasing knowledge and understanding, inspiring visual reasoning
- **Stretch**—developing children's artistic imagination and skills in their ability to reflect, respond, and create
- **Spark**—enabling children to discover meaning by building connections among themselves and their ability to see relationships among various knowledge disciplines

> Every child is an artist. The problem is how to remain an artist once he grows up.
>
> – Pablo Picasso



*Artistic explorations begin with what children know, and then open new doors.*

## Development of Artistry in Childhood

Artistry in children is not a straight path, nor is the developmental curve one that easily moves from simple to complex. Gardner (1982) identified a U-shaped progression (Figure 1-48).

*Figure 1-48.* **Progression of artistry development** (Gardner, 1982).

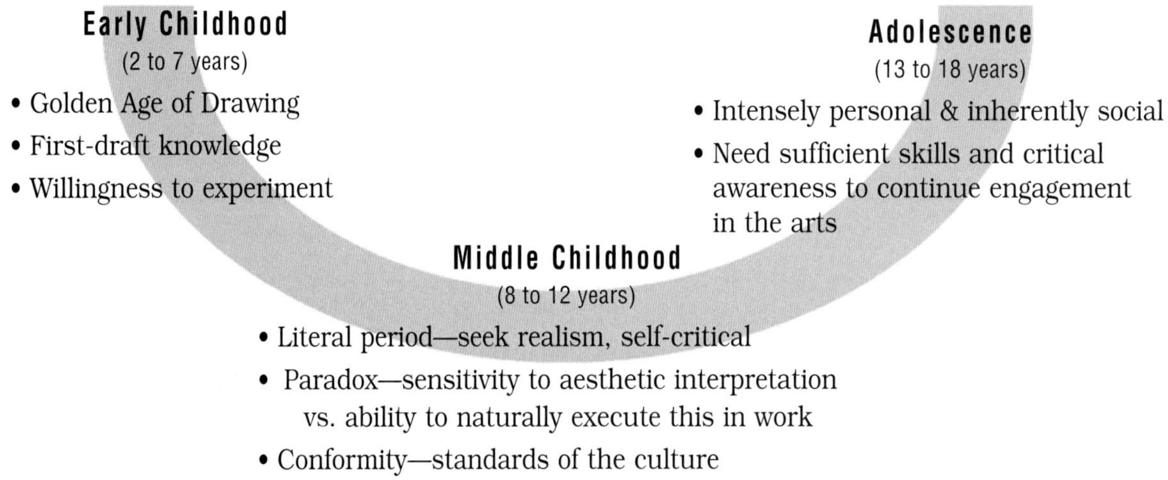


Early Childhood
(2 to 7 years)

• Willingness to experiment
Adolescence
(13 to 18 years)
• Intensely personal & inherently social
• Need sufficient skills and critical awareness to continue engagement in the arts
Middle Childhood
(8 to 12 years)
• Literal period—seek realism, self-critical
• Paradox—sensitivity to aesthetic interpretation vs. ability to naturally execute this in work
• Conformity—standards of the culture

***Note:*** Adapted from *Art, Mind, & Brain,* (p. 86-90), by H. Gardner, 1982, New York: Basic Books. Copyright © 1982 by Howard Gardner. Reprinted with permission.

### Golden Age of Drawing

Gardner (1982) refers to the initial level of children's artistry development (birth through 8 years) as the Golden Age of Drawing. Children's enthusiasm to acquire the structural and functional aspects of art's symbol system are exciting. Many families and teachers remark that, "If I let them, they would draw all day."

This observation highlights the importance of opportunity for young children to explore the rules and functions of the visual language often and through many different types of media. Children's excitement with representation demonstrates their "first-draft knowledge" of many structural aspects of the visual language and their spontaneous, expressive use of aesthetic form.

## Literal Phase

Children's enthusiasm for the visual arts drops as they move into a literal phase of artistic development between the ages of 8 and 12 years. In their quest to master the rules of the language, the results are often stilted, over-stylized drawings. When they compare their work to that of their peers, they begin to feel that they are less able. Many children start to think that they do not have access to the language, and lament "I can't draw."

In light of this shift in children's perceived competence, it is imperative that educators support experiences for children that stretch and refine their skills and move them further into aesthetic, meaningful ways of representation.

*Stimulate, stretch, and refine children's skills. Move them further into aesthetic ways of representation.*

During this period, children's ability to interpret art perceptually and use cognitive reasoning when viewing other work continues to grow. Their ability to understand and assess artwork becomes more sophisticated at the same time that their creative thinking and production seems to be challenged. The guiding roles of both classroom teacher and art specialist remain crucial throughout this sensitive stage of artistic development.

## Adolescence

Adolescents come to "confront firsthand the full range of alternatives in an art form, as well as the peaks of excellence achieved by selected elders and peers" (Gardner, 1982, p.102). Continuation of some form of artistic engagement requires a level of skill and a feeling of competence. Their art, which often has strong personal and social meaning, must demonstrate a self-imposed standard or artistic activity may cease altogether. Opportunity, guidance, and technical skills are prerequisites for entering this fragile period of artistic development.

## Guiding Questions

These guiding questions will help you recognize your artistic development knowledge base and ability to observe children at work with the visual language.

- What do you believe and understand about children's artistic development?
- How are children's interests, skills, and enthusiasm for the visual language supported in your school? Your classroom?
- How has your experience with children at different ages shaped what you know about artistic learning?
- How do children transfer information and skills from art instruction to the classroom?

## Explorations: Characteristics of Children's Artistry

Characteristics of children's artistry—what and how they are learning as they become visual artists (just like they become writers)—can be described in four ways. These four characteristics give us a comprehensive look at the growth of an individual child's visual language, and thus are referred to throughout *Art as a Way of Learning*®.

**Characteristics of children's artistry**

- development and knowing—the pattern of change over time, gained through actual experiences
- artistic learning—the knowledge, skills, and dispositions acquired through instruction
- perception and style—the individual's unique perceptual sensitivities and pattern of learning and creating
- understanding and personal meaning—the ability to convey intention and render experiences intelligible through a representation

### Development and Knowing

Observant adults realize that children constantly demonstrate their knowledge about themselves and their experiences. Patterns of change are related to age, passage of time, and the practical skills gained by experience. Just as one story cannot give a whole picture of a child's writing ability, so too, no one drawing can give a full picture of what a child knows and is able to do visually. However, individual pictures or sculptures may give us an indication of new schemas or visual ideas that are emerging from experience. A set of a child's work collected over time helps us see an emerging developmental picture.

*Figure 1-49.* A child's drawing made in early childhood, during which time children are willing to experiment.

Researchers in children's artistic development have related both two- and three-dimensional artwork (drawings and sculpture) to typical levels of children's cognitive development (Fein, 1993; Gardner, 1980; Golomb, 1992; Kellogg, 1970, 1979; Lowenfeld & Brittain, 1987; Taunton, 1982). Their insights give us a broad picture of what children know and how they use media to demonstrate their knowledge, but they do not prescribe practice.

We know, for example, that young children's visual language is evolving and images are flexible (Figure 1-49). Both need time and opportunity to develop. In middle childhood, children are more constrained by social standards (Figure 1-50), and may be extremely critical of their own work, while appreciating that of others. Share expertise about child development and artistic representation by looking together at children's work. Suggestions for looking at children's work, created over a length of time, are found in *Art as a Way of Learning*® Component Four: Teaching Strategies.

*Figure 1-50.* A child's drawing made in middle childhood, when children are more realistic and conforming to cultural standards.

*Figure 1-51a.* These three drawings (FIgures 1-51a, b, and c) depict one child's work over time, at 4-1/2, 11, and 17 years of age. Notice the impact of artistic learning on his ability to draw and represent realistically.

## Artistic Learning

Some children are able to use the elements and principles of visual organization at an early age and with great success. Often these children are strong visual learners who are naturally observant, or they have had abundant opportunities to learn what the other children are just beginning to experience. Artistic skills, knowledge, and creative dispositions are nurtured and modeled by family members or informed teachers. These experiential differences partially explain the widening artistic gap, found from about age 8 on, between children's abilities to use visual language even at a functional level.

**Many of us in the United States seriously underestimate preprimary school children's graphical capabilities and the quality of intellectual effort and growth it can stimulate.**

**– Lilian Katz (1993, pp. 20-21)**

Ms. Vista and Mr. Angelo (we first met them in the Explorations in Teaching section) were mindful of *Art as a Way of Learning.* They and other good teachers guide students to acquire the knowledge and skills they need to express and communicate their visual ideas. Educators and parents are well aware that children can and should be taught strategies to become increasingly better readers. So too, technical strategies for successful and creative use of materials should be taught.

Challenging questions about content and expression pull children's artistic learning forward (see Figure 1-51). Sometimes teachers are reluctant to assess student's artwork, or to ask students to consider each other's efforts. Such considerations are essential for children to grow in their visual literacy. *Art as a Way of Learning*® art specialists and classroom teachers plan for and assess children's artistic learning as they guide children's perceiving, thinking, and creating. State and national art standards can serve as a guide in the process.

*Figure 1-51b.*

## Perception and Style

Children are highly individual in their perceptions and ability to express ideas and feelings. A child's unique perceptual strengths and style of learning become evident in creative work. Biology, family, culture, and community play major roles in determining what and how children perceive and to what they attend. Calley's and Matthew's paintings, songs, and dances can be as different as paintings by Claude Monet, Diego Riveras, and Aboriginal artists from Australia or movements by Margot Fonteyn, Alvin Ailey, or Balinese dancers!

*Figure 1-51c.*

*Figure 1-52.* ***Lion***, c. 1614. Sir Peter Paul Rubens, 1572-1640. Black and yellow chalk heightened with white. © Board of Trustees, National Gallery of Art, Washington, D.C. Ailsa Mellon Bruce Fund.

Observe children at work and play. You can see differences in the ways they think, move, approach a task, and interact with others. They attend to perceptual aspects and artistic elements differently as well. Josh uses line to show movement, while Arianna chooses color to embellish feelings. Some dramatic differences in artistic style are portrayed in Figures 1-52 through 55.

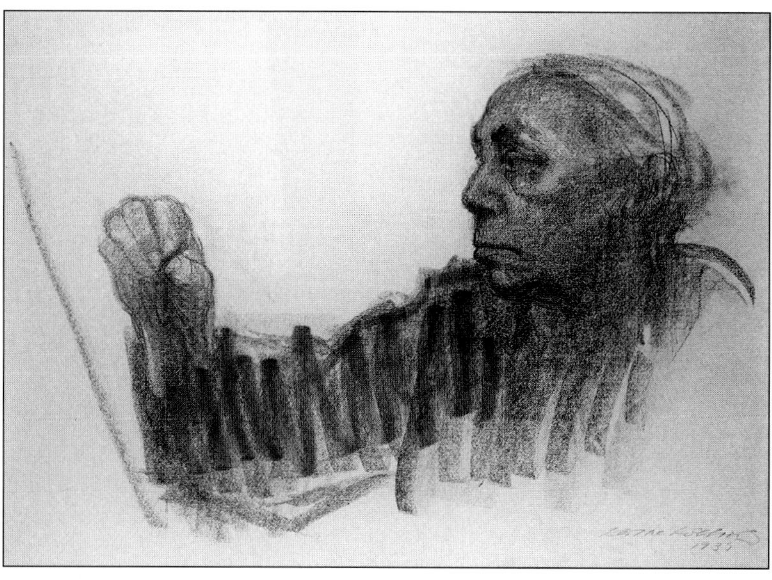

*Figure 1-53.* ***Self-Portrait,*** 1933. Kathe Kollwitz, 1867-1945, German. Charcoal drawing on brown laid Ingres paper. © Board of Trustees, National Gallery of Art, Washington, D.C. Rosenwald Collection.

Gardner's theory of multiple intelligences (1983b) provides an overriding structure for understanding the intelligence strengths individuals bring to learning, knowing, and remembering in the *Art as a Way of Learning*® framework. Learning style models, of which there are many, broaden and inform our abilities to look at how we teach, learn, and understand individual learners, as well as measure our self-knowledge related to how we teach, learn, and understand.

*Figure 1-54.* ***My Bedroom***. Kelsey Fritz, age 7. Tempera paint. Courtesy Crayola® Dream-Makers® Program.

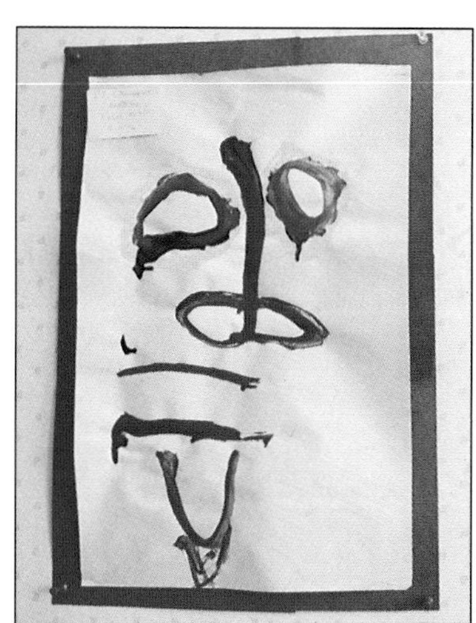

*Figure 1-55.* Preschool child's self-portrait. Northampton Community College Child Development Center, Bethlehem, Pennsylvania.

## Understanding and Personal Meaning

Pablo Picasso's comment that "Once I drew like Raphael, but it has taken me a whole lifetime to learn to draw like children" refers to the expressive, meaningful way in which children use line or color or shape to express an idea or feeling. Picasso could see the depth of understanding in children's marks.

The ability to express the essence of a person, the movement of a bicycle, or the fluffiness of a cat is rooted in prior knowledge, depth of personal understanding, and the ability to visually articulate that knowing. The power to convey intention and render personal experiences through symbolic form is the hallmark of the aesthetic use of language. Through your experiences with *Art as a Way of Learning*®, you will become increasingly skilled in guiding children to find connections, to pose artistic questions, and to value and recognize meaning.

*The power to convey intention and render personal experiences through symbolic form is the hallmark of the aesthetic use of language.*

Children take ownership of knowledge and discover new connections and deeper understanding through visual representation (recall Nicole's sports drawings in Figures E-7 through 13). This process happens as they interact with people who are willing to think together, and by working with various media to discover unique qualities about their knowledge. This self-discovery process requires children to thoughtfully work at something over time and continually evaluate and connect their knowing. This is the process of constructing knowledge, thinking critically, and creating understanding.

### Challenges

If you have not done so before, now is the time to closely observe children at work and look at their efforts with great care. Begin to collect examples that highlight various stages and types of artistic learning, perceptual variations, and individual meaning. Share your discoveries—about children's growing competence with visual language—with their families. This is one of the joys of teaching! Adults see children in a new light. The process validates families' knowledge about their children and demonstrates the value you place on visual language development.

***Collect photos or slides***—Most art specialists already have an extensive collection of children's work. Get tips from your art partner about how to select representative samples and take photos of children's work. Create a system to record different stages of development and use of different media. Share these during back-to-school night and at parent conferences.

***Share thoughts with families***—Through responsive interactions with children, you come to know the unique ways in which they construct meaning. Families often know this about their children, but schools rarely validate their unique perspectives. Every parent wants to know what is special and unique about his or her child. Discuss how you see the child as an artist in your class. Many *Art as a Way of Learning®* teachers have received thank-you notes for sharing that special kind of knowing with families.

***Showcase children's artwork***—How can you validate children's work in a way that communicates its learning value? Begin now to showcase students' artwork. Display it in the community. You'll find it strengthens advocacy for the arts and creates good will.

## Reflections

The ability to learn from children's work increases as you think about what you have observed.

- How does your art partner describe a group of children developmentally? Compare and contrast your thoughts on the same group of children.
- How do you see children's artwork differently now?
- What observations of their work coincide with your beliefs? Which challenge them?
- How will this knowledge change the way you display and document children's learning?
- Consider these stories about how three children solved the developmental challenge on the path to drawing people (Figures 1-56 to 1-59).

**Zak,** age 4-1/2, had a basic way that he drew people (Figure 1-56). Then his uncle engaged him in an observational drawing activity. He and Zak looked carefully at each other and then drew the other's portrait (Figure 1-57). The very next day Zak announced, "I can draw bodies now" and he proceeded to draw a person (Figure 1-58).

When you look at Zak's drawing, what do you think the two of them paid close attention to while looking at each other? What did Zak include in his portrait that is not in his earlier people drawing? What did Zak learn and how did it happen?

*Figure 1-56.* How Zak drew people before interaction with his uncle.

*Figure 1-57.* Zak's observation drawing of his uncle.

*Figure 1-58.* Zak's drawing of a person the next day.

**Andrew** is a beginning reader at age 5, and a strong auditory learner. He makes wonderful mandala designs, but has avoided drawing people. Through step-by-step drawing of birds guided by an adult, he makes the following analogy, "This is just like reading, putting sounds together to make words." After the lesson he moves to the print-making area, draws a person on a Styrofoam™ plate, and prints it.

What did Andrew need to move his learning forward? How was this similar to or different than Zak's?

**Lizzie** is a busy 3-1/2 year old, and spends lots of time playing with her baby doll, Emily. Lizzie's drawings are highly organized line scribbles, and on one occasion she exclaimed, "Baby bed!" She then embarked on a progression of drawings (Figure 1-59), with total absorption, moving from 1) a baby in a bed (#4), 2) a baby behind crib bars under covers (#5), 3) a mommy in a sideways position but without the crib (#6), and 4) a final line design (#7) topped off with an intense sigh before quitting. From then on Lizzie drew people.

How did Lizzie use personal meaning to move development forward? What can you conclude about her learning strengths? What aspects of her artistic ability remained the same? What changed?

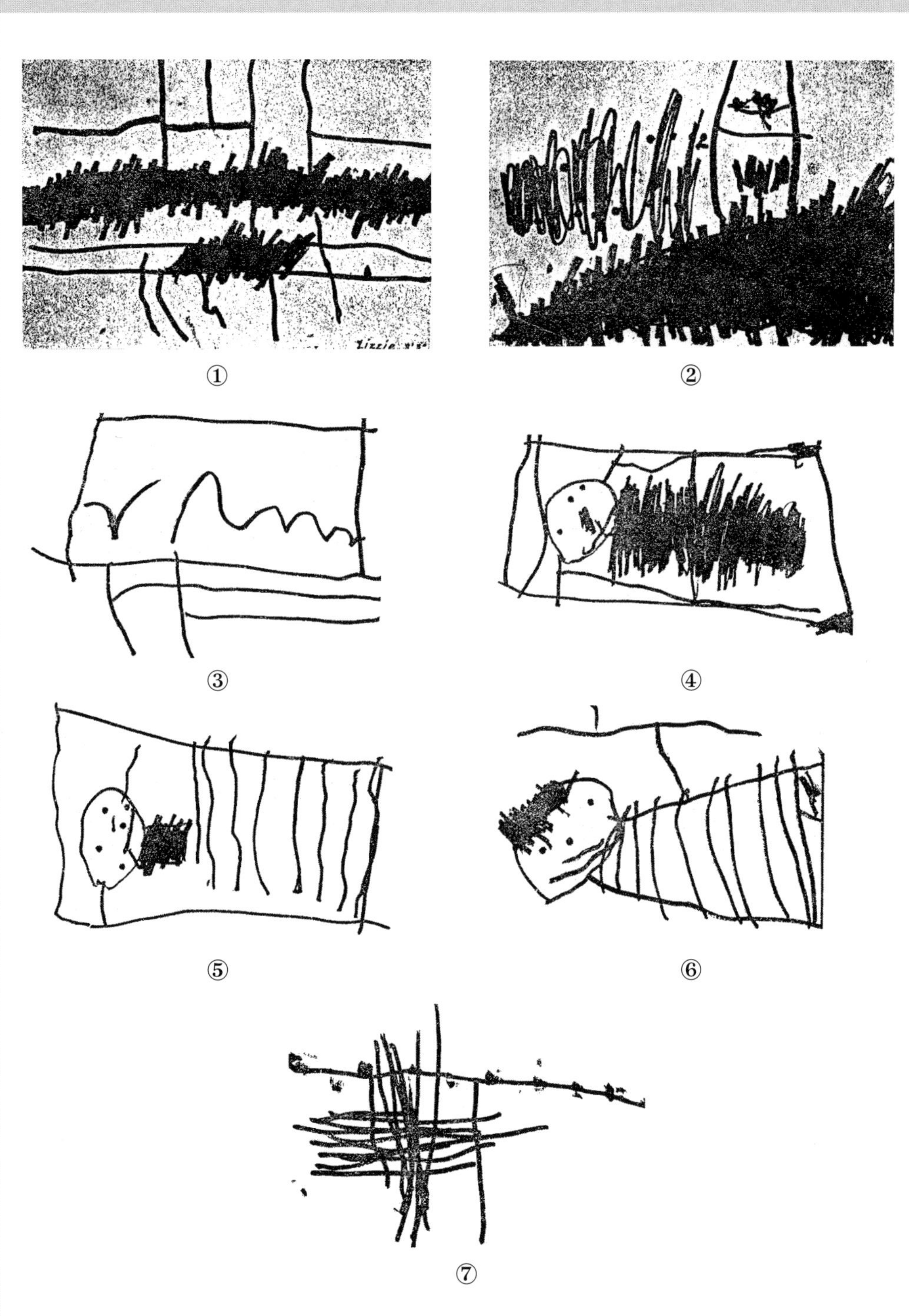

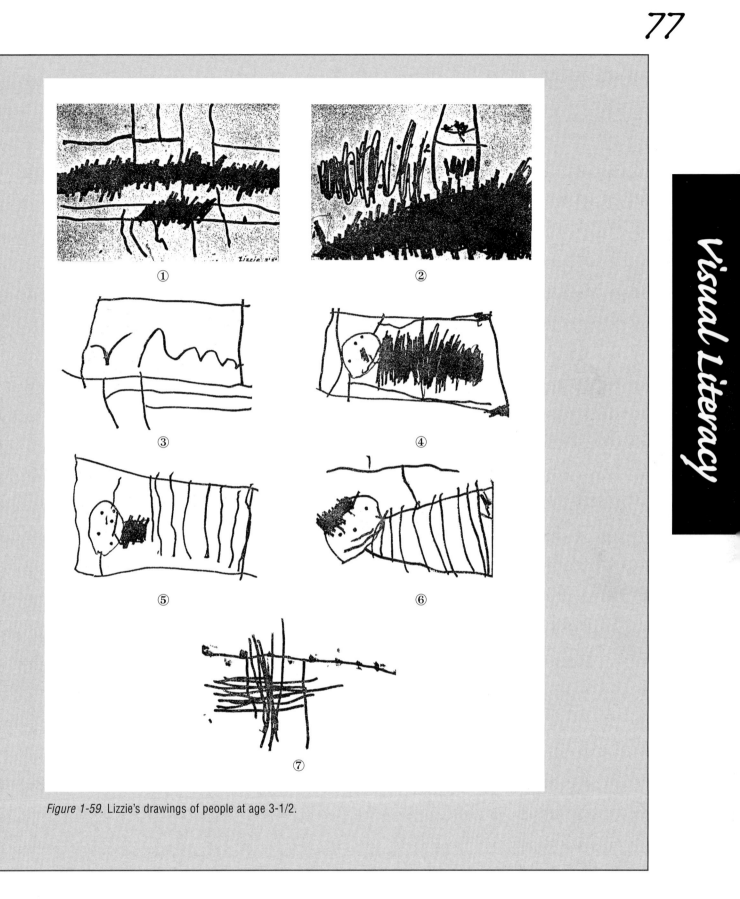

*Figure 1-59.* Lizzie's drawings of people at age 3-1/2.

# MODULE 4
# VISUAL ARTS CURRICULUM DESIGN



Painting is a thundering collision of different worlds, intended to create a new world in, and from, the struggle with one another, a new world which is the work of art. Each work originates just as does the cosmos— through catastrophes which out of the chaotic din of instruments ultimately creates a symphony, the music of the spheres. The creation of works of art is the creation of the world.

—Wassily Kandinsky

Aesthetic content abounds in the curriculum, both in the arts and in the classroom. It is found in every discipline and in every culture. The job of art partners is to find commonalties among the disciplines, to understand each other's areas of expertise, to use creative and critical thinking skills for learning, and to explore aesthetic content with each other and the children.

The possibilities for arts integration are virtually limitless; however, the integrity of the art curriculum and the classroom discipline must be equally valued and maintained. A coherent, sequential art curriculum is an essential requirement for collaborative planning and arts integration. A strong art curriculum is built on the structural, functional, and aesthetic aspects of the visual language and encompasses art production, art criticism, art history, and aesthetic experiences.

Take time to reflect upon the content of your art curriculum within and across grades before you begin collaboration. This is a prerequisite for learning more about each other's daily curriculum, and will ultimately benefit the children.

## Understanding Curriculum

*Value children's unique artistic interpretations.*

*Art as a Way of Learning*® is not an arts curriculum, but rather is a way for teachers, administrators, and art specialists—as partners—to think about curriculum and then to implement ideas with children. Together you plan and organize children's learning in the visual language. The ultimate goals are to (1) design artistic opportunities for children to enhance their understanding, (2) be able to assess children's understanding, and (3) plan learning experiences to guide understanding and personal meaning making.

How do we know if children truly understand? The arts provide unique opportunities for children to demonstrate understanding through their actions. These specific actions provide important links that enable children to transfer their learning to other curriculum areas. When children truly understand art as a visual language, they:

- Can **explain** processes, individual actions, or phenomena in a thorough, substantial manner.
- Can **interpret** works of art by telling meaningful stories or sharing personal images or experiences.
- Can **apply** information, skills, or attitudes to different learning contexts or situations.
- Have **perspective** by looking at something in another way, or taking a critical stance toward an idea or experience.
- Can **empathize** and sensitively perceive and value what others may not see, based on their own prior knowledge.
- Have **self-knowledge** in relation to visual reasoning and artistic behaviors, and are aware of their own personal style and habits of mind (McTighue & Wiggins, 1998).

You can look to a variety of resources and guidelines to determine visual art outcomes and art explorations. These resources assist art specialists in planning curriculum within and across grade levels and provide a solid foundation for artistic learning. Every art specialist should be aware of and have access to the following resources which can inform and shape your art curriculum.

- ***National Standards for Arts Education*** (MENC, 1994) provide broad goals that identify what students should know and be able to do in the visual arts, giving a focus for curriculum, instruction, and assessment.
- All curriculum areas (such as math, science, and language arts) have voluntary standards and educational frameworks that have been developed by national professional organizations. These documents, such as *Reaching Potentials: Transforming Early Childhood Curriculum and Assessment* (Bredekamp & Rosegrant, 1995) are valuable resources for curriculum design. Use them to help identify commonalties in various areas of children's learning.
- **State art education frameworks** are documents prepared by educators and art specialists in your state who have selected and organized instructional content so it relates to your state's curriculum standards. This framework identifies segments of instruction; categories of content; and the depth, breadth, and sequence of art content.
- **School district curriculum guides** for the visual arts and other curriculum areas outline explicit content relevant to your local area's characteristics. These guides typically

describe appropriate teaching methods, materials, equipment, and other resources.

- **Children's interests and ideas** may be the catalyst for curriculum development. Being open and responsive to their questions may lead curriculum into interesting areas of study.
- **Art specialists, classroom teachers, and/or community artists'** expertise and interests are another resource. Art specialists and some classroom teachers have specific areas of art expertise that should be shared with children. Incorporate community artists through artist-in-residence programs to extend your school's artistic knowledge base.
- **Regional resources** often offer unique opportunities for children to explore the arts. Take advantage of museums, local artists, businesses, and raw materials that may be special to your location.

*Value the excitement that comes from individual discovery, collaborative understanding, and artistic production.*

Nearly all of these resources address the language of art and contain a wealth of knowledge and skills to integrate into the curriculum. The National Assessment Governing Board (1994) developed a wide range of authentic assessment tools in the visual arts to evaluate the creating and responding process. This work can also be used to direct your thinking and planning of curriculum.

Explorations throughout *Art as a Way of Learning*® develop skills, attitudes, and understandings related to the structural, functional, and aesthetic aspects of the visual symbol system. Through your experiences with *Art as a Way of Learning*, we anticipate that you will come to value the unique artistic interpretations of each child and the excitement which comes from individual discovery, collaborative understanding, and artistic production.

## Guiding Questions

Examine the content, processes, and types of assessment involved in creating and responding in the visual arts as you review your arts curriculum and begin to design integrated curriculum with your art partner.

- Which standards or resources do you use to build your curriculum?
- What essential questions or enduring understandings do you promote?
- What knowledge and skills are the basis for this discipline, art form, or topic?

- Which cultures, artists, or art works can contribute to our understanding?
- How can you assess and document children's understanding?
- How can you design instruction, guided art explorations, and aesthetic environments to enhance children's learning?

## Explorations: Curriculum Design

The arts, like any discipline, benefit from good curriculum design. McTighue and Wiggins (1998) delineate a backward thinking approach to curriculum development. Using this process assists both art specialists and classroom teachers in building meaningful curriculum in their respective content areas. Follow these steps to design curriculum for your own discipline first. This will be especially helpful when you begin to think together about integrated planning in the next component, Creative Collaboration, Module 3.

## Planning Resources: Identify Desired Results

The **first step** in designing arts curricula is to identify the **key knowledge and skills** students will acquire as a result of their study of a topic or unit. What is it you want children to know and be able to do? Thinking about curriculum backwards takes you away from building your art curriculum around activities and moves it toward more powerful learning. When curriculum is a set of different, albeit interesting, activities, students do

**Visual arts**

- traditional fine arts such as drawing, painting, printmaking, sculpture
- communication and design arts such as film, television, graphics, product design
- architecture and environment arts such as urban, interior, and landscape design
- folk arts such as quilting, tin sculpture, and tie-dyeing
- works of art such as ceramics, fibers, jewelry, works in wood, paper, and other materials

not make connections to other bodies of knowledge nor do they transfer skills from one discipline to another. Identifying the desired results must be the first step to meaningful curriculum design and collaboration.

The visual arts cover a wide range of knowledge and experiences, so it is helpful for art partners to focus students' attention on a specific aspect of the art curriculum, such as media, art style, or a particular culture. During the early childhood and elementary years, the curriculum should explore a range of media and materials, along with a variety of cultures, artistic styles, and themes, thus providing opportunities with all the visual variations in the language.

*Explore a range of media and materials, along with a variety of cultures, artistic styles, and themes.*

**The content of the art curriculum might include study in:**

- Artists
- Art styles
- Art from various cultures
- Themes
- Art forms and media
- Famous art works
- Periods of history
- Aesthetic topics
- Elements and principles of visual organization

> As a class we have been exploring the art form of painting throughout this fall. We began by experimenting with texture and different painting tools, such as our hands, leaves, string, and even corn cobs! We used our art prints to explore aspects of painting, such as color, line, texture, and shapes. We were surprised how quickly the children responded to the various artists and could "read" and interpret to make meaning for themselves individually. Children now openly ask for painting time and talk about ideas for their next painting. Children stand and look at the various works created by their classmates that are hung in our gallery. We are beginning to see their confidence with painting increase, they experiment more on their own, and they easily recognize artistic elements in each other's work.
>
> – Nancy Fogel, toddler teacher, Northampton Community College Child Development Center, Bethlehem, Pennsylvania

Use the accompanying **Art Scan** (Figure 1-60) to identify the range of art content, processes, media, aesthetic, and cultural topics which can be explored during any classroom curriculum theme. Together, select the most salient, appropriate, or aesthetically exciting connections. Doing an Art Scan before beginning a unit of study in the classroom gives you a wide range of ideas with which to engage children. This allows for flexibility and greater inclusion of the arts into children's teachable moments.

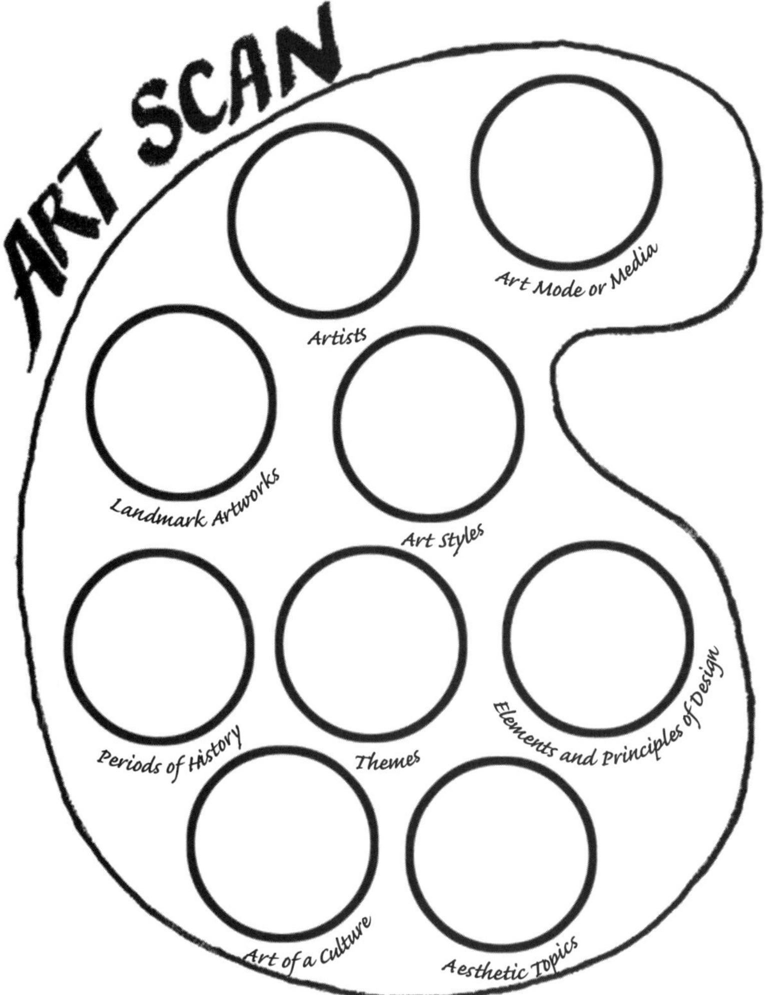


*Figure 1-60.* Art Scan, used to identify the range of topics that can be explored within a curriculum theme.

After you have determined what you want the students to know and do, the **second step** is to select the most **enduring understanding** that you want students to realize for this area of study. An enduring understanding enables students to answer essential questions inherent in the topic. It is something that is important to know as an adult, because it represents a "big idea" with value outside the classroom. Students need to grapple and work with the big idea, which is posed in the enduring understanding, and in doing so they uncover something meaningful.

Professionals in the field (painters, printmakers, weavers, sculptors) pose and solve problems about this understanding. The enduring understanding should result in the design of engaging learning experiences for children, which in turn often lead to other questions or connections (McTighue & Wiggins, 1998). A powerful enduring understanding ties together knowledge and skills and provides a meaningful link for learning.

## Planning Assessment: Determine Acceptable Evidence

You have just identified the outcomes for your area of study. Now, how will you know if the students understand the content and have acquired the skills? The next stage is to determine how you will assess student learning. This is often the last thing teachers think about when planning curriculum. However, there must be a direct relation between outcomes and assessment to determine the success of instruction.

For the arts to be valued both as a discipline and as important learning, the work children do must be assessed. Different kinds of assessment and ways to document learning are introduced in each module of this book. The arts have always assessed understanding through more authentic measures, currently called performance-based assessment. Portfolios, demonstrations, projects, and performances are the hallmarks of arts assessment. These art assessment practices are now being used in many other fields as well.

*If you are using class time for any activity, you should be able to assess its value.*

When planning for assessment, first take into account the characteristics of the learners. Consider children's ages, developmental levels, backgrounds, experiences, and learning types. You must also determine the purpose of assessment, and decide when the assessment method will be used. Children are typically assessed formally at one or more of these times:

*prescriptively*—before instruction beings
*formatively*—during the teaching and learning process, or
*summatively*—at the completion of instruction

Teachers are always assessing student learning, often informally. If you are using class time for any activity, you should be able to assess its value. In *Art as a Way of Learning*®, assessment of both the art and classroom discipline outcomes is an essential part of integrated planning. For both disciplines to be valued, students must be able to demonstrate understanding in each one and in their combination.

There are many interesting and informative assessment methods and ways to organize evaluative criteria (Table 1-2) that can be used in both art and the regular classroom (Beatty, 1998; Council of Chief State School Officers, 1994). Art partners can share these methods and criteria for assessment. Select a variety of performance methods (work samples, portfolios, journals) supplemented by more traditional types of measures (tests or quizzes).

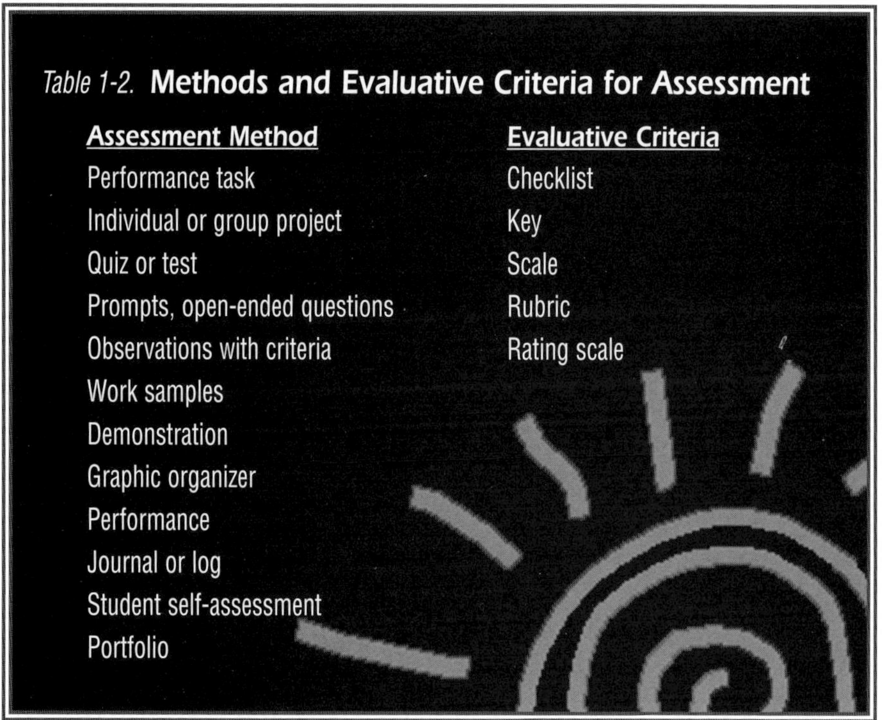

*Table 1-2.* **Methods and Evaluative Criteria for Assessment**

| Assessment Method | Evaluative Criteria |
|---|---|
| Performance task | Checklist |
| Individual or group project | Key |
| Quiz or test | Scale |
| Prompts, open-ended questions | Rubric |
| Observations with criteria | Rating scale |
| Work samples | |
| Demonstration | |
| Graphic organizer | |
| Performance | |
| Journal or log | |
| Student self-assessment | |
| Portfolio | |

Use the information in Table 1-2 to select the types of assessment methods you will use. Then, for each method, choose a corresponding way to organize your evaluative criteria. After that, specify the criteria you will use to evaluate whether students have achieved the previously-selected

- key knowledge and skills and
- enduring understanding.

## Planning Instruction: Guided Explorations and Aesthetic Environment

Now, individually or in collaboration with your art partner, you can begin to think about instruction. Activities are put at the end of the curriculum planning process because a "cool" or "cute" art activity should not drive the curriculum. This approach perpetuates the view of arts as a frill, and diminishes the role of the arts as a core area of study. Also, guided art explorations are more than just an art activity. They are a way to scaffold artistic learning.

There are many exciting, engaging art explorations, but they are only meaningful if they are connected to your outcomes and assessment. After you and your art partner have identified your outcomes and assessment methods, you are ready to create the sequence of learning experiences that will equip students to develop and demonstrate the targeted understanding(s). A sequential list of experiences or a block plan may be a way to demonstrate when and what kinds of instruction will occur.

Your classroom environment must also support this learning. Refer to Component Three, Aesthetic Environment, and select ways to

- *support* communication,
- *stimulate* inquiry,
- *stretch* problem solving, and
- *spark!* imagination.

The modules in the Teaching Strategies Component also contain a variety of ideas.

## Challenges

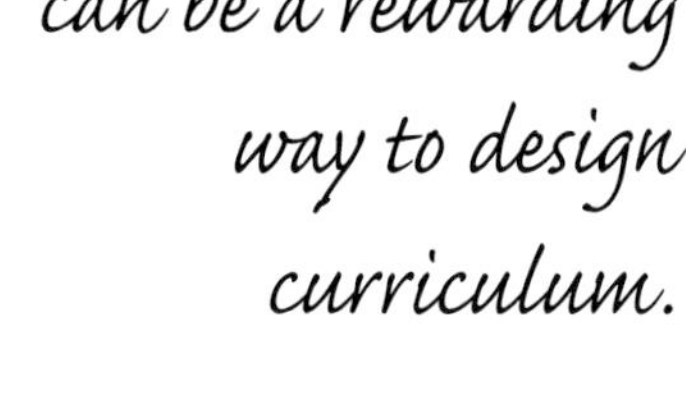
Thinking backwards can be a rewarding way to design curriculum.

Thinking backwards can be a rewarding way to design your own curriculum as well as a model to use in collaborative planning (see Component Two, Module 3 on Collaboration in Action). You and your art partner will want to use Art Scans to explore the aesthetic content and processes of classroom topics more fully. Make the most of the artistic challenges inherent in a topic and to decide upon your strategies for teaching curriculum content in areas such as science and language arts. Work to create curriculum that is built around understandings and is supported by performance assessment and engaging learning experiences.

- Fill in an Art Scan prior to meeting. Share and plan.
- Find the richest art topic to explore, one that will engage children fully in **guided explorations** into the structural and aesthetic use of art.
- Use your curriculum resources to create a coherent curriculum plan.

## Reflections

When classroom teachers, administrators, and art specialists work together, they often find gaps and discrepancies in district and school expectations for the visual arts. You are gaining a unique perspective on using art as a language and tool to develop personal meaning and understanding. Accept the challenge. Make change.

- How is your plan consistent with national, state, and district guidelines?
- What values are reinforced in your school and district in relation to art curriculum?
- What have the two of you learned in planning curriculum this way?
- To which aspects of the curriculum content on the Art Scan do you predict that children will respond with enthusiasm and engagement?

## Bibliographies

### Creative and Visual Thinking

Arnhiem, R. (1969). *Visual thinking.* Berkeley: University of California Press.

Arnhiem, R. (1974). *Art and visual perception.* Berkeley: University of California Press.

Arnhiem, R. (1986). *New essays on the psychology of art.* Berkeley: University of California Press.

Berger, J. (1977). *Ways of seeing.* New York: Penguin.

Berk, L.E. (1996). *Infants, children, and adolescents.* Needham Heights, MA: Allyn & Bacon.

Brosterman, N. (1997). *Inventing kindergarten.* New York: Abrams.

Engel, B.S. (1995). *Considering children's art: Why and how to value their works.* Washington, DC: National Association for the Education of Young Children.

Henri, R. (1923). *The art spirit.* New York: Harper & Row.

Kowalchuk, E. (1996). Promoting higher order teaching and understanding in art education. *Translations From Theory to Practice, 6*(1), 1-6.

Langer, E. (1997). *The power of mindful learning.* New York: Addison-Wesley.

Madeja, S.S. (Ed.). (1983). *Gifted and talented in art education.* Reston, VA: National Art Education Association.

Marks-Tarlow, T. (1996). *Creativity inside out: Learning through multiple intelligences.* New York: Addison-Wesley.

Piirto, J. (1992). *Understanding those who create.* Dayton: Ohio Psychology Press.

Rosenberg, H.S. (1987). *Creative drama and imagination.* New York: Holt, Rinehart & Winston.

Santrock, N.W. (1995). *Children.* Madison, WI: WCB Brown & Benchmark.

Starko, A.J. (1995). *Creativity in the classroom: Schools of curious delight.* New York: Longman.

Sternberg, R.J., & Williams, W. (1996). *How to develop student creativity.* Alexandria, VA: Association for Supervision and Curriculum Development.

Tegano, D.W., Moran, J.D., & Sawyers, J.K. (1991). *Creativity in early childhood classrooms.* Washington, DC: National Education Association.



### Artistic Development

Brittain, W.L. (1979). *Creativity, art, and the young child.* New York: Macmillan.

Cherry, C. (1972). *Creative art for the developing child.* Belmont, CA: Fearon.

Cole, R. (1992). *Their eyes meeting the world: The drawings and paintings of children.* Boston: Houghton Mifflin.

Cox, M. (1992). *Children's drawings.* New York: Penguin.

Dyson, A.H. (1986). Transitions and tensions: Interrelationships between the drawing, talking, and dictating of young children. *Research in the Teaching of English,* 20, 379-409.

Fein, S. (1993). *First drawings: Genesis of visual thinking.* Pleasant Hill, CA: Exelrod Press.

Freeman, N.H. (1980). *Strategies of representation in young children.* London: Academic.

Gardner, H. (1980). *Artful scribbles: The significance of children's drawings.* New York: Basic Books.

Gardner, H. (1982). *Art, mind, & brain.* New York: Basic Books.

Gardner, H. (1983a). Artistic intelligences. *Art Education, 36,* 47-49.

Gardner, H. (1993b). *Frames of mind.* New York: Basic Books.

Golomb, C. (1992). *The child's creation of a pictorial world.* Berkeley: University of California Press.

Goodnow, J. (1977). *Children drawing.* Cambridge: Harvard University Press.

Herberholz, D., & Herberholz, B. (1994). *Artworks for elementary teachers: Developing artistic and perceptual awareness.* Madison, WI: WCB Brown & Benchmark.

Hurwitz, A. (Ed.). (1994). *The arts in their infancy.* Baltimore: Symposium at The Maryland Institute College of Art.

Kellogg, R. (1970). *Analyzing children's art.* Palo Alto, CA: Mayfield.

Kellogg, R. (1979). *Children's drawings, children's minds.* New York: Avon.

Kindler, A. (1995). Significance of adult input in early childhood artistic development. In C.M. Thompson (Ed.), *The visual arts and early childhood learning* (pp. 10-14). Reston, VA: National Art Education Association.

Kindler, A. (1998). *Child development in art.* Reston, VA: National Art Education Association.

Lark-Horovitz, B. (1976). *The art of the very young: An indicator of individuality.* Columbus, OH: Merrill.

Lowenfeld, V., & Brittain, W.L. (1987). *Creative and mental growth* (8th ed.). New York: Macmillan.

National Art Education Association (NAEA). (1995). *Visual arts education reform handbook.* Reston, VA: Author.

Robinson, G. (1996). *Sketchbook: Explore and store.* Portsmouth, NH: Heinemann.

Taunton, M. (1982). Aesthetic responses of young children to the visual arts: A review of the literature. *Journal of Aesthetic Education, 16*(3), 93-109.

Thomas, G.V., & Silk, A.M.J. (1990). *An introduction to the psychology of children's drawings.* New York: New York University Press.

Thompson, C.M. (1990). "I make a mark": The significance of talk in young children's artistic development. *Early Childhood Research Quarterly, 5*(2), 215-232.

Thompson, C.M. (1995b). "What should I draw today?" Sketchbooks in early childhood. *Art Education,* September, 1-11.

Zurmuehlen, C.M. (1990). *Studio art: Praxis, symbols, presence.* Reston, VA: National Art Education Association.

**Curriculum**

Beattie, D.K. (1997). *Assessment in art education.* Worcester, MA: Davis Publications.

Bredekamp, S., & Rosegrant, T. (Eds.). (1992). *Reaching potentials: Appropriate curriculum and assessment for young children* (Vol. 1). Washington, DC: National Association for the Education of Young Children.

Bredekamp, S., & Rosegrant, T. (Eds.). (1995). *Reaching potentials: Transforming early childhood curriculum and assessment* (Vol. 2). Washington, DC: National Association for the Education of Young Children.

Cecil, N.L., & Lauritzen, P. (1994). *Literacy and the arts for the integrated classroom: Alternative ways of knowing.* New York: Longman.

Council of Chief State School Officers, with the College Board and the Council for Basic Education. (1994). *Arts education assessment framework* [prepublication edition]. Washington, DC: Author.

Dunn, P.C. (1995). *Creating curriculum in art.* Reston, VA: National Art Education Association.

Edwards, L.C. (1997). *The creative arts: A process approach for teachers and children.* Upper Saddle River, NJ: Prentice-Hall.

Gardner, H., & Perkins, D. (1989). *Art, mind & education.* Chicago: University of Illinois Press.

Getty Education Institute for the Arts, The. (1985). *Beyond creating: The place for art in America's schools.* Los Angeles: Getty Center for Arts in Education.

Getty Education Institute for the Arts, The. (1992). *The DBAE handbook: An overview of discipline-based art education.* Santa Monica, CA: The J. Paul Getty Trust.

Getty Education Institute for the Arts, The. (1993). *Discipline-based art education and cultural diversity.* Santa Monica, CA: The J. Paul Getty Trust.

Johnson, A. (Ed.). (1992). *Art education: Elementary.* Reston, VA: National Art Education Association.

Katz, J. (Ed.). (1988). *Arts and education handbook: A guide to productive collaborations.* Washington, DC: National Assembly of State Arts Agencies.

Katz, L. (1993). What can we learn from Reggio Emilia? In C.P. Edwards, G. Forman, & L. Gandini (Eds.), *The hundred languages of children: The Reggio Emilia approach to early childhood* (pp. 19-37). Norwood, NJ: Ablex.

McTighue, J., & Wiggins, G. (1998). *Understanding by design.* Alexandria, VA: Association for Supervision and Curriculum Development.

Music Educators National Conference (MENC). (1994). *National standards for arts education.* Reston, VA: Author.

National Art Education Association (NAEA). (1995). *Visual arts education reform handbook: Suggested policy perspectives on art content and student learning in art education, maintaining a substantive focus.* Reston, VA: Author.

National Assessment Governing Board. (1994). *Arts education assessment framework.* Washington, DC: Author.

Thompson, C.M. (1995a). Transforming curriculum in the visual arts. In S. Bredekamp & T. Rosegrant (Eds.), *Reaching potentials: Transforming early childhood curriculum and assessment* (Vol. 2 ) (pp. 81-98). Washington, DC: National Association for the Education of Young Children.

COMPONENT TWO

# Creative Collaboration

## MODULES

- Discovering Your Art Partner
- Ways Administrators Support Collaboration
- Collaboration in Action: Planning for Arts-Integrated Learning
- Developing Arts Advocates: Communicate and Network

# MODULE 1 DISCOVERING YOUR ART PARTNER

A supportive and challenging **art partner**—teacher, administrator, art specialist, artist-in-residence—with whom you can collaborate is essential for *Art as a Way of Learning®* to fully succeed. Your art partner is someone with whom you will stretch and elaborate your professional skills as you plan for children's experiences. The benefits of these partnerships are immeasurable, both for your relationship and for student learning.

Collaboration is an interactive process that enables people with diverse expertise to generate creative solutions to mutually defined problems.
– Idol, Nevin, & Paolucci-Whitcomb (1994, p. 1)

Creative Collaboration

## Finding a Collaborator

Each art partner is expected to contribute equally to the exchange of ideas and techniques, so it is important that partners are willing to share and be open to new challenges. Respect for the ways individuals think and work is inherent in this approach to teaching and learning. Through a respectful, honest exchange of beliefs and expectations you will experience personal and professional growth that will enable you to offer more arts-integrated experiences for children.

*Art as a Way of Learning* partners work as cognitive apprentices, learning about and experiencing more depth within each other's professional domain. As you collaborate, you too will scaffold what you learn, much in the same way children's learning is scaffolded. You will build upon what you already know, and integrate the new knowledge into your work and life.

Each of you is an expert in your own teaching field, and you have some skills relevant to your art partner's area. An attitude of respect and willingness to pose and solve problems together permeates effective partnerships. You will model for and learn from each other, bringing a renewed respect for education, and reawakening the artists within yourselves.

*Respect for individuals is inherent in this approach.*

An administrator, art specialist, classroom teacher, parent, or school board member can initiate the building of an *Art as a Way of Learning* team because art partners may come from many different sources, inside and outside the school.

The best art partner for **administrators** may be a classroom teacher, your school's art specialist, an artist-in-residence, museum personnel, staff at a local arts agency, a college art student, or a student's parent with expertise in art. If your school does not have an interested or available art specialist, community arts organizations may be a source for art partners.

**Classroom teachers and art specialists** might choose as your art partners another teacher or a group of teachers from various grade levels, a librarian, media specialist, or support teacher. Make sure your administrator is involved to facilitate the partnering process by providing common planning time and resources (see Module 3).

Art partners come from inside and outside school.

Wherever you search, the goal is to discover an art partner who is willing to grow with you in a collaborative relationship based on respect and trust. Early childhood programs often need to contact community agencies to identify an art partner and possible funding sources. Local arts councils, museums, or colleges may have someone in their education or art department who would be interested.

Would-be collaborators face a number of challenges. First, of course, you need to find an art partner who wants to try the *Art as a Way of Learning®* approach. Both of you will identify your own gifts and weaknesses in relation to your knowledge and skills in your teaching domain. The next challenge is to work together in ways that lead to true collaboration, while accepting and learning from each other's different teaching, planning, and creating styles.

## Guiding Questions

As you begin to discover how you and your art partner can best use your gifts to grow together, personally and professionally, use the following questions to stimulate your discoveries about each other. Come to your first meeting prepared to ask and answer:

- How would we describe our personal styles? What are our hobbies and interests?
- What are our beliefs about teaching and learning? How do we each like to plan and implement a lesson? How much time do we each have for these processes?
- In which areas of our curriculum knowledge and skills do we each feel strong? In which areas of our curriculum do we each feel weak?
- How best can we share our information and techniques with our collaborator? What do we need to ask each other? What do we need to know as a team to be successful collaborators?

## Explorations: Stages of a Collaborative Relationship

Building a relationship with your art partner is at the heart of *Art as a Way of Learning*®. A good working relationship almost assures success in developing knowledge and skills in each other's areas of expertise.

> Two heads are better than one. As far as I am concerned, I still feel I have a lot of knowledge to learn. However, I feel the collaboration process makes me more daring to try new techniques. Without Louise's expertise, I wouldn't be doing the art in my classroom that I am doing at this point, and the children are the beneficiaries of this new teaching emphasis.
>
> The most significant changes in my teaching are in the implementation of the project approach. We don't do small, isolated studies anymore. We select a rich topic and move through it deeply and completely, looking at all integrated areas. The children decide where we will go with the topic, webbing all our thoughts and questions. We research, read, and study, and of course, the culminating way of demonstrating what has been learned is the art project.
>
> –Mary Richards, first grade teacher,
> Truman Elementary School,
> Salisbury School District, Pennsylvania

### Developing a Collaborative Relationship

New art partners usually go through four stages: coexist, cooperate, coordinate, and collaborate. As you work through these stages, toward true collaboration, you will discover the joy of sharing ideas and planning together to enhance children's learning—and your own professional growth.

**Stages of Partnerships**

- **coexist**—to exist together in the same place and the same time
- **cooperate**—to operate together for a common objective
- **coordinate**—to harmonize or adjust in relation to another
- **collaborate**—to develop a reciprocal relationship working toward the same goal

**Coexist**—In many schools, art specialists, administrators, and teachers coexist, which is the first stage of a partnership (Figure 2-1). Classroom teachers leave the room or drop off the children at the art room door with a cheerful, "Have fun." Teachers and administrators are sociable, yet they do not fully value the learning happening in the school, nor do they share information about children's experiences. They simply coexist.

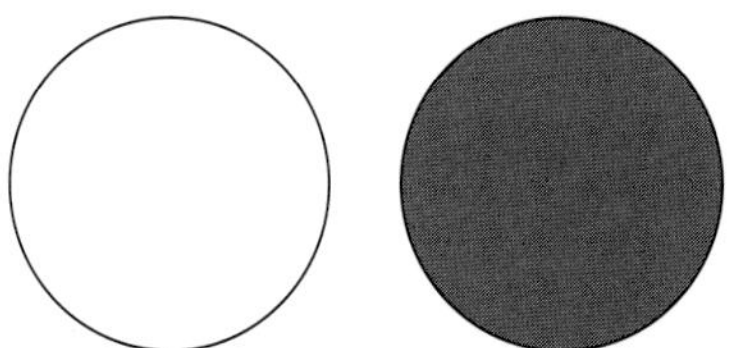

*Figure 2-1.* ***Coexist***—the first stage of a partnership.

**Cooperate**—When professionals begin to see some value in each other's skills or knowledge, they are open to the second stage—cooperation (Figure 2-2). At this level, there is a minimal amount of one-way sharing. Administrators may support art pro classroom, and the classroom teacher usually cannot seem to stimulate as much creativity with children as the art specialist does, this is an important level in the formation of a partnership because trust and respect are developing in each exchange.

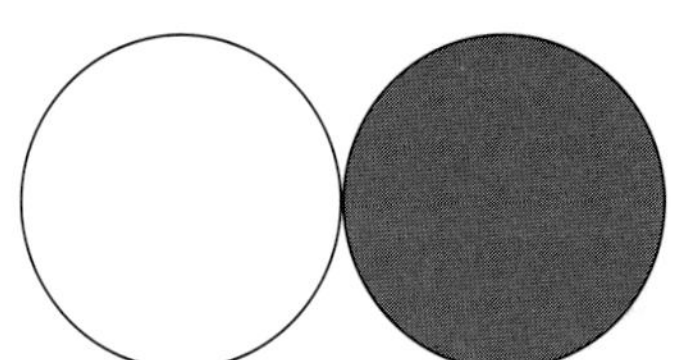

*Figure 2-2.* ***Cooperate***—the second stage of a partnership.



**Coordinate**—The third level of partnerships is the most time-consuming stage. Coordination begins as the art partners start to harmonize their work (Figure 2-3). Time is needed to share ideas, values, goals, and feelings while discovering each other's strengths. This stage is exciting because educators discover the commonalties in their disciplines, find a true partner in the process of teaching, and build a supportive relationship. Teachers, administrators, and art specialists at this stage will find renewed interest and enthusiasm for education and their relationship.

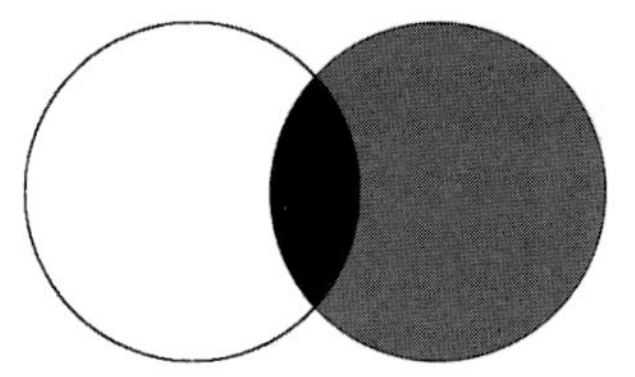

*Figure 2-3.* ***Coordinate***—the third stage of a partnership.

**Collaborate**—The highest stage of working together is collaboration (Figure 2-4). A relationship is established and the dialogue focuses on children's learning and ways to enhance each art partner's work. Team collaboration allows teachers, administrators, and artists to build curriculum together. Children easily work with the knowledge and skills of various disciplines, so learning is connected, meaningful, and powerful. The enthusiasm for collaboration is contagious, and spills out into the school and community.

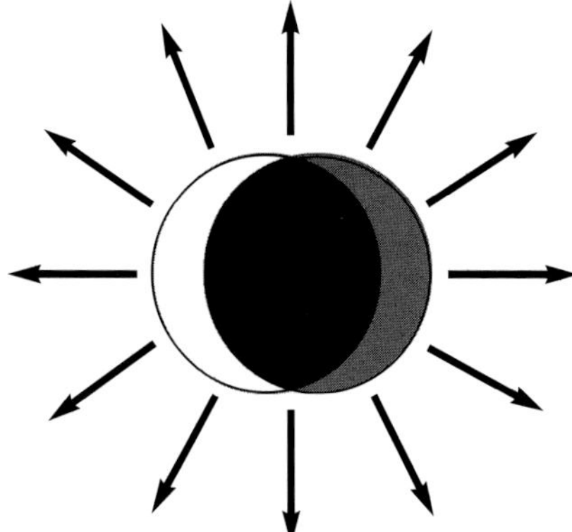

*Figure 2-4.* ***Collaborate***—the highest stage of a partnership.

The following description of an actual relationship looks at each partnership level and at the challenges both art partners (Figure 2-5) faced as they restructured their teaching and learning.

## Our Collaborative Journey

*Figure 2-5.* Louise and Mary are experienced collaborators. You, too, will discover the joy of sharing ideas and planning together to enhance learning for children.

The goal of our collaboration as first grade teacher (Mary Richards) and art teacher (Louise Cosgrove) was to integrate art across the curriculum and increase the use of visual expression.

Prior to our collaborative efforts, we coexisted in isolation. We both felt responsible for what took place in our own classrooms, yet we didn't value the learning that was going on in the other person's classroom. There was no awareness of connections that were possible across the curriculum. We didn't really share information about the children or their learning. We never used each other as resources. Mary would simply drop her students off at the art room door and say, "Have fun!" (Louise never actually knew whether that was meant for her or the students.) Then Mary would return to her classroom for a prep period.

So, what brought about a change? In our first year of *Art as a Way of Learning*® we started asking each other, "What do you teach?" Through that beginning dialogue, our stage of making connections developed. We met primarily at the end of the school day, but often on our own time. We got on each other's turf, meeting in the classroom and the art room. Our first collaborative effort was a combination of social studies (Native American Indians), language arts (experience stories), and art (illustrating the text). All were combined in a book that was read by the children to a kindergarten class. The project actually traveled back and forth from the first grade room to the art room as it was being created.

While making connections like this, we woke up to the fact that we needed a lot more education in each other's content area. This became the most time-consuming stage as our learning became more in-depth. Mary stimulated the children's interest by having them generate a web of prior knowledge on a particular topic. She asked Louise, "How can art be used to teach this unit? What are ways I can incorporate art in this unit?" Louise asked, "What do you expect children to know and be able to do at the conclusion of this unit?"

Mary's visual art literacy increased through dialogue with Louise, as Louise learned more about the curriculum in science, math, social studies, and language arts. Mary initiated an arts center in her classroom. It integrated a math theme, incorporating art prints that evidenced geometric patterns, basic shapes, and symmetry to stimulate the wondering process. The art center, with its hand-on activities, became another place to stretch learning, as children constructed and demonstrated their knowledge. Learning was also supported with other resources such as artifacts, supplies, and reference books. Louise modeled techniques and terminology for Mary and the children, and they began to use art vocabulary in both classrooms.

Many projects were developed that traveled between what we now refer to as our "lab" classrooms. Along with intensive coordination, we realized the value of an assessment component. This necessitated the need for our presence in each other's classrooms, periodically "child-watching" and conducting one-on-one interviews to spark thinking, trying to document all we could. At the same time, we were committed to a philosophy of modeling metacognitive thinking skills that focused on work in progress. This was an exciting stage because we discovered the commonalties in our disciplines while building a wonderful, supportive relationship.

The stage of collaboration is still being fine-tuned. Nearly every art lesson links various content areas with the national standards for the visual arts. Art is being used as an integral component in building a classroom curriculum that supports all areas. This collaborative process now allows for full exploration of a topic or theme, providing a unique form of communication and demonstration of learning. Our reciprocal relationship has established ways of maximizing and enhancing teaching as children share knowledge and skills between our classrooms.

## P.S. Reflections on a Journey...

Do art partners for collaboration need to have the same teaching and learning style? Or do opposites attract? Mary is an extrovert. Louise is an introvert. Mary is bubbly; Louise is quiet. And yet we demonstrate a willingness to share ideas, are open to suggestions, show flexibility, and have an unabating enthusiasm for our work. Louise values her partnership with Mary because she no longer feels isolated as an art specialist. Mary has gained immeasurable confidence in working with art materials and knowing how to look at and talk about art with her students. In building this relationship, we feel secure in fostering attitudes of collaboration because we don't push or own ideas, but dialogue and choose techniques and concepts that we are comfortable with.

We found it was okay to be a physical teaching presence in another teacher's classroom; that it's okay to be a risk taker; that it takes time to change. We learned to be patient and to start with baby steps and take one thing at a time, reflecting and assessing constantly. And the journey continues....

–Mary Richards, first grade teacher;
Louise Cosgrove, art teacher,
Truman Elementary School,
Salisbury School District, Pennsylvania



**Nothing is as empowering as making change happen, the change that you own and champion.**

**–Unknown**

## Challenges

Your challenge for this module is to identify your art partner and begin to collaborate. For the relationship to work, both of you must be willing to make allowance for differences in how you think, work, and feel. You each will learn from your art partner and expand your repertoire of personal and professional behaviors.

*Learning is connected, meaningful, and powerful.*

***Twenty Questions***—Whether you already have a friendly relationship or are just beginning to work together, here is a fun way to begin to share. Design a set of questions related to art, children, and teaching to ask each other over a cup of tea or soda. Consider questions such as: Who is your favorite artist? What is it about her or his work that you love? Describe an environment which makes you feel and work creatively. How would your students describe you as a teacher? How do you learn best?

Make your questions fun and funny. They will break the ice and begin to give you insight into the wonderful things you will learn from your relationship.

***Thoughtful Questions***—Assessment in the Creative Collaboration component consists primarily of taking time to reflect and discuss ideas with your art partner, administrators, and community resource people. Frame your questions to "explore the possible" and initiate trust, respect, and two-way communication. These open-ended and thought-full (full of thought) questions set a tone for communication that can open your minds to the potential in *Art as a Way of Learning*®.

***Time Is on Your Side***—There never seems to be enough of this precious commodity, so schedule time on a regular basis to ensure a good start for the collaboration. Arrange your schedules so collaboration is consistent and easy for both art partners. Administrative support is critical to make the scheduling process go smoothly. Be creative to find time.

- Eat lunch together and discuss plans.
- Call each other at home at a set time each week.

- Send outlines back and forth with student messengers moving between your classes. Give them an important name.

***A Picture Is Worth a Thousand Words***—Create a sculpture, collage, print, or painting which demonstrates the partnering relationship. How do you see yourself, your art partner, and your relationship? Capture your levels of change visually.

> I used to be concerned that if I taught classroom teachers what I knew, they wouldn't need me as much and when the budget cuts came ... I'd be gone. But just the opposite happens. When the entire school is focused on art, and classroom teachers, parents, and administrators realize the importance of art as a special discipline and as a tool for teaching all subjects, the art budget is the last line item that could get cut. I've taught a team of converted believers who will fight every battle with and for me, to save the arts in school.
>
> –Jane Oplinger, visual art specialist,
> Resica Elementary School,
> East Stroudsburg, Pennsylvania

## Reflections

Learning to work with a collaborative partner takes time and effort. It means learning to do some things differently or seeing some things from another perspective. Assess your progress by asking yourselves:

- Were we able to feel comfortable finding a common ground for planning? Were we able to discuss our time constraints and come up with a plan with which we could both live?
- Could we identify ways that we could complement each others' weaknesses and strengths?
- What areas do we need to work on to become successful collaborators?

# MODULE 2
# WAYS ADMINISTRATORS SUPPORT COLLABORATION

by Greg Naudascher

**Administrators need to support teachers' co-planning and co-teaching and rework schedules to foster collaboration.**

**–Greg Naudascher, principal, Resica Elementary School, East Stroudsburg, Pennsylvania**



Each school's instructional program holds a unique potential to integrate the arts in the curriculum. Building principals and early childhood program directors—all of whom are administrators—make it possible to turn this potential into opportunities for learning. This module is addressed to administrators who oversee educational programs for children ranging from the early years in child care and Head Start through elementary school.

## Administrators Articulate the Vision

As an administrator, you are in a position to establish the overall vision of *Art as a Way of Learning*®. In your work with teachers, children, families, and the community, you articulate this vision daily, developing an environment for advocacy that:

- emphasizes the centrality of the arts
- identifies and allocates resources
- assesses and evaluates the effectiveness of the vision's implementation in the aesthetic environment

Administrators who perceive the arts as a multifaceted vehicle for student learning are most likely to encourage staff to match instructional strategies to students. Your commitment to include the arts as an equal element in the curriculum may require significant changes to enhance, not replace, programs already in place. As teachers use the arts to broaden children's learning opportunities, they in turn empower students with a variety of tools and languages with which to demonstrate and express their knowledge.

*Turn your school's potential into opportunities for learning.*

### Guiding Questions

Administrators seeking to support teacher collaboration for integrating the arts are encouraged to consider these questions:

- What are our basic goals for staff development? How are these goals integrated into the current program and staff responsibilities?

- What support systems will staff need in addition to their formal participation in *Art as a Way of Learning*®? What resources–time and funding–are needed to assure full involvement? What community resources–organizations, artists, partnerships–are possibilities? What budgetary concerns are relevant?
- How can our school reflect the vision of *Art as a Way of Learning*? How can administrators publicly support the importance of the aesthetic environment? How do displays of students' work demonstrate learning that stretches and stimulates both doer and viewer? How can we spark a sense of aesthetic awareness in our building?

*Encourage staff to match instructional strategies to students.*

## Explorations: Administrators as Arts Advocates

Your work as an administrator means that you are a curriculum leader. You assure that staff development is an ongoing process, develop a schedule to enhance collaborative efforts, and identify curricular links–all of which are part of arts advocacy. When you identify and allocate resources, you empower teachers and specialists who are striving to do the best job possible. Your ultimate goal as an advocate of *Art as a Way of Learning* is to communicate its aesthetic, artistic, and learning results to parents and community. As these changes unfold with your leadership, the curriculum is transformed.

> As I walk into classrooms or through the hallways, I can gain an incredible sense of what's happening by looking at the display of students' work. Seeing their projects, artwork, writing, etc., everywhere you look, says that the building is alive, a learner-friendly place, where children have many different opportunities to show what they know.
>
> –Greg Naudascher, principal,
> Resica Elementary School,
> East Stroudsburg, Pennsylvania

### Orchestrating an Arts-Friendly Environment

Collegial interaction among staff—talking, planning, sharing knowledge and skills, organizing ideas and resources—unleashes creative energy. As the principal or program director, more than any other individual, you are responsible for orchestrating professional interactions. In doing so, you send the clear message that

*Collegial interaction among staff unleashes creative energy.*

The morale and creative energy in this building have improved tremendously! I sense that the teachers have become learners again, open to sharing ideas, successes, and questions. My specialists contribute their expertise freely in staff meetings and are sought out as resources. There is energy right down to the last day of school; planning has already spontaneously begun for next year.

–Greg Naudascher, principal,
Resica Elementary School,
East Stroudsburg, Pennsylvania



inclusion of the arts is a real instructional priority, not merely something to do if time and resources allow. You play three key roles in the process: to encourage staff development, to help identify curricular links, and to schedule shared planning time.

### Encourage Staff Development

Seek out resources and opportunities for staff to add to their knowledge about the potential for the arts to enhance curriculum for a broader range of learners. In the process, you will forge strong connections with community resources in the arts, education, business, and other areas.

Keep the staff development process focused and regular, attuned to and responsive to teachers' needs. As you facilitate their ability to reach students through the arts, consider your overall staff development goals, program demands, time and funding resources, and support systems. Investment in sound staff development initiatives will pay off not only for teachers, but the entire learning community.

*Figure 2-6.* (detail of Figure 2-7 sculpture) Although primarily an arts residency, this work coincided with the first grade language arts unit entitled "Scared Silly." Three-dimensional skills coupled with creative expression make this a powerful and imaginative sculpture.

*Figure 2-7.* This sculpture, done with first graders, was a collaborative effort between artist-in-residence Jonathan Hertzell and art teacher Jane Oplinger, Resica Elementary School, East Stroudsburg, Pennsylvania. Hertzell incorporated his sculpture with the children's to create a new work of art.

## Identify Curricular Links

Successful integration of the arts in education depends largely upon the ease with which teachers can grasp connections between the arts and other areas of the curriculum. You can facilitate the linking of the arts within the curriculum by making sure that staff have a generic framework with which to conceptualize these connections.

The curriculum planning outlines included later in Component Two of *Art as a Way of Learning®* are models, but it is important that teachers and art specialists design their own planning format. Their framework will establish a common language and approach to including the arts.

*Art partners design their own planning format.*

Encourage teachers to approach curriculum restructuring in a way that is realistic, perhaps by one core unit at first. Initially limiting the scope of arts integration gives participants an opportunity to collaborate with less chance for burnout.

Classroom teachers and art specialists will approach the planning process with very different perspectives. Many classroom teachers will be uncertain of their ability to integrate various media, techniques, and concepts, while art specialists may face a body of skills and content that may be unfamiliar. The wise administrator adopts a motto of "Slower is better ... less is more."

## Schedule Shared Planning Time

Most classroom teachers typically approach inclusion of the arts with some reservation. They may seek the support of colleagues who are formally trained in the arts or have more experience integrating the arts in their curricula. Art specialists have the expertise in their discipline, but may not informed as to the learning outcomes required and subject matter content taught in the regular classroom.

**It is possible to carve out time together. It is easier and more productive when the administration is supportive and schedules time for teachers to plan with specialists.**

**–The consensus of art specialists and classroom teachers at Resica Elementary School, East Stroudsburg, Pennsylvania**

Some schedule juggling may be necessary to assure that teams have time to plan together. Creative collaboration is most effective when shared planning time can take place on a regular schedule within the school day. Groupings for shared planning time are based on a combination of factors including partnerships, individual function, expertise, and personality.

One way to free up grade-level planning time is to consolidate specialists' (art, music, physical education) assignments. If itinerant art specialists are involved, cooperate on scheduling with fellow administrators in other buildings.

## Allocating Arts Resources

Every teacher in your building is concerned about the budget and how resources will be doled out. *Art as a Way of Learning*® may bring new requests, but it also provides systems of communication and a shared vision to facilitate the allocation of resources for learning. Administrators play a pivotal role in making sure resources are allocated in ways that promote children's learning.

### Involve Teachers in the Budget Process

When classroom teachers begin to integrate the arts, you may need to make changes in how and what materials are ordered. Requests for art items, media and visuals, and reference sources are likely to increase, so both classroom teachers and art specialists must be involved in the materials selection process.

*Encourage classroom teachers and art specialists to make joint decisions on resources.*

Art specialists often voice concern that there will be a drain on art supplies as classroom teachers diversify their instructional planning to integrate arts-related activities. Therefore, it is important that you establish a budget planning process that encourages classroom teachers and art specialists to make joint decisions on resources. Grade-level teams that use the same themes should also be encouraged to work together on budget requests. When teams of classroom teachers and specialists collaborate, they find that resources can support each other's programs, rather than compete with each other.

As teachers begin to enhance children's learning through integration of the arts, administrators:

- Allocate sufficient funds to balance materials available to classroom teachers and art specialists.
- Share your budget restructuring thinking with staff as early as possible. Schedule staff planning sessions and make catalogs and ordering information available.
- Distribute and store materials so they are readily accessible. Shared resources, such as art history books, prints, courseware, and specialized media should be stored in central locations with a method to ensure their accessibility and circulation.

### Plan Artist-in-Residence Programs

Artist-in-residence programs can be a stimulating addition to your school. Artists who may not be a part of the staff are often available for a limited time. These artists or performers offer classroom teachers and specialists the opportunity to work with an allied professional to implement unique art experiences that can greatly enrich children's learning.

There are three types of collaborative residencies:

- **Classroom residency**—Artist collaborates with classroom teacher or grade-level teams to connect residency to classroom content.
- **Arts residency**—Collaboration between the art specialist and visiting artist is driven by art curriculum (Figures 2-6 and 2-7). Connections may or may not be made to classroom curriculum.
- **Integrated arts residency**—Usually the most comprehensive. The artist, art specialist, and classroom teachers work as a team to design an arts-integrated thematic unit involving all partners (Figure 2-8).

You will want to make sure that the activities and goals of the residency are closely linked to your school's long-term instructional goals. Build in plenty of time for artists and staff to share their expertise and plan for integrated experiences for children.

*Figure 2-8.* Maxwell Donkur, artist-in-residence from Ghana, Resica Elementary School, East Stroudsburg, Pennsylvania. Artists- or performers-in-residence can greatly enrich children's learning and collaborative teaching.



### Establish Partnerships in the Arts

Community partnerships have the potential to expand your school's resources, increase staff development, fund residencies and arts programs, acquire additional materials, and gain access to community arts resources. Your primary roles as an administrator who recognizes the value of the arts are to foster an attitude of receptiveness for seeking support and to develop rapport with community groups.

*Foster an attitude of receptiveness for community support.*

In addition, get to know local, state, and national arts resources. Encourage membership and participation, and get involved yourself. Your connections might include:

- PTA/PTO projects
- University professional development programs
- Business partnerships
- Local, state, and national arts organizations

## Communicating Aesthetic, Artistic, and Learning Results

Your building's environment and each classroom's decor confirm your school's values and beliefs about learning. Administrators communicate strong messages about the value of visual learning by encouraging the prominent display of students' artwork. This visual link helps communicate essential, yet sometimes intangible, components of learning such as sensory learning, visual thinking, observation, comprehension, and reflection, all of which are components of students' knowledge.

You will find that displays of student work frequently enable teachers and families to reflect upon an individual students' learning, as well as the whole class's accomplishments. Some of these achievements may not be fully demonstrated through conventional writing or discussion. Students realize a sense of success as individuals and members of a classroom community. In addition, displays of students' work can act as a catalyst for other teachers to generate ideas, broadening their repertoire of instructional strategies (see Aesthetic Environment, Component Three).

We realize that your administrative functions and responsibilities are demanding, and that you face a daily challenge to maintain a sense of the learning that is going on in the school. By actively encouraging teachers and students to demonstrate their knowledge through displaying artwork, you implement a powerful tool for continually assessing learning.

*Figure 2-9.* Encourage the prominent display of students' art explorations to communicate essential components of learning. Japanese scroll paintings, watercolors, Resica Elementary School, East Stroudsburg, Pennsylvania.

## Challenges

Your flexibility and leadership are essential to create an artistic vision for your school. Review the research by Bray and Pinciotti (1997) about the impact of teaching on an arts-integrated curriculum that is reported in the Explorations section of this guide. Find resources such as these to support you in your efforts to improve children's educational progress.

***The Big Picture***—Write a vision of what you would like to see happen in your school with implementation of *Art as a Way of Learning*®. List three initial steps toward your vision and share these with your staff to obtain their comments.

***Wish Upon a Star***—Start an *Art as a Way of Learning* dream list. This may include new facilities, more resources, and unlimited time. Periodically review your list and compare it to possible opportunities in the district, community, state, or regional level. Dreams do come true!

***A Research Agenda***—Create a partnership with a local college or university to conduct research. Examination of the changes that take place is likely to validate your staff's growth and children's learning. Research could look at teachers, families, and children, and even the overall changes in the use and look of your facilities (Arts Education Research Agenda for the Future, 1994).

***Create Partnerships***—The collaborative model extends to principals and program directors, too. The more ways you discover to support your educational program and stretch your resources, the stronger it will become.

***Roll Out the Carpet***—Take every opportunity to promote your arts-integrated program by inviting visitors to your school and sending information about events, performances, and student successes to newspapers and local businesses. You never know who will take notice.

## Reflections

Reaching your administrative goals with *Art as a Way of Learning* takes time, so regularly evaluate what you have done and what still needs to be accomplished by reviewing these assessment questions.

- How realistic are our goals for staff development? How are these goals being integrated into the program, considering the responsibilities the staff already handle? What are some additional support systems we can seek?
- Do staff have ample time to develop *Art as a Way of Learning*? What funding sources support development of this program? Are we staying within our budget? What community resources—organizations, artists, partnerships—support the program, both in time and funding?
- How does our learning environment reflect *Art as a Way of Learning*? Do we display students' work as evidence of learning? Are we on schedule for introducing a firmer sense of aesthetic awareness in our building?

MODULE 3

# COLLABORATION IN ACTION: PLANNING FOR ARTS-INTEGRATED LEARNING



"There can be no curriculum development without teacher development and therefore no curriculum development without institutional change."

– Helen Simons (in Bressler, 1993, p. 33)

A survey of 949 art educators conducted by Binney & Smith Inc. at the National Art Education Association conference in 1993 yielded the following information:

- 85% of the respondents do some type of collaboration with classroom teachers
- 81% would like to do more art-based activities

These results demonstrate both interest and commitment on the part of most art educators to work with classroom teachers.

> My collaboration with Mary has impacted me in a tremendous way. Working so closely with her has shown me the vast scope of work she does with her students. I never realized how much is covered in a classroom and the many ways I could plug into her curriculum. We put a great deal of time into collaborating to meet the needs of our students and because it really enhanced our teaching.
>
> Now I see collaboration as imperative. If I don't connect my content with the classroom teachers, I won't know if what I am teaching is even relevant to what the students need. How could I expect students to transfer and apply what they are learning from me into any meaningful context in their lives? Now I enrich their understanding of their world, because I am more informed about their world.
>
> –Louise Cosgrove, art teacher,
> Truman Elementary,
> Salisbury School District, Pennsylvania

## Sharing Planning and Teaching

*Take time—to talk, plan, and share knowledge and skills.*

The *Art as a Way of Learning*® approach is based on collaboration among classroom teachers, administrators, and art specialists. The key to its success is taking time—to talk, plan, and share knowledge and skills; to organize ideas, materials, and resources; and to assess and document outcomes for all participants. The entire collaboration process is depicted in Figure 2-10.

*Figure 2-10.*
**Planning, Implementing, and Documenting.**

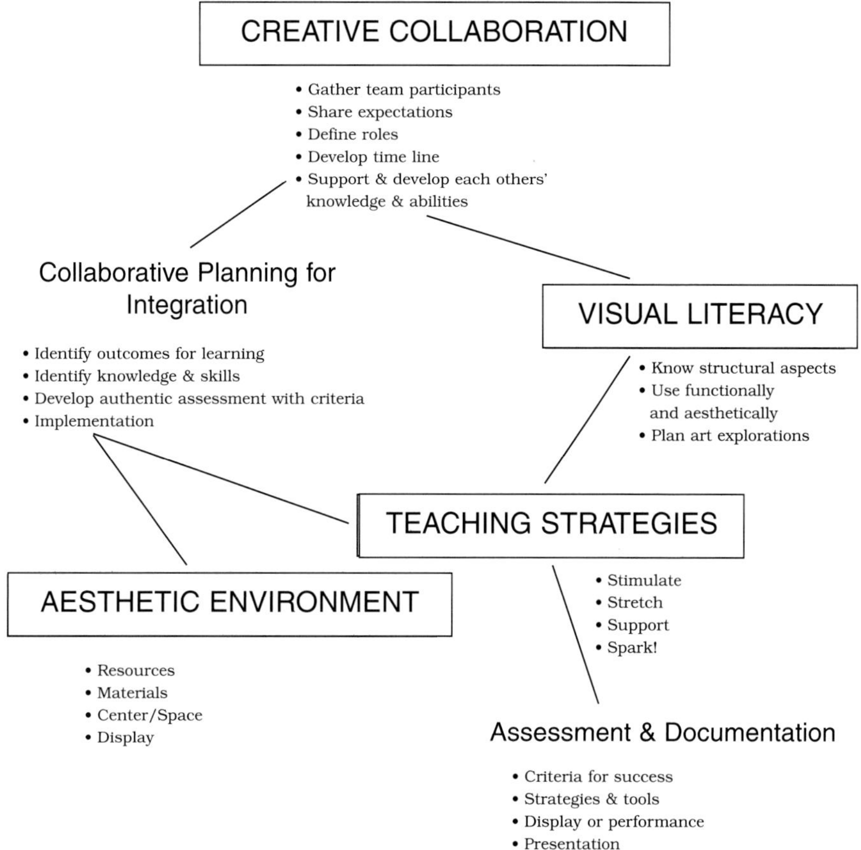




In our vision of creative collaboration, art partners who work with groups of children share ideas and responsibilities for teaching and planning activities that integrate the arts in a meaningful way. Initially this may consume a fair amount of time, but as communication lines are established and you become comfortable with and confident in each others' abilities, planning time becomes shorter and more productive. Children become more fully engaged as learners.

In order to plan well collaboratively, it is helpful to start with a common language, a place to begin, and some basic planning strategies. This module, therefore, includes a set of Curriculum Planning Frames (Figure 2-11) and an Integrated Arts Curriculum Planning Form (Figure 2-15).

*Clarify your separate curriculum outcomes and connect them in a comprehensive plan.*

The **Curriculum Planning Frames** urge you to look at the four ways the arts can be integrated into the curriculum. Consider children's experiences and ideas, aesthetic connections, and what you want them to know and be able to do. Incorporate curriculum standards and guidelines, from the national recommendations to your local curriculum.

As you integrate the arts with *Art as a Way of Learning*®, you are likely to further explore the constructivist model of learning. The **Integrated Arts Curriculum Planning Form** provides places for you and your art partner to clarify your separate curriculum outcomes and connect them in a comprehensive plan for each theme you choose. When you use the thinking backwards approach to curriculum planning, you will integrate the classroom content and art content into a coherent, meaningful plan for teaching and learning. It can also highlight the unique perspective and knowledge base that each of you, and all of the children, bring to the learning experience.

## Guiding Questions

As you and your art partner master use of these planning frames on your own, you make choices based on the learning outcomes you each have in mind. The frames stimulate you to build children's learning experiences.

- How can we integrate teaching experiences using the planning frames?
- How can we evoke responses to support perceptual awareness or analytical thinking about art? How can we stretch art skills as a way of knowing? In what ways can we stimulate knowledge about a topic through art or art history? How can we spark the aesthetic or conceptual aspect?

## Explorations: Planning Frames to Integrate Art

In an *Art as a Way of Learning* classroom, children use the arts as a language which encompasses and facilitates communication, inquiry, curriculum development, and self-discovery. There are different ways to approach or frame a place to begin planning for arts integration. In each frame, children gain the essential knowledge, skills, feelings, and dispositions necessary for developing understanding and meaning. One goal of the *Art as a Way of Learning* approach is to include aspects of all of these in your planning, but where will you begin?

Each of you has curriculum outcomes that must be met for the quarter, semester, or year, based on your district's curricu-

*Figure 2-11.*

**Curriculum Planning Frames**

## STRETCH CURRICULUM

**SPRINGBOARD:** Art and classroom curriculum standards. Curriculum content reinforces and extends problem-solving skills.

**FOCUS:** How? When? Children demonstrate understanding of both content areas and connections between them.

**TEACHING STRATEGY:** Mentor or demonstrator. Foster success and mastery. Generate problem-solving strategies and performance to support enduring understanding.

**ASSESSMENT:** Production/Performance. Children's original creations are indicators of mastery and curriculum connections.

## SUPPORT COMMUNICATION

**SPRINGBOARD:** Students' ideas, imaginations, or interactions.

**FOCUS:** Who? Why? Children engage in artful conversations and art explorations to support visual and verbal interaction.

**TEACHING STRATEGY:** Coach or nurturer. Support self-esteem, expression, and competence.

**ASSESSMENT:** Art criticism/Reflection. Children see themselves and each other as collaborators, communicators, and creators.

## STIMULATE INQUIRY

**SPRINGBOARD:** Curriculum and artistic knowledge, art references. Activities increase knowledge, inquiry methods, and looking behaviors.

**FOCUS:** What? Where? Children gain knowledge and information about both discipline areas. Develop curiosity. Present inquiry formats for gaining knowledge from art.

**TEACHING STRATEGY:** Instructor or research guide. Encourage construction and integration of knowledge.

**ASSESSMENT:** History/Theory. Children see themselves as apprentices to experts

## SPARK! SELF-DISCOVERY

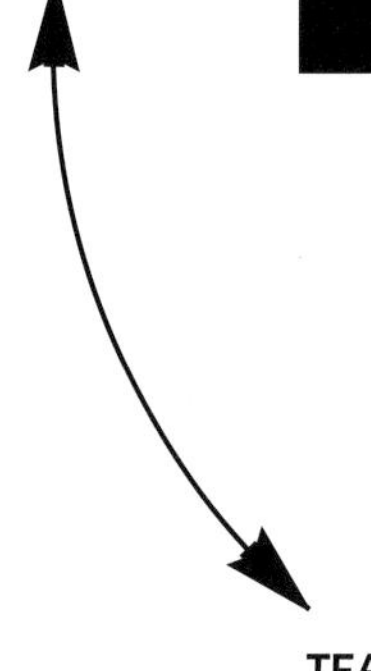

**SPRINGBOARD:** Unifying aesthetic concept. Assessment and curriculum intertwined. Metacognitive and connective.

**FOCUS:** What if? I wonder? Children are curious, seek answers to complex questions, and discover connections among experiences. Pose problems to solve.

**TEACHING STRATEGY:** Challenger or questioner. Facilitate learning and dispositions such as originality, connections, creativity, flow, synthesis.

**ASSESSMENT:** Aesthetic/Creative/Risk. Children construct knowledge and see themselves as resourceful learners.

lum guides and the state and national standards for individual disciplines (MENC, 1994; NAS, 1996; NCTE & IRA, 1996; NCTM, 1989; NCSS, 1994). These objectives should be identified at the beginning of the planning process. Classroom teachers may need to complete certain content in which students can demonstrate knowledge and skills. Art specialists may require the wedding of artistic explorations with the curriculum-inspired artistic skills and knowledge. Students, through their work, demonstrate their understanding and mastery of various skills in multiple disciplines, including the arts.

Next, in dialogue with your art partner, decide in which frame you want to begin your arts integration. Do your objectives lead you to support children's visual communication skills, stimulate inquiry through the arts, stretch curriculum by designing an integrated teaching plan, or find the spark! to facilitate self-discovery? You will probably discover all of these frames have merit in your classroom and art room. Each embodies valuable strategies to help children become creative and critical thinkers, able to make connections and transfer learning across disciplines.

*S-T-R-E-T-C-H students' mental connections and visual thinking.*

Then think through your plans by using one of these four Planning Frames—**Communication, Inquiry, Curriculum, and Self-Discovery**—which enable you to see ideas from three perspectives: yours, your art partner's, and students'. (Teaching strategies for each of these planning frames are described in detail in Component Four of this book: Module 1—Support; Module 2—Stimulate; Module 3—Stretch; and Module 4—Spark!)

> I let the children be the experts and teach me the art techniques and art vocabulary they learned. They would demonstrate and review the art class, which served as an excellent reinforcer for them and a nice update for me. I would probe them on the problems they encountered as they created their pieces and what problem-solving techniques they used. I asked how they decided to use the colors they used and how they got the various effects.
>
> We discussed cultural and scientific references that could help them with their work. We evaluated the processes they used, discussed how additional knowledge of the subject matter could be incorporated into the image, and students made plans on how to continue their artwork in their next class. It was collaboration at its best!
>
> –Jan Steigerwalt, third grade teacher,
> Resica Elementary School,
> East Stroudsburg, Pennsylvania

Each of the frames provides a place to start making curriculum connections by addressing the ways students learn and teachers teach. Within each frame there are four areas for planning and organizing: springboard, focus, teaching strategy, and assessment.

You can begin at any place, with any Planning Frame. As you plan, you will probably find new ways to think about how and what you teach. Some frames may evoke larger themes or conceptual projects that address the big questions of a constructivist curriculum. Together, you and your art partner can develop an engaging, integrated learning experience.

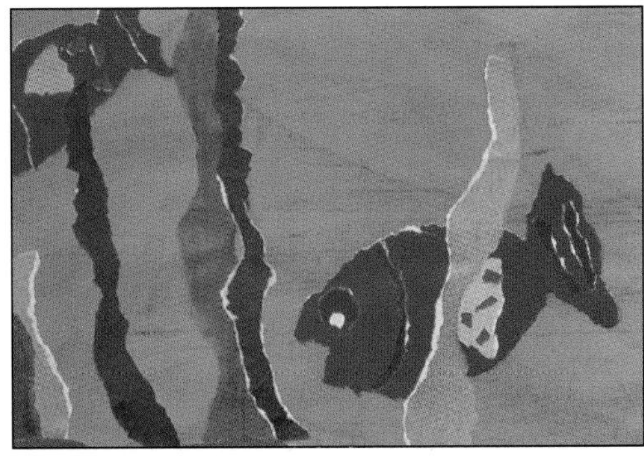

*Figure 2-12.* ***Dive.*** Sophal Cin, age 11, crayon rubbing over torn paper collage.

*Figure 2-13.* ***Adventures of the Ocean.*** Javier Pasos, age 10, crayon marker and oil pastel.

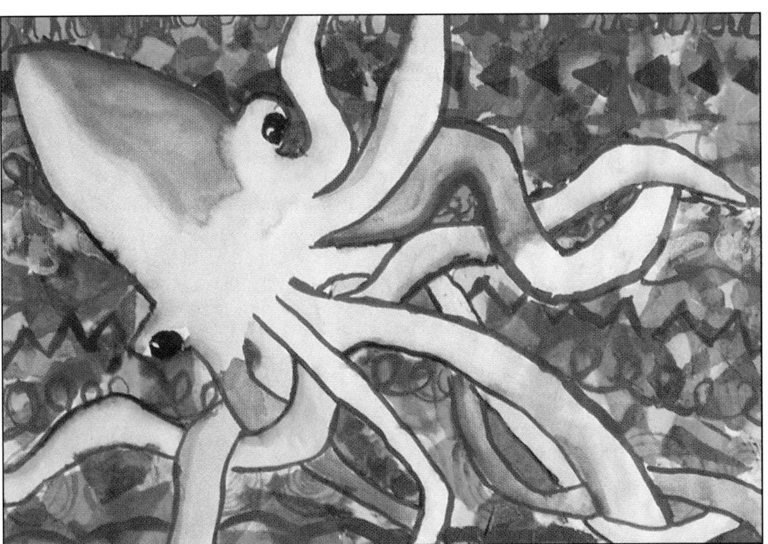

*Figure 2-14.* ***Octosquid.*** Josy Conklin, age 10, tissue, watercolor, and tempera.

## Communication Frame

With the Communication Frame, you and your art partner use children's ideas and interests as a springboard to precipitate the simultaneous interaction of art and curriculum. **Support** for children's feelings and questions evoked by a work of art, a topic, or learning experience is essential. Art specialists encourage students to recognize the validity of their perceptual responses as a basis for considering artworks, thus building the foundation of the skill called **art criticism**.

**I learned about reflection. Never before had I closed a unit with the students reflecting on their experience. This is self-evaluation, part about the learning and part about how it felt.**

**–Fourth grade classroom teacher**

Teachers also support students as they solve artistic challenges by exploring feelings that are inspired by their ideas, culture, experiences, a work of art, aspects of media, or a theme. You act as a coach to encourage children to explore and elaborate on their ideas and feelings. Your interactions with children nurture their freedom to experiment, elaborate, explore, and develop their capacity for more astute perceptual awareness and art criticism. A few suggestions for beginning a Response Frame are listed here.

*Nurture children's freedom to experiment, elaborate, explore.*

**SPRINGBOARD—** Children's ideas, interests, and imagination regarding (topic).

**FOCUS—** Ask children to reflect upon how the feeling conveyed by a work affects them. When have they had this feeling before? How would they demonstrate the same feeling in their artwork?

**TEACHING STRATEGY—** Encourage children to respond to artworks and topics through (list techniques). Encourage interaction with art and curriculum by (describe activities). Foster development of children's feelings as a valid response to artistic competency, perceptual awareness, and art criticism.

**ASSESSMENT—** Children work independently to express and share their unique perceptions with others.

## Inquiry Frame

The springboard of the Inquiry Frame is the questioning strategies to wonder about art and curriculum content. Teachers activate students' prior knowledge and perceptual awareness while providing, or prompting them to seek, new information. You **stimulate** the children's imaginations and reasoning abilities by including art references and research possibilities using artistic language. The art specialist helps children apply their knowledge through art to better understand a topic or discipline.

**SPRINGBOARD**— Curriculum and art knowledge inquiry strategies.

**FOCUS**— Children use webbing, brainstorming, research, and discussion to gain knowledge in (discipline or area).

**TEACHING STRATEGY**— Stimulate children's imaginations and whet their curiosity by finding relationships between art and other topics (e.g., knowledge of cities from the perspective of Arthur Dove, Romare Bearden, and Faith Ringold). Support study with art references that highlight knowledge and understanding in the curriculum area.

**ASSESSMENT**— Children acquire knowledge and understanding about (curriculum topic or theme) through art-related explorations and vice versa.

*Help children apply their knowledge through art.*



## Curriculum Frame

The Curriculum Frame uses the structural content of the visual language and the skills related to the classroom theme as its springboard. Art specialists usually begin this frame with the content of the art curriculum—to reinforce and extend art knowledge, skills, techniques, and artistic reasoning (see the Art Scan, Figure 1-60). Teachers typically use the Curriculum Frame to stretch students' mental connections, physical learning skills, and visual thinking. Through these activities, children develop the skills and analytic thinking processes needed to represent ideas. Here are some suggestions to get you started.

**SPRINGBOARD**— Identify an enduring understanding that will lead learning on the topic, stretching children's interest and skills. Use what children are learning about (topic) to reinforce and extend a range of vocabulary, skills, and art techniques.

**FOCUS**— How did the artist do this work? Explore the artistic and problem-solving skills. Relate art skills to learning skills about topic.

**TEACHING STRATEGY**— Introduce children to several artworks related to the topic and/or created using the techniques children will apply. Demonstrate how to apply these techniques. Discuss problem-solving strategies and curriculum connections.

**ASSESSMENT**— Children develop skills, mentally and physically. Children use their knowledge and skills to represent what they are learning about (topic) and demonstrate performance understanding.

Children develop artistic knowledge and skills as well as critical and creative thinking needed to represent ideas in art.

> Dawn told me they were doing the planets. I had some ideas of how I could link the art curriculum with that, but wanted to build on what the kids knew about planets. So, I told them that I didn't know much about planets and since they were the experts, they had to teach me what they had learned in Mrs. Dubbs' room. They shocked me! They told me about sizes, coloring, and individual characteristics of each planet. We made a chart on the wall of all the facts they knew about planets. That in itself served as an assessment of what they learned in class.
>
> –Sylvia Radvansky, art teacher,
> Clearview Elementary,
> Bethlehem School District, Pennsylvania

*Focus on learning artistic dispositions: curiosity, creativity, artistic sensitivity, synthesis, and aesthetics.*



### Self-Discovery Frame

In the Self-Discovery Frame, the springboard is a unifying aesthetic concept that connects art exploration to personal meaning making. Classroom teachers spark connections and relationships, and engage children in critical, creative thinking—you challenge children to investigate possibilities. Art specialists use the aesthetic aspect of the language—you urge students to find artistic problems and discover connections between experiences and themselves. The focus with the Concept Frame is on learning artistic dispositions such as curiosity, connection, creativity, artistic sensitivity, synthesis, and aesthetics, which impact all learning.

**SPRINGBOARD**— Identify unifying aesthetic concepts. Discuss ways art and curriculum can intertwine. Find the personal connections.

**FOCUS**— What if I applied that knowledge to (create an experience)? I wonder if this idea is valid when (find artistic problems to solve)? Discover personal connections between experiences to create meaning.

**TEACHING STRATEGY**— Spark! Challenge unique combinations. Help students find their own images and personal meaning.

**ASSESSMENT**— Children develop learning and artistic dispositions such as curiosity, connections, creativity, artistic sensitivity, synthesis, and aesthetics. Demonstrate personal meaning.

**There was a combined ownership in making it work, a combined spirit for the importance of art and a doable plan to make it happen!**

**–Elementary art specialist**

*Figure 2-15.*

# Integrated Arts Curriculum Planning Form

| Teams/Project | Essential Questions | Knowledge and Skills | Assessment | Projects |
|---|---|---|---|---|
| **Team members** | **Students will wonder about**<br>*Curriculum focus:*<br><br>*Art focus:* | **Students will know and do** | **Criteria for evaluation** | **Explorations** |
| **Title:**<br><br>**Enduring Understanding:** | | | | |

I wonder now how I used to decide what topics to cover to teach the art curriculum. Now, I am more sensitive to what the kids are learning in the classrooms and using the subject matter to teach the curriculum.

–Ray Hamilton,
Palisades School District,
Pennsylvania

Our curriculum focus at Clearview is total integration of all subject areas; and to this end, there is common planning time for each grade level, as well as 30 minutes daily for all faculty to meet. This is necessary for effective communications among all areas. Classroom teachers are able to meet with specialists weekly. Other than good scheduling and communication among the staff, there is no secret to having our plan work.

–Carol Sham, principal,
Clearview Elementary School,
Bethlehem School District, Pennsylvania



***Remember***—These planning frames are tools to help you achieve your collaborative teaching goals. As your relationship develops, you may come up with some tools of your own. They should demonstrate how all learning is connected, and that you can begin at whatever point excites you or your children!

*Figure 2-16.* **The Alien.** David Matthews, age 8, construction paper and glitter glue. Courtesy Crayola ® Dream-Makers® Program.

## Challenges

### Integrated Arts Curriculum Planning

How do you pull together your exciting ideas to create an integrated teaching plan? This is the thinking and working challenge in this module. The steps for designing curriculum, outlined in Visual Literacy, Module 4, afford a unique way to integrate art and classroom teaching. In collaboration with your art partner, work through the three stages of curriculum planning to create a picture of your integrated unit.

*Begin at whatever point excites you or your children!*

*Figure 2-17.* **Explorer.** Shannon Kuprewicz, age 11, poly plate print and crayon. Courtesy Crayola ® Dream-Makers® Program.

Figure 2-18.

# Integrated Arts Curriculum Planning Form

| Teams/Project | Essential Questions | Knowledge and Skills | Assessment | Projects |
|---|---|---|---|---|
| **Team members**<br><br>Third grade teachers<br><br>Visual art specialist<br><br>Librarian<br><br>**Title:**<br>Mysteries of the Deep<br><br>**Enduring Understanding:**<br>The oceans are an ever-changing sculptural landscape. | **Students will wonder about**<br><br>*Science focus:*<br>**The Ocean**<br>What do we know about the oceans?<br>How do we know about the ocean?<br>What mysteries still remain?<br>What is an underwater landscape and how can we best describe it?<br><br>*Art focus:* **Sculpture**<br>How can drawings appear three dimensional?<br>How can we move from a two-dimensional drawing to a three-dimensional sculpture?<br>What images reflect sculptures in an underwater landscape?<br>Which artists depict the ocean in their art?<br>Who are sculpture artists and what techniques do they use for their sculptures? | **Students will know and do**<br><br>Types of animals:<br>≤ fishes ≤ anemones<br>≤ sea urchins ≤ plant life<br>Adaptations/protection:<br>≤ camouflage ≤ color<br>≤ movement ≤ texture<br>≤ body parts<br>Ocean depth:<br>≤ coral reef<br>≤ levels of sea life<br>Writing skill focus:<br>≤ main idea and details<br>Observational drawing focus<br>Organizing principles<br>≤ space ≤ balance<br>≤ symmetry ≤ color<br>≤ form<br>Types of sculpture and various 3-D techniques<br>≤ kinetic sculptures<br>≤ stuffed sculptures<br>≤ armature sculptures<br>Exploration of techniques and materials including armatures, Model Magic®, and collage materials.<br>Artists: Alexander Calder, Red Grooms, Henry Moore, Winslow Homer | **Criteria for evaluation**<br><br>**Observation:**<br>Ongoing manipulation, dialogue, and evaluation of ocean floor mural.<br>**Writing/drawing project with rubric including:**<br>≤ check for inclusion of details and consistency<br>≤ scientific depiction of sea life and animal camouflage through color, drawing, and highlighting<br>≤ accurately draw scales, fins, gills for animals<br>≤ depict water depth through color<br>**Sculpture projects with rubrics including:**<br>≤ attention to size, shape, color, form, and texture<br>≤ use of drawing, painting, and different paper techniques that add sculptural details<br>≤ attention to symmetry, space, movement, and form<br>**Open-ended questions:**<br>Problem-solving questions to assess science/sculpture knowledge.<br>**Vocabulary quiz** | **Explorations**<br><br>Ocean floor mural labeling the various levels of the sea with realistic drawings of the plants and animals which inhabit each layer.<br><br>Predict, research, write, and illustrate an ocean report attending to main ideas and scientific details of ocean life.<br><br>Field trip to aquarium<br><br>Integrated science and sculpture center on the mysteries of the deep<br><br>Art explorations:<br>≤ Stuffed fish<br>≤ Box sea creature<br>≤ Coral reef sculpture<br><br>Library research |

Use Figure 2-15, the Integrated Arts Curriculum Planning Form, as a guide. This planning form provides a focus to present the curriculum requirements for both partners and assures that you build a curriculum that values, connects, and deepens children's understandings in each discipline.

*Build a curriculum that values, connects, and deepens children's learning in each discipline.*

Both partners first determine what is **important to know and do** for their topic or unit. The content of the topics is guided by one of the resources discussed in Visual Literacy, Module 4. Remember to observe and listen to children. Their conversations or book selections, for example, may reveal topics that especially intrigue them. Perhaps a major event such as a space mission or a local archeological dig captures their imaginations. Ask children their topic recommendations.

Using the Art Scan (Figure 1-60), the art specialist can suggest a content area that connects aesthetically with the curriculum unit. For example, if the unit is dinosaurs in science, possibly printmaking or sculpture would be a good connection. Or in studying patterns and geometry in math, an artistic connect could be the artist M.C. Escher or quilting.

After you have determined the outcomes for both disciplines, generate an **enduring understanding** that connects both bodies of knowledge. For example: "The print of our past" could be an enduring understanding for the dinosaur/printmaking unit. The overarching questions and enduring understanding should both inspire imagination and deepen children's learning. Ask yourself these questions:

- Is this important to know as an adult?
- Is there really something here to uncover?
- Do scientists and artists work in this way?
- Is this enduring understanding inherently engaging?

The next stage is to identifying the **assessment methods** and **evaluative criteria** to determine student learning. What will be the best ways to demonstrate performance understanding? Which traditional assessment methods will be incorporated to support authentic learning? How will you document and share student success with parents and the rest of the school?

As you work through this backward process, resist the temptation to let a nifty activity stop your work. Keep an **activity log,** write down those ideas, and finish stages one and two before you think of **instruction** and the **learning environment.** You may uncover some new ideas, untried explorations, or learning experiences you have never implemented before! List your activities, who is doing which ones, and what resources you need to deliver arts-integrated instruction. Finally, generate ideas for an environment that demonstrates your shared creative energy and ideas (see Aesthetic Environment). You have done good work, celebrate the moment!

Using the Integrated Curriculum Planning Form (Figure 2-15) as an organizational tool promotes collaboration because all goals and options are identified in advance and art partners are aware of each other's constraints and guidelines. See Figure 2-18 for a sample completed form. As you complete your own forms, keep in mind children's interests, ideas, knowledge, and skills. Ensure that their cultures, personal styles, and development are respected. This is the kind of information you will include in each section.

- **Team members.** Identify all art partners: The classroom teacher and art specialist or any other partner such as the librarian, artist-in-residence, music specialist.
- **Enduring understanding.** Highlight the enduring understanding that forms the core of the integrated unit.
- **Outcomes: Knowledge and skills.** Identify what you want the children to know and do in each discipline, classroom and art.
- **Assessment: Methods and criteria.** Determine the acceptable evidence for student success.
- **Instruction: Experiences and environment.** Generate the order of experiences and type of aesthetic environment you will create to support, stimulate, stretch, and spark! children's learning.
- **Resources and responsibilities.** What will you need and how will the teaching responsibilities be shared?

Keep in mind children's interests, ideas, knowledge, and skills. Ensure that their cultures, personal styles, and development are respected.

> By collaborating on this new, intense level with classroom teachers, I am able to determine what units of study students are presently working on and build that into my art program. I have a copy of the particular unit and time frame to work with. This has helped me to develop correlating art projects that build on the students' knowledge and enrich the experience on all ends. The students gain a tremendous amount of knowledge in the unit of study and are even more excited when they come into the art room. They come ready to work, with ideas and information. This new sharing has made me feel more 'in tune' with what is going on with the school as a whole, rather than being the isolated specialist, doing my own little thing in my own little world.
>
> –Jane Oplinger, art teacher,<br>Resica Elementary School,<br>East Stroudsburg, Pennsylvania

## Reflections

To assess your progress on your first collaborative planning project, you and your art partner can ask yourselves these questions.

- Which frame was the most comfortable starting place? Which was most difficult? Why?
- How successful do you feel you were in preparing a plan that develops children's perceptual awareness or art criticism, builds ways of knowing in the curriculum area, increases knowledge about a topic using art or art history, and explores the aesthetic or conceptual aspects of a topic or theme?
- How well have you planned an integrated experience for children that values both disciplines and makes learning meaningful and powerful?
- What have you learned from each other?

> The collaboration not only happens between my art teacher partner and myself, when we meet and plan. The collaboration now happens internally in me, in my mind. I used to think of art as a separate subject. I don't even think that way anymore. Everything I do with my students has art as an integral part. Now I look at my past years' lesson plans and laugh. I teach art, all day, every day. We just did our bees/honey unit. I used to read, lecture, and verbally quiz. Instead, we observe the illustrations in the book closely as we read them. I don't lecture; we question, discover ... and they draw the process; they make a cardboard beehive; they create three-dimensional flowers and bees. We turn our room into the process. They get it in a big way!
>
> –Dawn Dubbs, classroom teacher,<br>Bethlehem School District,<br>Pennsylvania

MODULE 4

# DEVELOPING ARTS ADVOCATES: COMMUNICATE AND NETWORK

*Art as a Way of Learning*® is based on an awareness that the arts are entering a new age in education. Research on children's brain growth, learning, and development consistently substantiates the value of the arts as a medium, tool, and language for children to use to construct meaning. Arts advocates from many disciplines–psychology, education, business, sociology, early childhood education, and many others–demonstrate the need for and importance of the arts in education.

> This school is an exciting place to learn. Here the arts are a big part of the learning for everyone. Walking around and looking at all the children's work from the art class or in the classroom, I get a sense of who learns here; who works here. I wish I could come back to elementary school.
>
> –Parent

**It is difficult to imagine a human society without the arts. What dark and empty souls would populate such ... an environment without paintings, statues, music, architecture, drama, music, dances, or poems. The arts define ... civilization.**

**–Harold Williams (1995, p. 66)**



## Building Momentum for the Arts

Organizations are banding together to advocate for the arts in schools. The arts organizations that undertook the monumental task of developing national standards have succeeded in bringing together not only diverse ideas but different arts forms as well. In addition, the Internet is making it possible to communicate about, and advocate for, the arts in exciting new ways. Online resources include a wealth of information and ideas. The energy generated by these activities creates a vision of what learning can be for children–our challenge is to inspire more advocates to support the vision.

*Inspire advocates for an arts-integrated curriculum.*

As you begin to seek out new advocates, research the availability of advocacy resources in your area. Community arts councils generally welcome involvement in the schools. Families can become good-will ambassadors for the arts if you communicate with them about your program's benefits for their children. Invite them to experience with their children the exciting learning possibilities that the arts foster.

> My son is the student who is doodling all day in the corner on the backs of his work. [In this school] his need to doodle is given a real place, with many opportunities to include his love for drawing in class assignments. He is a happier student because he has so many more chances to make something he is proud of. He has always been short on words, an action kid. He loves the doing and making things, which help him learn and show what he knows. He really shines at this school.
>
> –Parent

Develop arts resources by networking in your school and community. Build partnerships which foster the arts. Find funding resources through grants. Document child, teacher, and school benefits. Changes in education are assured when people grasp how *Art as a Way of Learning*® integrates children's learning and promotes professional growth.

## Guiding Questions

As you begin to develop arts education advocates, focus on these questions:

- What does your school's mission statement say in relation to the arts? How can it become the basis for your advocacy goals? What strategies will you implement? On what time line? Who will be responsible for what?
- What organizations in the community already support the arts? What resources might each organization provide—materials, money, referrals for artists-in-residence?
- How can your school support an organization's advocacy efforts on behalf of the arts in your school—displays or slides of children's work, presentations by children, time for an open house?
- How can you demonstrate the value of the arts in the curriculum to the community? To children's families? To other educators?
- How can you recruit the support of your principal or program director? What school organizations can you enlist?
- How will your school's arts advocacy achievements be assessed? How often? Who will follow through to make improvements?

# Explorations: Generating New Support

You can find resources and develop ways to network for integrating the arts in education. We encourage you to gather information about the arts, and to put together a questionnaire to learn more about your community. Your ability to become a strong advocate for arts in education depends upon how well you know your arts community and understand the value of the arts for children's learning. You have the power to speak for the arts!

## Make a Strong Case

Individual memberships in professional art associations at the local, state, and national level are one of the best ways to magnify your voice as an advocate for the arts in education. The importance and role of arts in education is delineated in various documents related to the arts and Goals 2000 (The Goals 2000 Arts Education Partnership, 1995), state and national standards (MENC, 1994), and national assessment projects (Council of Chief State School Officers, 1994).

This mainstream view of the essential nature of the arts in children's schooling is supported by various programs, advocacy efforts, and numerous publications from the U.S. Department of Education, Office of Educational Research and Improvement; National Endowment for the Arts, Arts in Education Program; Center for Arts in the Basic Curriculum; Harvard's Graduate School of Education's Project Zero; and The Getty Education Institute for the Arts. Every document or position paper reinforces the power of the arts to transform American education. These publications make a positive case for the arts as integral to learning, teaching, and educational reform.

*Figure 2-19.*

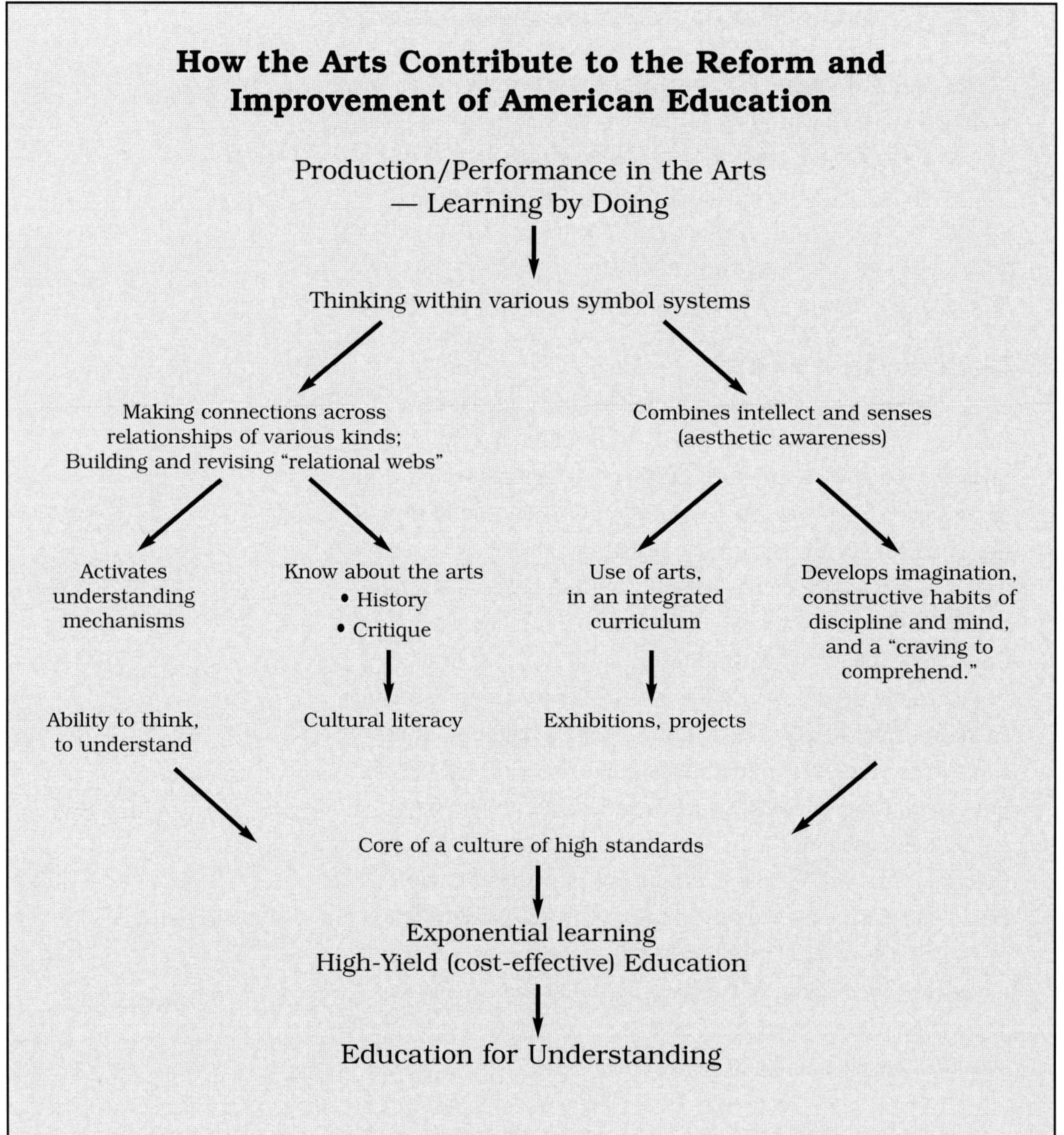


***Note.*** From *Asking the Right Question* (p. 10), The Center for Arts in the Basic Curriculum, ©1992, Higham, MA: Author. Reprinted by permission.

Examine the relationships that are outlined in Figure 2-19 and compare them to your school's progress in implementing the *Art as a Way of Learning*® approach. Keep up to date with current ideas and research on the arts and learning. Share this convincing information whenever you speak with people in your school district or in the community.

There are many other resources available to assist in your journey with using art as a way to learn. Many national organizations have materials to share with families, board members, and interested staff. Foundations and organizations at all levels may offer grants for arts education. Also, the Internet is a place to find resources, arts happenings, legislation at the state and national level, as well as grant possibilities and teaching ideas. The content at any Web site, and groups' addresses, are subject to change. If you enjoy surfing the Net or finding groups to support your arts advocacy efforts, check the resources at the end of this module.

> At the end of every year the school has an Arts Celebration (Figure 2-20) to thank everyone for all that they have done. What an event. The children's work is exceptional and you have a felt sense of the learning that goes on. On this evening, parents perform, children sing and dance, local artists demonstrate art techniques, and the children get to try their hand at different art activities. It's a great evening and just one of the ways the school comes together as a community.
>
> –Parent

*Figure 2-20.* A Celebration of the Arts—a yearly event involving families, students, faculty, and community in an evening of artistic enjoyment, Resica Elementary School, East Stroudsburg, Pennsylvania.

# Using Arts Research for Advocacy Efforts



The arts have been a subject of serious research and inquiry since the 1970s. Many of the initial studies were part of doctoral dissertations. Findings showing positive arts impact were often spotty due to overzealous hypotheses, inadequate designs, or failure to examine essential characteristics of the arts or the unique nature of artistic reasoning. Nevertheless, some important ideas surfaced.

These studies demonstrated that the arts are worthy of study and that they provide challenging research problems unique to the arts, such as measuring creativity, perception, problem-solving, and the art products themselves. Some of this research suggested that the arts have an impact on learning habits and aesthetic perceptions that may increase academic success. In addition, these studies began to interest a diverse group of researchers including cognitive psychologists; neuroscientists; arts educators in music, visual arts, dance, and theater; as well as educators from different fields of study such as measurement, literacy, and administration.

Today, the wellspring of inquiry into the arts contributes to the general understanding of learning, teaching, brain development, literacy, and assessment. This knowledge base is supported by a collaborative spirit and a broad base of arts research activities and organizations. Familiarity with and intelligent use of these resources can lend valuable support to a school's arts program and educational reform efforts.

## Learning, Cognition, and Intelligence

Through continuing collaborative research and exciting exchanges of scholarly ideas at interdisciplinary conferences, studies and recommendations for best practices related to the arts and learning, cognition, and intelligence have been prolific. With each study, understanding of the arts as both unique and familiar emerge.

Gardner's theory of multiple intelligences (1983) grew out his work in the arts at Harvard University's Project Zero. Studies across the nation explore the impact of arts engagement on academic success (Welch & Greene, 1995) and shed light on the reasons for the arts success (Fowler, 1996; Dorn, 1999; Task Force on Children's Learning and the Arts, 1998; Zimmerman, 1998). The arts opened the door to authentic assessment and performance-based learning (Lewin & Shoemaker, 1998; McTighe & Wiggins, 1998) which is grounded in constructivist theory.

## Language and Literacy

The arts are unique symbol systems that allow people to communicate meaning and express ideas, feelings, and understanding. Research findings in the last two decades shed light on verbal literacy and the individual and integrative processes of reading, writing, speaking, and listening. These studies provide models of inquiry for visual, musical, dramatic, and movement systems of communication.

Research on visual art development (Gardner, 1990; Kindler, 1997) provides a more comprehensive picture of this unique symbol system and its uses in making meaning. Comparative studies of verbal to artistic language systems and transfer studies attempt to identify parallel constructs, interactive processes, and educational benefits (Burton, Horowitz, & Abeles, 1999; Cornett, 1999; Piazza, 1999).

## Brain Development

Probably the newest and most exciting area of research has been in relation to brain development and the arts (Caine & Caine, 1994; Scherer, 1998; Sylwester, 1995). Research on the brain is truly in its infancy, so major implications for instruction are even more tenuous. However, it is clear that the arts can provide unique experiences which engage children in powerful ways that may affect brain activity and connectivity.

Jensen (1998) cites a number of studies which begin to address the impact arts experiences have on brain activity, memory, and emotions. Art explorations offer a direct path to seeking patterns and making meaning, which constitute the essential work of the brain. Learning in the arts engages the body's entire physiology. Feelings and the resulting images become the glue that helps people remember past experiences and create original and expressive works of art.

The arts provide novel, constructive challenges with a built-in feedback loop which generates self-discovery, possibly "wiring" the brain for future learning and success. The arts, most notably music (Rauscher, et al., 1997; Weinberger, 1998), suggest a special role the arts might play in brain development throughout a lifetime, from the prenatal stage to old age.

Educators are encouraged to become familiar with this work and look for future studies and valid recommendations for educational practice.

## Model Programs

Schools with a strong arts base often are highlighted in national, regional, or state publications (President's Council on the Arts and the Humanities and Arts Education Partnership, 1999). These schools may use different models or program designs to infuse the arts in learning and teaching and have differing ways to document success, but they are always a testimony to best practices in education.

School leaders cite increased attendance, test scores, student attitude, and a sense of respect and community that appear to accompany the arts infusion. The arts have become partners in the school reform movement and are a way to address educational objectives and meet standards (Getty Center for Education in the Arts, 1993; National Endowment for the Arts, 1995).

Business and community leaders have also taken an interest in the gains made in learning, creative thinking, adaptability, and cooperation among students when schools fully embrace the arts (U.S. Department of Labor, 1991).

Classroom teachers, arts specialists, and administrators are encouraged to document their arts journeys and to share their stories with others.

## Fan the Flame

Now that the arts have been recognized as a core subject and state and national standards have been articulated, we need to continue the movement and advocacy for the arts in education. Standards are still voluntary, and the arts are still an underutilized resource in many schools. Individuals in your school and community may still not fully understand the arts' benefits. Our work has just begun.

Our task is to keep the arts in the forefront of thinking, planning, and decision making at the local, state, and national levels. Developing advocates from your school that extend out into the community will strengthen this base. Encourage families, teachers, business leaders, and students to become active participants in guiding educational reform.

Here are three action-oriented tasks to magnify your advocacy efforts: conduct a survey, form a partnership, apply for grants. They go hand-in-hand with arts integration and curriculum reform. However, they are not a substitute either for high standards throughout the curriculum or for professional development.

### Conduct a Survey

Your school district or early childhood program may already conduct periodic community surveys. Before you start to gather information about your school's needs and strengths in the arts, check to see whether recent results on the topic are already available. If a survey is needed to reveal local potential for support for the arts, work with the designated officials to design and distribute your questionnaire to your community—schools for all ages, businesses, leaders, organizations, and artists. A few suggestions for planning a survey are offered here.

**Plan—**What do you want to know? Review the literature or ask if anyone has collected this type of data. Who must clear your plans for a survey or other activity before you implement them? Who can help with the distribution, tallying, and analysis?

**Choose a sample—**Who will you survey? How will you identify these people?

**Construct a questionnaire—**Is there a survey instrument available? If not, the art specialist, principal, and classroom teachers can develop one. What form will you use (survey, interviews, phone calls)? How will the results be recorded (computer, hand tally)? Design the form accordingly. Try it out; revise questions if needed.

**Collect data—**Ask the questions, and send reminders to boost the number of responses.

**Translate the results—**Tabulate the responses and prepare them for analysis. Could students or families assist?

**Analyze results—**Separately analyze individual items and groups of related items. Interpret what the responses mean.

**Report—**Look at the results from many angles. Was your initial question answered? What other information did you receive? What follow-up is needed to capture the energy of potential advocates for the arts? Share your findings with the school board, families, and other faculty. How will the results affect your goals for arts advocacy?

### Form a Partnership

Today schools, as with other institutions, cannot remain isolated from the resources and interactions in the surrounding community. Effective schools initiate relationships with local institutions and businesses to build advocates for education and the arts (Irwin & Kindler, 1999; Katz, 1988). These mutual partnerships strengthen programs, build resources, and establish a dialogue with the community about learning. They create new patterns of working together.

Partnerships can be designed for various reasons, with different groups, and with diverse benefits to students and teachers. The experiences may be cultural and educational, have a service focus, or introduce students to the world of work. Partners may come from businesses, large or small, or institutions that may have a vested interest in education, such as museums, colleges and universities, arts organizations, and cultural institutions.

Partnerships expand horizons. Children and teachers have the opportunity to work with experts from other fields. These role models demonstrate the critical and creative thinking cycle as they engage children in hands-on experiences that capture the imagination. Learning becomes situated in the context of the real world. Partnerships often narrow cultural gaps.

Professional development is another important aspect of partnering. Teachers and art specialists benefit from workshops, training, and internships provided by the partner. In turn, teachers and art specialists provide valuable insights into the teaching, learning, and creating process. A renewed respect and a feeling of investment and ownership are often results.

Documentation and research should be built into every partnership. Schools need to quantitatively demonstrate the impact of arts integration on learning and teaching (National Endowment for the Arts, 1994). Include this aspect into your partnership proposal from the beginning. The results can be used when applying for grants or advocating the arts in education.

A partnership requires planning, team building, negotiation, trial, and effort. Begin by assessing your needs related to arts integration and informally reviewing community sources. Design a proposal which covers at least a 3-year span. Use a team approach to delineate responsibilities. Be sure everyone involved is kept up to date regularly. Have a flexible plan of action that is changed as needed. Evaluate the program and celebrate its successes yearly.



### Apply for Grants

Grants for the arts, curriculum integration, assessment, and educational reform can be found at the district, state, and national levels. Resources for writing grants are available along with sources for funding (NAEA, 1995a; 1995b). Each grant application has specific requirements and timetables to be followed closely.

Know your facts by familiarizing yourself with research in arts education and learning (Welch & Greene, 1995). Understand and use the standards. Highlight the role of the arts to improve learning and assessment. Reflect the strong positive relationship that exists between the arts and arts education and workplace skills and preparation for college (U.S. Department of Labor, 1991). Emphasize the use of creative and critical thinking and the interactive, problem-solving nature of making art.

Here are some overall general maxims to consider when writing grants:

- **Sound like a winner—**Success is what grantors want to see, so be positive. Instill confidence with your thoroughness and clarity. Make sure the evaluation section of your proposal is strong.
- **Go to the library—**Your school or community librarian has access to grant sources and tips on writing successful proposals. Libraries may even have a person who can assist in writing and editing grants.
- **Be brief, clear, and direct—**A pile of proposals sits on a reviewer's desk. Where to start, with the 200 page albatross or the succinct, visually appealing, readable 30-page proposal?
- **Make it visual—**Use headings to break apart the text for the review. This helps you organize main ideas and present understandable content.

- **Get in touch—**A call to the agency giving the grant can be very helpful. Often a representative will answer specific questions, possibly divulge additional information, and send samples of successful proposals. This also allows the agency to get to know you as well.
- **Build in collaboration—**Clearly a partnership can originate or be enhanced with a grant. Make sure all participants know and agree to their responsibilities. Write them down and keep everyone well-informed.

## Challenges

Successful school-wide advocacy for the arts can build a sense of community and generate spontaneous enthusiasm for extending the efforts. After your advocacy efforts take off at your school, extend them to local, state, and national arenas. Activate the growing arts advocacy among families in your school through advocacy teams. Here are some other ways to promote advocacy within and beyond the school.

- Ask for a spot on the PTA/PTO program to explain *Art as a Way of Learning*®. Use project resources. Bring a beautiful display of children's thinking and work. Encourage children to speak about their experiences or demonstrate what they are learning.
- Write letters to your state's education leaders, including local legislators. Ask students to send artwork and describe the importance of this type of learning. Invite decision makers to visit your school and see *Art as a Way of Learning* in action.
- Write a news release about your successes for the local newspaper. Invite a photographer to add to the story.
- Feature student work with documentation at a school board meeting.
- Apply for a grant, no matter how small. Consider submitting proposals to local businesses, foundations, museums, parent groups, organizations. Ask for donations of materials, learning resources, and/or funding. When the grant is awarded, announce it in school district communications and in the local paper.
- Find key families who can explain *Art as a Way of Learning* to their friends.
- Plan a public event showcasing your students' work—perhaps an open house at a Senior Center, an art exhibit at a public

library or business, or an art fair in conjunction with the Week of the Young Child. Be sure to document the learning process.

- Plan an Arts Celebration for parents and community. Ask children and families to display or perform.
- Involve other teachers and administrators to initiate school-wide or grade-level art projects. Share your expertise in another teacher's classroom.
- Invite families and others in the community to share the arts and crafts of their own culture. Ask them to help amount and hang student artwork.

## Reflections

It takes a firm commitment, thoughtful reflection, and a willingness to listen to be able to make the most of surveys and questionnaires, or to create and sustain a network of interested individuals. Think about your progress as an arts advocate by considering these questions periodically.

- What arts organizations might provide support for your program? What resources do these groups have that could benefit your program? What new groups or leaders should be contacted?
- How can you regularly demonstrate the value of the arts to the community? To children's families in the PTA/PTO? To school board members, administrators, and other teachers?
- How supportive is your principal as an advocate for the arts? What can you do to increase that support?

## Resources

*Web site addresses are constantly changing. If an address is not available, a search for the key words may help you locate the site.*

### Organizations

**American Alliance for Theatre in Education (AATE)**
Arizona State University
Dept. of Theatre
Tempe, AZ 95287-3411
(602) 965-6064

**American Arts Alliance**
1319 F St., N.W., Suite 500
Washington, DC 20004
(202) 289-1776

**American Council for the Arts (ACA)**
1 E. 53rd St.
New York, NY 10022-4201
(212) 223-2787
www.artsusa.org/

**Center for Arts in the Basic Curriculum**
58 Fearing Road
Hingham, MA 02043
(617) 740-0114
www.newhorizons.org

**Council for Basic Education**
725 15th St., N.W.
Washington, DC 20005
(202) 347-4171
www.C-B-E.org

**ERIC Clearinghouse for Social Studies/Social Science Education (includes art education)**
Indiana University
Social Studies Development Center
2805 East 10th St., Suite 120
Bloomington, IN 47408
(812) 855-3838
(800) 266-3815
www.indiana.edu/~ssdc/eric_chess.htm

**Getty Education Institute for the Arts, The**
1200 Getty Center Drive, Suite 600
Los Angeles, CA 90049-1683
(310) 440-7315
www.artsednet.edu
www.ahip.getty.edu/

**Harvard Project Zero**
Graduate School of Education
323 Longfellow Hall
Appian Way
Cambridge, MA 02138
(617) 495-4342
http://pzweb.harvard.edu

**John F. Kennedy Center Alliance for Arts Education Network**
Education Department
Washington, DC 20566
(202) 797-0083
www.artsedge.kennedy-center.org

**Music Educators National Conference (MENC)**
National Arts Standards
1806 Robert Fulton Dr.
Reston, VA 22091
(703) 860-4000

**National Art Education Association (NAEA)**
1916 Association Dr.
Reston, VA 22091-1590
(703) 860-8000
www.NAEA-RESTON.org

**National Assembly of Local Arts Agencies**
927 15th St., N.W., 12th Floor
Washington, DC 20005
(202) 371-2830

**National Dance Association (NDA)**
1900 Association Drive
Reston, VA 22091
(703) 476-3436

**National Endowment for the Arts**
Arts in Education Program
Division of Educational Programs or Museums and Historical Organizations Programs
1100 Pennsylvania Ave., N.W.
Washington, DC 20506
(202) 682-5426
www.artsedge.kennedy-center.org

**National Endowment for the Humanities**
Division of Education Programs or
Museums and Historical Organizations Programs
1100 Pennsylvania Ave., N.W.
Washington, DC 20506
(202) 606-8428

**Pennsylvania Coalition for the Arts in Education**
P.O. Box 987
Frazer, PA 19355

**Very Special Arts**
1300 Connecticut Ave., N.W., Suite 700
Washington, DC 20036
(202) 628-2800

**U.S. Department of Education**
Office of Educational Research and Improvement
555 New Jersey Ave., N.W.
Washington, DC 20208
(202) 219-1385

## On-line resources

**American Council for the Arts**–http://www.artsusa.org/

**ArtsEdge**–A collaboration between the Kennedy Center and the National Endowment of the Arts at http://www.artsedge.kennedy-center.org

**ARTS EdNet**–Getty Center for Education in the Arts at http://www.artsednet.edu

**ArtServ**–More than 10,000 images primarily from Mediterranean cultures at http://rubens.anu.edu.au/

**Arts Wire**–http://gopher.tmn.com:70/1/Artswire

**Bayler Art Museum**–A Web version of the exhibit "African Art: Aesthetics and Meaning" at http://www.lib.viginia.edu/dic/exhib/93.ray.aa/African.html

**Binney & Smith**–Product information, resources, and educational information at www.crayola.com/crayola OR www.crayola.com/art_education

**EMIG**–The newsletter of Electronic Media Interest Group of the National Art Education Association at http://www.cgrg.ohio-state.edu/NAEA/emig.html

**ERIC**–National resource center at http:/ /ericir.sunsite.syr.edu

**Getty Art History Information Program**–Extensive database of architectural terms at http://www.ahip.getty.edu/

**Goals 2000 and the Arts**–http://gopher.tmn.com:70/1/NAEIN/menu.b16

**Goals 2000 legislation and related items**–http://www.ed.gov/legislation/GOALS2000/index.html

**Internet Art Resources**–http://www.ftgi.com/

**Library of Congress**–Archives and exhibits at www.loc.gov

**Mosaic**–Art prints on line at ftp://ftp.sunset.se/pub/pictures/Art
www.ncsa.uiuc.edu/SDG/Experimental/anu-art-history/prints.html

**National Endowment for the Arts**–educational programs at http://gopher.tmn.com.70/1/NAEIN/menu.b21

**National Museum of American Art**–at http://www.nmaa.si.edu/

**Smithsonian Institution**–Access its museums at http://www.si.sgi.com/sgistart.htm

**World Arts Resources**–at http://www.cgrg.ohio-state.edu/Newark/artsres.html

## International and unusual on-line art sites

**Ancient Palestine-Israel, Palestine, Syria:** Take a walk through the buildings of ancient Palestine. Take animated tours of various sites reconstructed by archaeologists at http://staff.Feldberg.brandeis.edu/~jacka/ANEPP.html

**Architecture of Islam:** Photos and a tour of doors, arches, and beautiful entryways to buildings in Middle Eastern styles at http://rubens.anu.edu.au/islam2/Part1.html

**Ardeche Cave Art Discovery–France:** Site of the 1994 discovery of prehistoric cave paintings. Only way to see it, because it is closed to nonscientists at http://www.culture.fr./culture/gvpda-en.html
www.ed.gov/offices/OERI

**Art Crimes:** Graffiti art gallery from the U.S., Brazil, and the Czech Republic at http://www.gatech.edu/desoto/graf/Index.Art_Crimes.html

**Auction Houses:** Turn your Web to one of the art auction houses to see what's on the docket: Sotheby's is at http://www.sothbys.com/ Christies is at http://www.christies.com/

**Book of Kells-Ireland:** Sample pages from this 8th-century illuminated gospel in Trinity College, Dublin at http://www.tcd.ie/kells.html

**Christo:** Loaded with facts, photos, and pictures of islands, fences, umbrellas, and a wrapped Reichstag at http://www.nbn.com/youcan/christo/

**Egyptian Artifacts–Egypt:** Want to see a mummy? See five Egyptian artifacts at the University of Memphis at http://www.memphis.edu/egypt/artifact.html

**Electronic Visualization Labs Gallery:** See 3-D, raytraced, digitally manipulated images. Have lots of memory, a fast modem, and a large crossword puzzle while image pages load at http://evlweb.eecs.vic.edu

**Folk Art and Craft Exchange**–Canada, U.S., Mexico, Central and South America: An online shop that includes items made by Native and indigenous peoples. Site also includes information about folk and craft museums at http://www.folkart.com

**Images from Japan:** A gallery of photos of shrines, temples, and other buildings in Japan at http://www.cs.uidaho.edu/~marac9442/japan.html

**Internet Movie Database–England:** Database covers 40,000 films, indexes of actors, by country, genre, and more at http://www.leo.org/Movies/welcome.html

**Javanese Masks–Indonesia:** This page has a display of Javanese masks in full color, with historical data at http://rs6000.bvis.uic.edu/museum/javamask/Javamask.html

**Leonardo Net–Italy:** A guide to Leonardo, his paintings and drawings at http://leonardo.net/

**Le WebLouvre–France:** The unofficial site. has more images (and of Paris, including the catacombs) than the official site at http://sunsite.unc.edu/louvre/

**OTIS:** An online gallery of a gigantic art site that includes performances, comics, video, digital art, sculpture, painting, cool T-shirts, and extensive links to world art sites at http://sunsite.unc.edu/otis/otis.html

**Pompeii Forum Project–Italy:** Images of reconstructions of buildings in Pompeii at http://jefferson.village.virginia.edu/pompeii/page-1.html

**Sistine Chapel:** 325 images from the ceiling! High-speed modem and lots of patience recommended at http://www.christusrex.org/wwwl/sistine/0-Tour.html

**Viking art and artifacts–Denmark, Norway, Sweden, Russia, England:** Runes, history, artifacts, and a runic font for Macs. Text is in Norweigian, Danish, Swedish, and some English. Take the links to the museums, especially the Tromso Museum at http://www.demon.co.uk/past/vikings

**Web Museum–France:** The web site for museum buffs. Scores of artist bios and images. Plus, take a tour of Paris online at http://www.emf.net.wm/

**World Art Resources:** Site connects you to hundreds of galleries, online exhibits, commercial, government, private links at http://www.concourse.com/wwar

## Grants and funding for the arts, on-line resources

**ARTSEDGE Funding Resources Directory:** http://artsedge.kennedy-center.org/sc/fn-index.html

**Catalog of Federal Domestic Assistance:** http://solar.rtd.utk.edu:70/11/Federal/CFDA

**Educational Testing Service:** http://gopher.ets.org/1/

**ERIC Clearinghouse on Assessment and Evaluation:** http://ericae2.cua.edu/

**Foundation Center:** http://www.fdncenter.org/

**GrantsWeb:** http://infoserv.rttonet.psu.edu/gweb.html

**National Center for Research on Evaluation, Standards, and Student Testing:**
http://cresst96.cse.ucla.edu/cresst.html
http://www.cse.ucla.edu/search/search.html

**North Central Regional Educational Laboratory:** http://www.ncrel.org/ncrel/

**School-to-Work Gateway:** http://www.stw.ed.gov

**Teachers Guide to U.S. Department of Education:** http://www.ed.gov/pubs/TeachersGuide/

**What Should I Know About ED Grants:** http://www.ed.gov/pubs/KnowAbtGrants/

## References


Binney & Smith Inc. (1993). Unpublished survey conducted at conference of the National Art Education Association.

Bray, J., & Pinciotti, P. (1997). Success in education: Creating a community of learners through the arts. *Arts and Learning Research, 13*(1), 79-92.

Burton, J., Horowitz, R., & Abeles, H. (1999). *Learning in and through the arts: Transfer and higher-order thinking.* New York: Center for Arts Education Research, Teachers College, Columbia University.

Caine, R.N., & Caine, G. (1994). *Making connections: Teaching and the human brain.* New York: Addison-Wesley.

Center for Arts in the Basic Curriculum, The. (1992). *Asking the right question.* Washington, DC: Author.

Cornett, C.E. (1999). *The arts as meaning makers: Integrating literature and the arts throughout the curriculum.* Upper Saddle River, NJ: Prentice-Hall.

Council of Chief State School Officers, The, with The College Board and The Council for Basic Education. (1994). *Arts education assessment framework.* Washington, DC: National Assessment Governing Board.

Dorn, C.M. (1999). *Mind in art: Cognitive foundations in art education.* Mahwah, NJ: Erlbaum.

Fowler, C. (1996). *Strong arts, strong schools.* New York: Oxford University Press.

Gardner, H. (1983). *Frames of mind.* New York: Basic Books.

Gardner, H. (1990). *Art education and human development.* Los Angeles: Getty Center for Education in the Arts.

Getty Center for Education in the Arts. (1993). *Perspectives on education reform: Arts education as catalyst.* Santa Monica, CA: Author.

Goals 2000 Arts Education Partnership, The. (1995). *The arts and education: Partners in achieving our national education goals.* Washington, DC: National Endowment for the Arts.

Idol, L., Nevin, A., & Paolucci-Whitcomb, P. (1994). *Collaborative consultation* (2nd ed.). Austin, TX: Pro-Ed.

Irwin, R.L., & Kindler, A.M. (Eds.). (1999). *Beyond the school: Community and institutional partnerships in art education.* Reston, VA: National Art Education Association.

Jensen, E. (1998). *Teaching with the brain in mind.* Alexandria, VA: Association for Supervision and Curriculum Development.

Katz, J. (Ed.). (1988). *Arts and education handbook: A guide to productive collaborations.* Washington, DC: National Assembly of State Arts Agencies.

Kindler, A. (Ed.). (1997). *Child development in art.* Reston, VA: National Art Education Association.

Lewin, L., & Shoemaker, B.J. (1998). *Great performances: Creating classroom-based assessment tasks.* Alexandria, VA: Association for Supervision and Curriculum Development.

McTighue, J., & Wiggins, G. (1998). *Understanding by design.* Alexandria, VA: Association for Supervision and Curriculum Development.

Music Educators National Conference (MENC). (1994). *National standards for arts education.* Reston, VA: Author.

National Academy of Sciences (NAS). (1996). *National science education standards.* Washington, DC: National Academy Press.

National Art Education Association. (1994). *Goals 2000 education reform handbook.* Reston, VA: Author.

National Art Education Association. (1995a, Fall). Funding for arts education through Internet services. *NAEA Advisory.* Reston, VA: Author.

National Art Education Association. (1995b, Fall). Keys to successful grant writing. *NAEA Advisory.* Reston, VA: Author.

National Council for the Social Studies (NCSS). (1994). *Curriculum standards for social studies: Expectations of excellence.* Washington, DC: Author.

National Council for the Teachers of English (NCTE) & International Reading Association (IRA). (1996). *Standards for the English language arts.* Washington, DC: Authors.

National Council of Teachers of Mathematics (NCTM). (1989). *Curriculum and evaluation standards for school mathematics.* Reston, VA: Author.

National Endowment for the Arts. (1995, January). *The arts and education: Partners in achieving our national education goals.* Washington, DC: Author.

National Endowment for the Arts & the U.S. Department of Education. (1994). *Arts education research agenda for the future.* Washington, DC: Author.

Piazza, C.L. (1999). *Multiple forms of literacy.* Upper Saddle River, NJ: Prentice-Hall.

President's Council on the Arts and the Humanities and Arts Education Partnership. (1999). *Gaining the arts advantage: Lessons from school districts that value arts education.* Washington, DC: Author.

Rauscher, F.H., Shaw, G.L., Levine, L.J., Wright, E.L., Dennis, W.R., & Newcomb, R.L. (1997). Music training causes long-term enhancement of preschool children's spatial-temporal reasoning. *Neurological Research, 19,* 2-8.

Scherer, M.M. (Ed.). (1998). How the brain learns (theme issue). *Educational Leadership, 56*(3). Alexandria, VA: Association for Supervision and Curriculum Development.

Sylwester, R. (1995). *A celebration of neurons: An educator's guide to the human brain.* Alexandria, VA: Association for Supervision and Curriculum Development.

Task Force on Children's Learning and the Arts: Birth to Age Eight. (1998). *Young children and the arts: Making creative connections.* Washington, DC: Arts Education Partnership.

U.S. Department of Labor. (1991). *What work requires of schools. A SCANS report for America 2000.* Washington, DC: Author.

Weinberger, N.M. (1998). The music in our minds. *Educational Leadership, 56*(3), 36-40.

Welch, N., & Greene, A. (Eds.). (1995). *School, communities, and the arts: A research compendium.* Tempe: Morrison Institute for Public Policy, Arizona State University.

Williams, H. (1995, September). Don't ignore the arts. *USA Today Magazine, 124* (2604), 66-69.

Zimmerman, E. (Ed). (1998). *The NAEA research task force: Status reports.* Reston, VA: National Art Education Association.

COMPONENT THREE

# Aesthetic Environment

## MODULES

- The Visual Learning Environment
- Developing an Art Materials Center
- Curriculum Connections: Imaginative Art Spaces
- Children's Art Explorations: Displays and Documentation

# MODULE 1
# THE VISUAL LEARNING ENVIRONMENT

**Every child has the right to know the beauty of the world, in order to deal with those who bleat, scream, and make the world a shrill place.**

**–Isaac Stern**

Something wonderful happens when children turn their classroom into a celestial galaxy; a school hallway into a prehistoric cave; the art room into a medieval castle with tapestries, manuscripts, and paintings; or the cafeteria into an undersea world. You can feel children's energy, curiosity, and enthusiasm for learning, the attention to detail and beauty, and the quality of engagement from the moment you walk into the building.

## Messages in Children's Surroundings

You, too, may be an educator who realizes that "For aesthetic development to occur, children need experience with beautiful environments within the school and outside of it, exposure to fine art, and opportunities to discuss art and beauty with thoughtful adults" (Feeney & Moravcik, 1987, p. 11).

The *National Standards for Arts Education* define aesthetics as "a branch of philosophy that focuses on the nature of beauty, the nature and value of art, and the inquiry processes and human responses associated with those topics" (MENC, 1994, p. 82). A visual learning environment implies deliberate and thoughtful choices made by administrators, art specialists, classroom teachers, and children to heighten aesthetic awareness.

*What messages are you sending about learning, the nature of art, and children?*

Your choices demonstrate the values and beliefs about the nature of art and types of learning experiences found throughout your building and community. You make a conscious effort to connect children's perceptual awareness of their surroundings with their visual thinking in every curriculum area. Your aesthetic choices engender curiosity, activate the creative and critical thinking cycle, and give pause for reflection.

Consider your building's environment.... Look around the school, down the halls, in and out of classrooms, the cafeteria, gym, playground, and library. Imagine how these places appear from the height and perspective of a preschooler, a second grader, a prospective parent, a business leader, or retiree in the community. What messages are you sending about learning, the nature of art, and children? What can you decipher about the explicit and implicit (hidden) curriculum?

The physical, cultural, and social characteristics of the school—or any other building—communicate visually to all who enter. The environment says, "See who works here, what there is to know and do, and how people and their work are valued and cherished."

It is harder to *see* than it is to express.

-Robert Henri (1923, p. 87)

## Guiding Questions

Consider the perceptual and cognitive outcomes as you develop your school or classroom environment. Plan displays and engage in thoughtful interactions to enhance children's visual thinking and to create an overall aesthetic sensibility.

- How is perception and visual thinking enhanced throughout the school and within the curriculum?
- What might be the environment's aesthetic focus? How can children be involved in aesthetic planning?
- What visual and verbal connections to the curriculum need to be identified through collaboration among staff? How will children's input be assured?

## Explorations: Visual Thinking Connections

Embedded in the belief that the visual arts are a language is an understanding that perception, construction, and performance require thinking. Reasoning in each phase of the Action Cycle of Creative and Critical Thinking (Figure 1-4) generates various kinds of visual thinking. Visual thinking uses images or mental pictures, which are rich in sensory detail, as material to record, analyze, select, and recall prior experiences or manipulate, transform, evaluate, and generate new imaginative images.

Contemporary understandings about learning and cognitive processes highlight the role of perception and visual thinking in higher-order reasoning.

Many people view visual thinking and cognition as separate, as two discontinuous and discrete educational processes. Therefore, the arts are often viewed as nonacademic "because they are based on perception, and perception is disdained because it is not assumed to involve thought" (Arnhiem, 1986, p. 135). Contemporary understandings about the function of the brain in learning and cognitive processes highlight the role of perception and visual thinking in higher-order reasoning processes.

We know that **perception** is an essential step in the reasoning process and functional use of any language. It is absolutely critical for aesthetic communication, because perception deals with the *qualities* of an experience. Vivid perceptions and visual

**Perception would be useless without thinking; thinking without perception would have nothing to think about!**
**-Rudolf Arnhiem (1984, p. 132)**

*Perceptual challenges are novel and rich in sensory information.*



*Visual thinking tools enhance learning and the transfer of knowledge.*

thinking enable children to produce the clearest, most powerful images in art. **Perception is visual thinking.** The process of perception involves a heightened sense of visual awareness, attention to details, ability to recall vivid, sensory images, and sensitivity to the affective content of images.

All of us are familiar with the barrage of visual stimuli in the media and at shopping malls, but there is an important distinction between sensory stimuli (sometimes to the point of overload) and **perceptual challenges**. Perceptual challenges are novel and rich in sensory information. They require people to "mobilize their capacities to grasp, to interpret, to unravel, to improve" (Arnhiem, 1986, p. 238). These challenges address the aesthetic aspect inherent and unique to each symbol system.

Adult guidance is crucial for children to perceive and process visual challenges encountered in their experiences. Joint attention—to visual changes in nature, or sensory characteristics of the physical world of objects and art materials—develops visual thinking strategies to enhance perception, construction, and performance. When teachers and art specialists link the perceptual and the communicative aspects of the learning environment, the impact on children's visual thinking and the school is dramatic!

Artists, writers, dancers, musicians, and actors each require certain individual environmental conditions to stimulate, order, and energize their work. Physical, cognitive, and affective needs are met by the arrangement of tools; type of lighting, work surfaces, and objects; and pictures or music gathered for inspiration. Each of you can probably identify the environmental qualities that facilitate the learning of new material or set the mood for creative work for yourself and groups of children.

Visual thinking and problem-solving strategies found in children's **construction** demand deliberate guidance from adults. Challenges in construction relate to the extent one can discover the visual possibilities in an idea, situation, or image. Through modeling and posing challenging questions, teachers, art specialists, and artists-in-residence can guide children to discover the potential in art making. Visual thinking in the construction phase encourages interpretation and the expression of individual style.

Visual thinking in the **performance** phase is self-reflective and evaluative. The habit of reflective visual thinking develops when adults and children participate in a continuous dialogue about art. Children monitor, interpret, and direct their actions as they converse about their work with others. The ability to describe, analyze, interpret, and judge both the cognitive and artistic processes clarifies intentions and continues the learning cycle. Visual thinking tools acquired at each phase of the cycle enhance learning and the transfer of knowledge.

As a proponent of *Art as a Way of Learning*®, you realize that an aesthetic environment reflects the ways children know; the context of their learning; the range of their feelings, ideas, curiosity, learning processes, and meaning. You recognize that children (and adults) think visually when we view displays of art work, watch the bustle of activity in art learning centers, and engage in thoughtful conversations about perceptual challenges. Educators relish these opportunities to observe, compare, understand, and reflect.

*The habit of reflective visual thinking develops when adults and children participate in a continuous dialogue about art.*

The elements and principles of visual organization (see Visual Literacy, Component One, Module 2), along with various display techniques (discussed in Module 4 of this component), visually command people's attention and focus us on active, perceptive learning. Indeed, an aesthetic environment makes a strong statement about the relationship between perception and thinking (Figure 3-1).

*Figure 3-1.* Art center in Mary Richards' first-grade classroom, Truman Elementary School, Salisbury School District, Pennsylvania. Drawing by Louise Cosgrove, art teacher.

The guided explorations that *Art as a Way of Learning*® teachers extend to children are related to the critical and creative aspects of an aesthetic environment. These explorations deal with both function and form. The arts are viewed, not merely as entertainment or precious individual expression (Bresler, 1993), but as ways to understand our own humanity (see Table E-1). Intelligent perception and visual thinking lead ultimately to understanding.

*Observe what children understand and how they make their knowledge meaningful.*

## What Are the Functions of Aesthetic Environments?

An aesthetic environment highlights the interconnected relationship between the creative and critical thinking cycle and visual thinking. In schools that incorporate *Art as a Way of Learning*, the aesthetic environment—indoor and outdoor space—communicates how teaching and learning occur. Children's artistic creations, evidence of their learning in a variety of content areas, abound throughout the building. By observing the setting and how children function within it, you can see what children understand and how they make their knowledge meaningful.

We have already seen that when learning is scaffolded (Berk & Winsler, 1995), children are curious about the connections that give any subject or idea its meaning. Children are far more likely to grasp a topic when it is pursued within the context of their knowledge and experiences. By guiding children to build coherent webs and visual connections, we challenge them to think more critically (Perkins, 1989). Visual thinking is essential for creating a web of related ideas.

Thus, when you use *Art as a Way of Learning*, you encourage children to look at the topic or subject longer, cast off stereotypes and obvious surface relations, and use visual thinking to discover coherent, interesting perceptual relations. In the process, children's visual comprehension develops and their functional use of visual language is enhanced.

*Pursue topics within the context of children's knowledge and experiences.*

Each of us, child and adult alike, is engaged in an endless quest to make visual thinking connections. Our ideas are forever being refined and elaborated upon by rich learning experiences and perceptual challenges. The function of an aesthetic environment is related directly to the structural, functional, and aesthetic aspects of visual language. Therefore, we must fully explore the elements and principles of creating and responding in the visual arts in order to have a more complete understanding of art, our experiences, and the environment.

Colleagues within your building may be willing to lend your class items that would add to a display. Art specialists are often aware of visual, natural, or artistic resources at the school, or within the district and community, and how they can be acquired. Check with the librarian for books on artists, art techniques, illustrations, and stories about art. Families often are willing to loan interesting artifacts—just ask, and encourage them to explain their significance to the group!

*Enlist the help of your principal, colleagues, and children's families.*

We are well aware that changes to enhance your aesthetic environment may take time, money, and resources. Enlist the help of your principal, colleagues, and children's families. Make sure the aesthetic environment is included in planning discussions. Regularly assess the form and function of your learning setting. Initially, it will take a bit of additional time and convincing conversation. However, eventually your commitment to maintain an aesthetic environment will catch on, and the community will realize its impact on the quality of education.

## Challenges

Think about the aesthetic diet children receive at school and in your classroom. Test your own perceptual awareness and aesthetic judgments by collecting objects that stretch your visual thinking and imagination.

***The aesthetic detective*** — Compare and contrast the aesthetic aspect of similar environments: banks, grocery stores, restaurants, shoe stores, flower shops, and other public places. What does the environment say about the setting? Are there any hidden messages in the advertising? Which one(s) "feels right" to you? Why?

***A visual collection*** — Decide on a visual theme such as a particular form, shape, color, texture, or line, and begin looking for examples in nature and manufactured items. A collection of spiral things might include: seashells, holiday ornaments, seed pods, pencils, abstract expressions postcards, sculptural toys. Organize these into a collection. Round it out by finding children's books, art postcards and posters, cultural artifacts, and other materials to enhance the visual connections inherent in your collection.

***A thing of beauty*** — A *tokonoma*, found in traditional Japanese homes, is a small space which holds a display of something beautiful. Create a space in your classroom to focus attention

*Figure 3-3.* Early childhood display, Elizabeth McKinley, art teacher, Westmont Montessori School, Chester, New Jersey.

on both natural and created beauty. Discuss with the children what kinds of things would be beautiful and how you could display them to draw attention to their perceptual qualities. Let children make as many decisions as possible and help set up the displays. Rotate the items often. Choose interesting visual connections.

***Thoughtful responses*** — Let children view parts of the school or another type of display and have them write what story or meaning they see. What do they decipher? What is confusing? Compare and discuss similarities and differences.

***A picture is worth a thousand words*** — Begin your own environment journal or notebook. Draw or photograph displays, both effective and nondescript, for comparison. Reflect upon the elements of displaying and principles of design with your art specialist. Ask for design suggestions and jot them down next to the pictures. Date and keep them to assess your personal aesthetic development.

## Reflections

These two questions can help you look back on your own aesthetic progress in using *Art as a Way of Learning*®.

- How has your perceptual awareness grown as you considered the ideas in this module?
- What do you look for, pay attention to, think of as essential for your aesthetic comfort?

# MODULE 2
# DEVELOPING AN ART MATERIALS CENTER

**I like the easel. It kinda makes me think I'm a real artist.**

**-Lauren, age 4**

Within perceptually rich environments such as those described in Module 1 of this component, children have regular and frequent opportunities to work with visual art materials in both the art room and their classroom. This module suggests some considerations for the design, materials, and use of the center, and connects directly to Teaching Strategies that are the focus in Component Four.

## Complementing and Extending Children's Learning

In *Art as a Way of Learning®* classrooms, art materials centers are an integral part of the learning environment. Classroom teachers set up these centers to encourage artistic expression, reinforce knowledge and skills, and promote visual thinking across curriculum areas. A classroom art center offers materials that provide choices for artistic representation, along with ample experiences for children to engage in artistic problem solving and visual thinking while enhancing their ability to make connections with other areas in the curriculum.

*Classroom art materials centers encourage artistic expression and visual thinking.*

In a basic classroom art materials center, students find a variety of high-quality, provocative art materials to stimulate their creative expression, avenues for visual representation, and opportunities for deeper understanding (Figures 3-4 and 3-5). Talk with the art specialist about where to obtain supplies such as those recommended in this module and art references for extending children's learning.

The art material center complements other classroom experiences by providing alternative forms of expression and diverse ways for teaching curriculum content. While working with art materials, students reinforce their knowledge of the elements and principles of art, further develop art techniques and composition skills introduced by the art specialist, engage in visual thinking, and increase their respect for other points of view. As with similar learning centers, you will use this basic material area flexibly to pique, strengthen, and extend children's learning. Find opportunities to involve children, the art specialist, families, and local businesses in its planning and implementation.

*Involve everyone in your material center.*

*Figure 3-4.* A material center in Jean Benfante's first grade classroom, Resica Elementary School, East Stroudsburg, Pennsylvania.

**By rearranging the physical environment in the classroom—agitating, reshuffling, and redesigning it—we are able to inspire the imagination and thinking in ourselves and in our students.**

**-George Szekely (1991, p. 14)**



## Guiding Questions

Use the following questions as you prepare to develop your classroom's art materials center.

- At the art materials center in your classroom, which artistic skills and techniques do you want to encourage? Which artistic elements and principles will it support and nurture? How will the activities and materials stimulate children's imaginations?
- Where will you set up the materials center? What materials will children use to represent, express, and link areas of the curriculum? How will the center be organized, used, and maintained?

*Figure 3-5.* The material center in a classroom for 3- to 6-year-olds at Children's House Montessori School, New Brunswick, New Jersey.

- How will you assess the effectiveness of your material center? How can productivity, movement, and material use be measured? How do children help shape the center design, materials, and use?

## Explorations: An Art Materials Center

The purpose of a material center is to encourage children's visual thinking and creative expression with a variety of materials and artistic media. Art materials are readily available in the art specialist's room as well as in each classroom.

### Location and Design

*Choose a space that allows for easy access.*

In the art specialist's room, most of the space is devoted to creative materials and work areas. But where do you find space for art materials in a classroom? Choose a space that has good lighting, ample storage, and allows for easy access for a number of children simultaneously. Open shelves make it easy for children to locate and return items. Cupboards, labeled with words or pictures, also can work well. Color makes a pleasing organizer.

An orderly material center assures that items are easy to reach and that children can handle clean-up. Use clear plastic bins, baskets, and plastic containers such as margarine or ice cream tubs to organize the items. Ask families, the school cafeteria staff, and local businesses to donate storage containers.

Students can use trays to transport materials from the shelf to their desks or a table with ease. A table and sink near the art center makes messier or larger explorations possible. Use a shower curtain, vinyl table cloth, or painter's drop cloth to protect carpeted floors from drips. Keep a mop and sponge nearby so children can clean up messes on washable surfaces.

*Student work predominates.*

Think about what kinds of table or floor space children need as they work and continue their projects from day to day. Children may prefer to stand while they work with clay or finger paint, for example. Some children may enjoy drawing with paper spread out on the floor. Reserve protected space—high shelves, closets—for unfinished projects.

Wall and table space are needed to display students' completed work. Gradually, the room and surrounding hallways may be transformed as student work predominates. Check for display possibilities in the school office, cafeteria, library, and other rooms as well.

## Material Selection

Your classroom's material center will surely be equipped with the drawing materials with which children are most familiar and comfortable, such as markers, pencils, and crayons. Teachers can invigorate the area by offering specialty crayons that glitter, shimmer and "glow" in the dark. Specialty markers, which produce shapes or change colors, add new excitement to familiar drawing tools. Colored pencils are becoming favorites for children who like to combine early writing and symbol making with colorful illustrations.

*Make sure the paper matches the art media and techniques children are learning to use.*

Select art materials that are tailored for children's capacities as they are gaining muscle control. Toddlers, who often hold their drawing tools with clenched fists rather than in a pincer grasp, are usually most successful with thick crayons that are less likely to break, and with washable markers to ease clean-up. Bright tempera colors or washable paints and wide brushes are popular with preschool children in many cultures. Preschool children may also enjoy thick colored pencils, and often choose regular-size crayons because of the wider range of color choices. Fine-point markers and pencils appeal to all children who desire even greater detail in their artistic creations.

Make sure the paper you choose matches the art media and techniques children are learning to use. Try various types of paper—Bristol, oak tag, manila, and others—to become familiar with the unique characteristics of each. For painting, chose a thick, absorbent paper. Finger paint paper has a slick surface which is best for that media. Very young children usually work best with large sheets of light-colored, fairly thick paper so they can make broad, visible marks and won't rip the paper. Older children should be offered a variety of paper sizes and types from which to choose.

Select a range of materials for two- and three-dimensional work, such as paints, brushes, different kinds of papers, yarn, scissors, collage materials, and modeling clay. Choose only good-quality materials so children can be artistically successful. Materials should stimulate children's visual thinking and imaginative connections, so it's a good idea to regularly add to and change the types of materials available.

*Figure 3-6.* Fall display of two- and three-dimensional work, Northampton Child Care Services, Northampton, Pennsylvania.

*Select only good-quality materials for children's success.*

Plan with your art partner to assure consistent rules, responsibilities, and ways to use materials. Take time to demonstrate essential skills, which include the use and storage of materials as well as various artistic techniques. For example, scissors for very young children are small and have rounded ends. When introducing scissors with points for older preschoolers, demonstrate how to carry and use them safely. Teach children to replace marker lids, how to wash paint from brushes, and other essential skills to assure that materials are cared for properly.

Individual attention and instruction when presenting new media is essential to support children's artistic growth. Even young preschoolers can successfully use watercolors when they are taught how to use them. Japanese mothers prefer to use watercolors as the introductory art material for their youngest children. They feel watercolors are even easier to use than crayons because they are so fluid and responsive.

Family members, student volunteers, and the children themselves could be in charge of the organization and upkeep of the material center. Discuss art resources and places to find materials and best buys with the art teacher. The librarian, media specialist, janitor, families, and local businesses are some of your best partners for planning and maintaining your classroom's art materials.

### Cooperative Learning At Its Best

My students use the art center during flex group time (when I am working with small groups), when they are finished with independent work, during center time, or as part of a whole group art activity. I've introduced the materials and how to use them throughout whole group activities and now they are basically on their own to use and experiment with the supplies that are available.

During the first quarter of the school year I had a student teacher and when she was teaching, I sat near the art center, where I could observe her and, at the same time, students using the art center. I was pleased with the way students used the materials and very excited about how they helped each other.

One of my favorite observations was during a small group activity. The group of four students had to design and build a model of the ship Columbus used. I observed the group read and look at pictures in the books provided in the center, and then I listened as they brainstormed and planned how to make the ship. They finally decided on a fairly large box as the main part, but were having trouble deciding on a mast that would stay upright and hold the sail (sheet). They experimented for a while and then Teryance, a special education student who is mainstreamed for science and social studies, said, "I've got an idea how this can work!" He was so excited to show them how to notch two wrapping paper rolls and fit them together to have something to support the sail (the previous one had sagged).

The group was so happy they clapped for Teryance and they decided to make him the "Captain" of the ship because he had solved the problem. Teryance beamed! An excellent example of cooperative learning at the art center (at its best!)

-Dawn Dubbs, classroom teacher,
Bethlehem School District, Pennsylvania

### Safe Centers on a Shoestring

Reuse and recycle! One key to a well-stocked art center is to collect whatever you can from homes, school, local businesses, and industry. Think beyond the traditional art materials. Set up a creative collaborative involving the entire community. Be imaginative in your search for recyclable materials or discards—everything from egg cartons, lumber scraps, fabric, cardboard boxes, product samples, overruns, to outdated stock may have possibilities. Children, families, and local organizations could regularly contribute magazines, for example, or could search for materials for a special project.

Before making any donations or materials available to children, make sure the items are clean, safe, and suitable. In some states, Styrofoam™ packing pieces cannot be used with young children because of the health risks. Loose glitter has been banned in many school districts because it can scratch people's corneas; only glitter immersed in a paint or glue is safe. Check with the art specialist on any questions regarding art product safety guidelines. Use of food products in art, such as pudding or macaroni which is rendered inedible, is discouraged in an effort to be respectful of natural resources and families who may not have enough food.

#### Safety First!

Toxicity, or poisoning, is one of the most important safety issues in selecting art supplies, particularly when working with young children who put everything into their mouths. Use only non-toxic art supplies. Check to be sure the paint, markers, glue, and crayons carry the AP or CP seal, assuring that independent testing showed they are safe for children, even if ingested. Responsible manufacturers register all product information with Poisindex® and local poison control centers (which can be reached in most areas by phoning 911) in the event of an accidental ingestion.

Choking is another major concern for young children. Although national standards require labeling of potential choking hazards for children under the age of 3, educators know there is no magical age when children stop putting small objects in their mouths, and people at any age choke if objects get stuck in their airways. Responsible manufacturers are working toward lessening the choking concern in classrooms by changing small parts (such as marker caps) that can be lengthened or widened and still serve their intended purpose, and reconfiguring them to a safer size.

*Make sure items are clean, safe, and suitable.*

No matter how many donations you amass, you will still need to regularly buy some supplies for your material center. Budgets for art supplies may be very limited, so it may be necessary to discuss the possibility of increasing art and classroom teachers' budgets for supplies. This is where your advocacy skills (Component Two, Module 4) come into play. Talk with the school administration about budget and distribution of resources. Consult with principals and directors (and perhaps the janitor) about your plans for sorting and storing materials. Enlist parent organizations as advocates for funds for the arts. Think in terms of enhancing the aesthetic environment of your school. You might recommend the purchase (or seek donations of) art history reproductions that can be shared with the library and media center.

### Art Center Basic Materials

Offer a range of high-quality materials at the center to extend children's skills and experiences. Vary the materials, changing them periodically. Demonstrate how to use and care for new products.

**Drawing supplies**
- crayons in a range of colors
- markers, thick and thin
- chalk
- oil pastels
- pencils—graphite, colored, watercolor

**Construction/collage supplies**
- different types of paper and materials, stored in divided trays
- stapler
- string
- glue and glue sticks
- brads
- hole punch
- scissors—straight and decorative edge in good working order
- tape—masking and cellophane

**Painting supplies**
- brushes
- watercolors—large pans for preschool and primary children, sets for primary and intermediate children
- tempera and washable paint
- finger paint

**3-D supplies (also see construction)**
- natural, homemade, or commercial modeling compounds

**Paper**
- a variety of newsprint, tissue, drawing, manila, oak tag board, construction, and other papers

## Challenges

Decide where the material center can be located in your classroom. Sketch your ideas. Make a list of resources and materials needed. After your center is established and children know how to use it, use one or more of these assessment tools at regular intervals to measure its success.

***Draw a movement map*** — Draw a floor plan of your classroom and make multiple copies so you can use this process easily and often. Track the children's use of space by picking as many as four children to follow during independent and small-group work periods. Using a different color, trace their movement in the room.

***Prepare a materials-in-use checklist*** — Make a list of all the art materials available for children's independent use. Periodically tally which materials children use while engaged in a visual activity. List any materials which children ask for because they are not accessible or available.

***Survey materials children use*** — Occasionally at the end of a day, give each child a checklist of all the art materials. Have children check off the materials they used throughout that day. Then have them circle the material they enjoyed using the most. Ask them to suggest materials that they would like to have available.

*Reuse and recycle.*

## Reflections

Focus your reflections on the material center's effects on teaching and learning in your classroom.

- ***Design*** — Is the area user friendly? Does it contain materials that children can use artistically? Can the children easily maintain the center by themselves? How do you know?
- ***Impact*** — How have you begun to incorporate the art center in your teaching? What evidence of visual planning and prob lem solving have you observed?

**It took 3 years, but now every classroom has a set of good working scissors and basic art materials.**

**-Greg Naudascher, principal,**
**Resica Elementary School,**
**East Stroudsburg, Pennsylvania**

# MODULE 3
# CURRICULUM CONNECTIONS: IMAGINATIVE ART SPACES

"Toto, I don't think we are in Kansas anymore."

-Dorothy in the *Wizard of Oz*

When space is used imaginatively to assure that the art and classroom curriculums are connected, the entire school benefits. An end of a hallway, or the corner of the library, for example, can be transformed to highlight integrated learning.

Picture an elaborate underwater mural filled with sea life surrounding a reading corner: Stuffed sculptures hang at appropriate ocean depths to reinforce concepts and connect an integrated unit on mysteries of the deep and sculpture. Visitors to the area learn about the ocean and sea life as well as sculpture techniques and individual interpretations of the underwater world. Students visually transformed the space by creating a total learning environment which demonstrates knowledge, skills, and feelings acquired during the integrated project.



## Finding Imaginative Spaces

Effective teachers—including art specialists and classroom teachers—situate children's learning in what they already know. Knowledge transfers from one discipline to another, so it is integrated within math, science, language arts, and social studies. You help children recognize the connections between bodies of knowledge and sets of skills.

*Help children recognize connections between knowledge and skills.*

In this module, we encourage you to extend children's learning beyond the art materials center in your classroom by looking for other spaces to visually connect facets of what children are learning. You might set up these art spaces in the art room, classroom, or in a gathering area such as a hallway or cafeteria. By bringing together a wealth of resources such as art reproductions, artifacts, reference books, various explorations, activities, games, and materials, children's extend and connect their knowledge.

Wherever the art center is established, it should include good quality, working art equipment, different types of art materials, and various art explorations for problem finding and solving. Imaginative space planning gives you a perfect opportunity to collaborate with other teachers and share learning resources. These transformed spaces should support original ideas, stimulate student thinking, stretch artistic expression, and spark individual interpretation and meaning making.

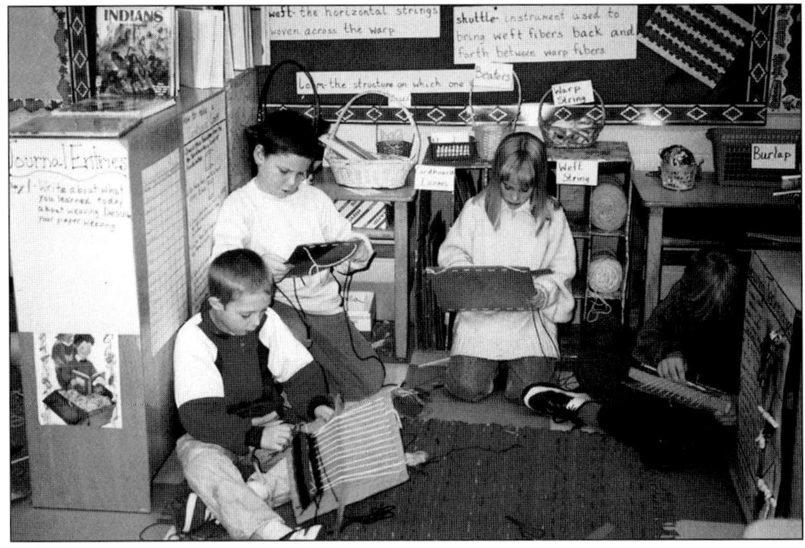


*Figure 3-7.* Second graders doing cardboard loom weaving at their weaving studio space, Stillwater, New Jersey.

**The art center is where you can make things and have fun. You can learn stuff there too!**

**-Travis, age 7**

*Collaborate and share learning resources.*

The art centers have really evolved throughout the year. The classroom teacher and I began very small, combining art and science activities on plants with works by artists. Now, I have at least one Art Studio Space in progress in my classroom, while the second grade teachers set up and share an Integrated Curriculum Area to complement their learning. I really feel art has become infused into school learning. At long last our classrooms are exciting studios for learning.

-Elementary art specialist

## Explorations: Transforming Learning Spaces

We have found two different ways in which educators feel comfortable in transforming classrooms and designing spaces for integrated learning.

1. The **Art Studio Space** highlights art content and stretches students' artistic knowledge and skills. It provides an indepth exploration of an art form or genre that links directly to the curriculum content being studied in a parallel fashion.
2. An **Integrated Curriculum Area** focuses on the connections between the classroom curriculum and art. It combines various aspects of art (history, production, and criticism) with another discipline (science, social studies) in one integrated learning center.

Both types of art centers, along with the Art Materials Center, engage students in visual imagery, creative problem solving, and critical thinking through guided explorations (Figure 3-8). These centers—which are so hands-on, attractive, and inspiring—make an excellent first step toward implementing an integrated curriculum.

As you design or transform teaching and learning spaces, we suggest you consider these steps in the planning process.

- Identify your partners—art specialists, teachers, children, families, businesses.
- Choose a theme. You might highlight art content or perhaps a curriculum concept.
- Define expected student outcomes for art and the discipline(s) which will be integrated or connected.
- Select a location—within a classroom, art room, or a central spot in the school—that has sufficient space for your needs.
- Identify resources (materials, artifacts, books, reproductions).
- Aesthetically arrange materials.
- Decide on a procedure to maintain, stock, rotate, and clean the center.

*Figure 3-8.* All three types of art centers—Art Materials Center, Art Studio Space, and Integrated Curriculum Area—are designed to provide students with the four Ss of *Art as a Way of Learning*®: Support, Stimulate, Stretch, Spark!

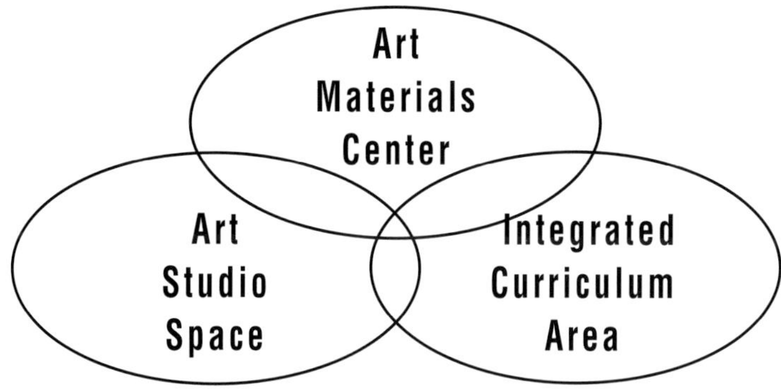


## Art Studio Space

The Art Studio Space establishes a "studio" feeling—a place to view, become inspired, and work—with numerous artistic explorations, art reference books, and reproductions to develop the specific artistic language. This type of center may be found in a number of places: in the art room, classroom, hallway, or library. It may be used with one class or shared with a number of classes.

An Art Studio Space offers children in-depth involvement with an area of the art curriculum (see Visual Literacy) such as media, an element or principle of visual organization, artists, art styles, or a period of art history. Your studio space might directly relate to the structural aspects of the visual language (Color Studio) or encourage a set of artistic problem-solving skills with a medium (Weaving Studio, Figure 3-9). This type of center might focus on an artistic period such as Impressionism, styles such as abstract and cubism, recycled art, or a particular artist (Matisse Studio).

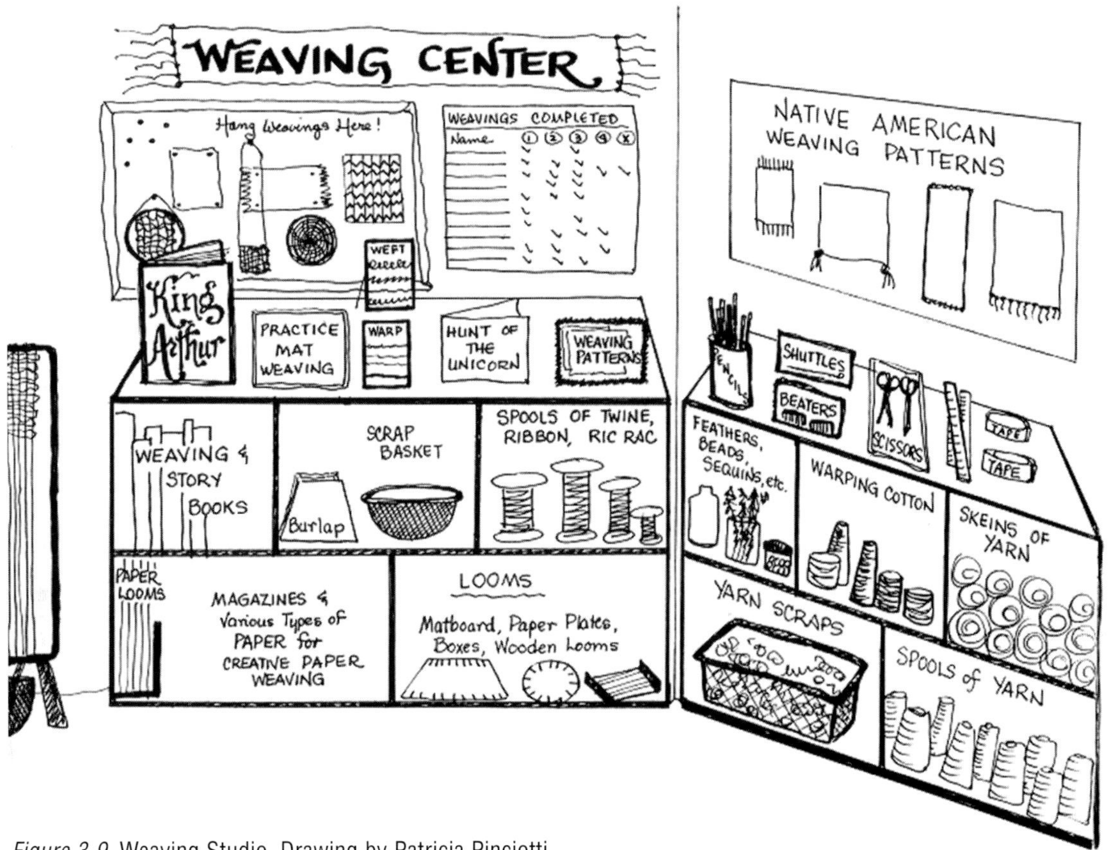


*Figure 3-9.* Weaving Studio. Drawing by Patricia Pinciotti.



Art Studios concentrate on the discipline of art, such as art production, criticism, history, and aesthetics, and powerfully focus artistic learning. In order to reinforce curriculum connections, a Studio should run parallel with a topic of study in the classroom. Use the Art Scan (Figure 1-60) to identify the range of art content, processes, media, aesthetic, and cultural topics. Here is a sample of connections—the possibilities are endless!

- Decorative Arts Studio while studying state history
- Art Studio on Weaving with a unit on farm animals

- Abstract Art Studio during the unit on geometry and shapes
- Romare Bearden Studio and the study of a city
- Book Studio and adventures in fantasy

## Integrated Curriculum Area

An Integrated Curriculum Area connects different types of experiences related to art content and a classroom curriculum concept or theme. You might select a topic for this center in response to children's interests, local or world events, or the curriculum. Children use their perceptual powers to explore the theme while using art to represent their understanding. The center includes materials and activities in two categories:

- **Art content**—art explorations, art games, art books, artifacts, and art references which develop artistic skills, perceptual awareness, and visual thinking
- **Curriculum content**—thematic connections including activities, books, games, and experiences which build a knowledge base and suggest the range and potential in the topic being studied

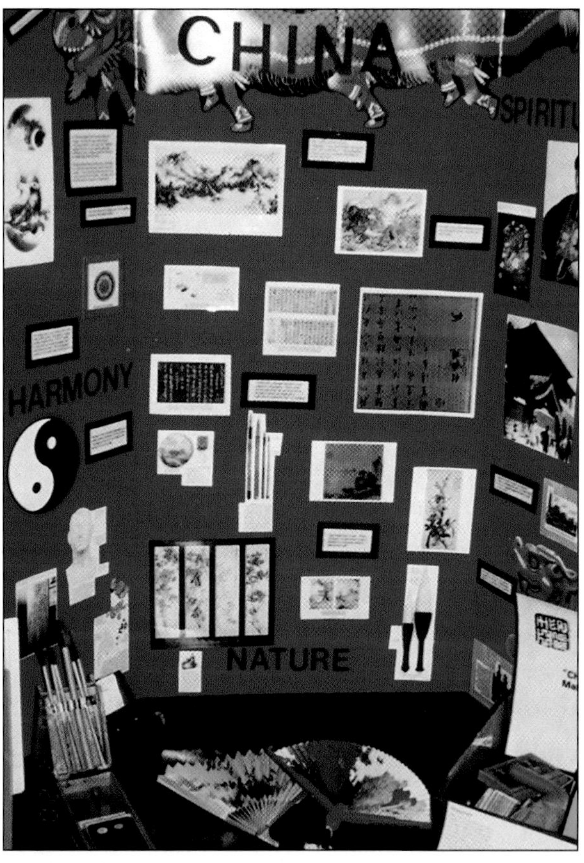


*Figure 3-10.* Chinese Integrated Curriculum Area. Teacher combines artifacts from her travel, student contributions from home, and art explorations supplied by the art specialist.

For example, an Integrated Curriculum Area on China could include artifacts and pictures from the country, books, games, puzzles, origami paper folding, oriental sumi painting, calligraphy brushes and ink sticks with which to write Chinese letters, art postcards of nature paintings, beautiful prints, and a number of printmaking possibilities. These are some of the many ways in which children can come to understand the Chinese people, their values, beliefs, and culture.

An Integrated Curriculum Area may be inspired by art from various cultures (art of Africa, contemporary American art), themes in art (the sea, art and nature, mythology), landmark artworks (van Gogh's *The Starry Night*, Egyptian pyramids), or it may begin with the content of the curriculum or ideas from the children. Table 3-1 outlines an Integrated Curriculum Area with art explorations, perceptual/looking-at activities, and knowledge related to the science and art on the topic of the human body.

Table 3-1. **Integrated Curriculum Area**

***The Human Body Resource List***

| ART CONTENT | CURRICULUM CONTENT | |
|---|---|---|
| Art exploration<br>• doll and paper doll making<br>• cartooning<br>• tracing and drawing details of body parts to be assembled into a "Frankenclass" figure<br>• fingerprint people<br>• wire figure sculpture<br>• silhouettes<br>• self-portraits<br>• mask-making forms | Art card matching games on people or masks from various cultures<br>Reproductions of artwork from several cultures<br>• Picasso, Cassatt, Van Gogh, Rembrandt, Hahlo<br>• Tical (Mayan ruins)<br>• Dancers from Burma<br>• Masks from Mexico<br>• Thai or Chinese figures | Science knowledge<br>• body parts, names and function<br>• taking care of your body: nutrition, health, and safety<br>• systems that work: muscles, bones, organs<br><br>Models<br>• skeletons, drawing dolls, masks |
| Book<br>• Zaidenburg: *How to Draw Heads and Faces* | Books<br>• Emberley: *Fingerprints*<br>• Gray: *Anatomy*<br>• DaVinci: *Anatomy* | Fingerprint match game<br>Sculpture sort game |

## Guiding Questions

Think about these questions as you begin to plan how you will enable students to make connections between curricular topics and concepts in the visual arts.

- Will your center be an Art Studio Space? If so, on which art curriculum area do you intend to focus? Which visual art standards (MENC, 1994) will your space address? How will children stretch their knowledge and skills? How will this center support the children's understanding of your shared curriculum goals?
- Is your center to be an Integrated Curriculum Area? What artifacts, art explorations, references, games, resources, books, and materials have you and your partner found to reinforce and connect to the curriculum? Will it provide enough re search material and exciting art explorations to engage children? How will you make direct connections between the transfer of learning skills and bodies of knowledge?
- Is your goal to transform a school space? What artistic techniques and principles can you use to create a total, imaginative environment? Will it spark children's imagination as both creator and viewer? How will both children's art and curriculum content be integrated in the space in an aesthetic manner?



**An Integrated Curriculum Area integrates different types of experiences related to art content and a curriculum concept.**

## Environmental Transformations

One class or an entire grade level might decide to collaborate with the art specialist to develop an exciting space to demonstrate arts integration and learning. Spaces such as a hallway, part of a library, cafeteria, or entryway can be transformed into a visual environment. These surroundings can highlight children's learning, curriculum content, and artistic connections in a more elaborate way. Such environments often come about as a culminating project to showcase the extent of knowledge and skills children acquired. Visitors to the environment are greeted with verbal information (from taped tours, written programs, or student docents) and a visual feast that transports viewers to another time or place.

*Figure 3-11.* ***Indian Desert.*** Christine Capra, age 7, wet brown bag and conté crayon.

Themes and topics for these environments can be found in social studies, literature, science, and math. An in-depth study of the rain forest, medieval times, prehistory, *The Secret Garden*, biomes, or geometric domes (to name a few) can stimulate realistic or imaginative environments. Generally, the space is transformed from floor to ceiling and contains work done primarily by children. Planning and implementation is done with the children and the art specialist. The technical work of transforming the space may include parents, older students, and volunteers. The school custodian is a wonderful source of ways to implement elaborate ideas.

*Figure 3-12.* ***The Old Rug.*** Darin Bigus, age 8, pencil and marker.

Planning provides ample problem-posing and -solving situations for you and your children as you consider:

- theme, expected outcomes, and ways to demonstrate what is learned and created
- location, ways to surround the visitor and transform the space
- materials, availability of resources and specific tasks
- public presentation: ways to communicate information to viewers



Take a trip to a science, art, or natural history museum to help visualize the overall display effect. Invite a museum display person to assist in the planning and technical issues (see the next module on displaying children's work). Don't forget to document the process and problems and make sure you get some positive press coverage from all your work.

*Figure 3-13.* A fourth grade Native American Integrated Curriculum Area.

## Challenges

After you have created your imaginative space, be it an Art Studio Space, Integrated Curriculum Area, or some other transformed environment, take time to extend children's learning and assess its impact. Select from the challenges below and keep a record of new ideas and suggestions in your sketchbook. The second time around is always easier.

### Visual Thinking

- Use art reproductions and artifacts from a variety of cultures that make a visual link to learning throughout the classroom (e.g., Renoir's *Girl With a Watering Can* hung near the plants).
- Encourage children to find new connections between art, nature, cultures, and the curriculum, sharing things from all of your homes or travels.

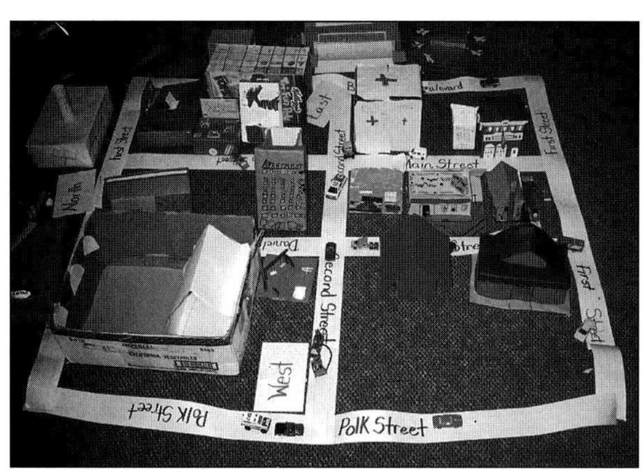


*Figure 3-14.* ***Our Town.*** Second grade, Resica Elementary School, East Stroudsburg, Pennsylvania.

- Increase perceptual awareness and reasoning with looking, touching, listening, and tasting experiences.
- Help children find connections between the art center and the curriculum content by playing games, questioning, and referring to the found relationships and coherent order.

### Visual Language

- Encourage children to use artistic language during the day. When you ask for assistance: "Would you please hand me the brayer?" When you make comments about what they are making: "Can you describe why these clouds look like they are moving?" Ask questions to encourage problem solving: "How could you make the duck's neck look smaller?"
- Reinforce the vocabulary of art to communicate what children know. Create artistic problems to solve, and ask artistic questions related to technique and skill.
- Emphasize the visual aspects found in books, nature, and the environment to develop a rich storehouse of perceptual images.

*Visitors are greeted with verbal information and a visual feast.*

### Extensions

- Provide time and opportunity for each child to extend and vary any projects at the center.
- Encourage artistic growth and visual literacy by adding new materials or demonstrating specific techniques, changing the art references, and incorporating children's suggestions for the art center.
- Ask questions, pose problems, and make direct connections while children work at the center.
- Include thought-provoking discussion or require written responses to questions to assess children's integration of knowledge or connections.

### Environment scan

- When the class seems to be using a lot of art materials (or none at all) for a few consecutive days, look around your environment and the centers. Consider the amount and types of materials, their condition, effects of rules, order, organization, need to introduce new materials or techniques. Engage the class in a discussion about what aspects of the center need to be changed or refurbished.

### Art Center survey

- Periodically put a sign-in sheet in the area. Tell the children you are doing a survey and you need them to sign their name each time they go to the area. Ask them to write the reason (or check off appropriate boxes) why they went to the center (to get information, just to look, show something to a friend).

*Teachers, children, and the art specialist plan together.*

*Figure 3-15.* ***Nature's Patterns.*** Brittany Esquibel, age 7, tempera and oil pastel.

## Reflections

Take the time to discuss with your partner the success of your art center. Explore any changes you would make and consider additions. Ask other teachers for input.

- Where do you find the best resources for an art center?
- How did you collaborate on the spaces?
- After using your imaginative area for a while, ask yourselves what you would do differently.
- What do the children remember about the space? How have they contributed to it?

# MODULE 4
# CHILDREN'S ART EXPLORATIONS: DISPLAYS AND DOCUMENTATION

**I like art for some reason, like whenever we have an idea inside, we get to put it down. When we have other assignments we only get to do one thing.**

**-Justin, age 8**

Children are very aware of whether or not we cherish their work. We demonstrate that we value young artists' critical thinking and creativity, and its products, when we provide them with sufficient materials and time to complete their creations. Our comments, made while children are working and about the finished product, communicate our interest and help children consider their progress (see Component Four on Teaching Strategies).

*Figure 3-16.* Young impressionist artist exploring watercolor at Northampton Community College Child Development Center, Bethlehem, Pennsylvania.

The attention we pay to creating and documenting displays of children's artistic work promotes visual and verbal messages. As children increase their capacity to communicate through art, our comments and exhibitions support the development of knowledge and skills, as well as their self-esteem. Shows of children's work clearly communicate that learning through art is a valuable endeavor. These exhibits can both guide and document their learning processes.



## Cherishing Children's Artistry

As her mom waited, Chloe said that her drawing was for me to DISPLAY. I asked her if there was anything she wanted to tell me about the picture that I should write. She said, "No. It's only for display."

I said, "Well, I'm going to make a little card that says, 'Chloe Martin' and should I put anything else on that card?"

She said, "No. It's only for *display* for you to keep!"

It hit me like a ton of bricks, of course. It needed no words; she was communicating to me that the visual was the message. Thank goodness that Chloe was so patient with me as I tried to insist otherwise (of course, gently!). I was wishing that Martha (artist-in-residence in this classroom) was there to share some of these moments today. It was truly an exciting day as so many "ah-ha" moments occurred in the classroom.

After Chloe left, I prepared a mat for her display piece and a card that read, "Chloe Martin 12-8-93" and hung it for *display* on the wall.

- Kathy Roberti, Child Care Services Coordinator,
Northampton Community College,
Bethlehem, Pennsylvania

Visual displays can be a memorable, public way in which we demonstrate the importance of *Art as a Way of Learning*®. Children develop respect for the work of others when they recognize that we value their work. This atmosphere builds a sense of community within the classroom and extends beyond the school walls into the neighborhood.

Displays that children create with their work can be learning experiences for the group as well as other children in the school (see Figure 3-17). Besides presenting children's creations, displays may also document a particular idea, artistic style, technique, the efforts of a small group, or an individual project. Whatever the objective of the display, the perception and belief that you value and cherish visual thinking and children's artistry will be evident.

*Figure 3-17.* Find a way to communicate details about students' visual thinking and learning. Sculpture display in hallway.

You also indicate your support for visual communication when children are expected to document their work with a title, artist's statement, or an explanation of the process. When you and the children prepare an exhibit of their work, find a way to communicate details about students' visual thinking and learning. Student documentation may also describe their thinking processes while they worked or indicate how their understanding has changed.

Interactive displays are a great way to extend children's learning. Perhaps children can demonstrate a technique as part of the display, or a student docent can explain how an art process works. These in-person experiences often elicit welcome responses from viewers and provide yet another dimension for student learning.

You can spark more connections in children's thinking by taking the show on the road. Local libraries, senior centers, shopping malls, and business often like to have displays. Call to arrange for a place and the period of time for the exhibit. To further integrate the student learning experience, take photos or slides of their display. Use these for back-to-school night presentations, parent conferences, student reference, and portfolio evenings.

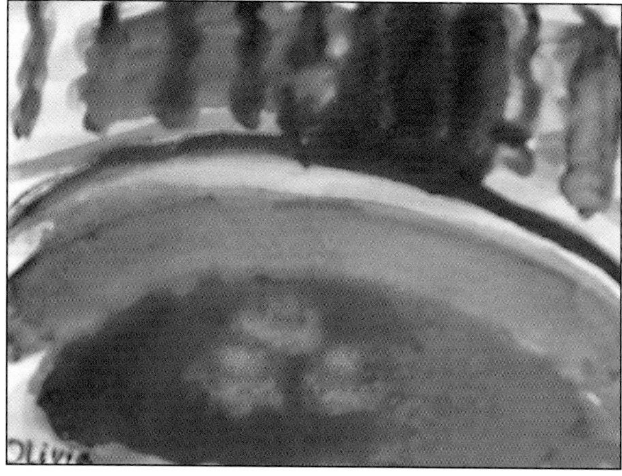

*Figure 3-18.* Interpretation of Monet's ***Water Lilies: Japanese Bridge*** (before defining purpose), Elizabeth McKinley, art teacher, Westmont Montessori School, Chester, New Jersey.

*Demonstrations or docents often elicit responses from viewers and provide yet another dimension to student learning.*

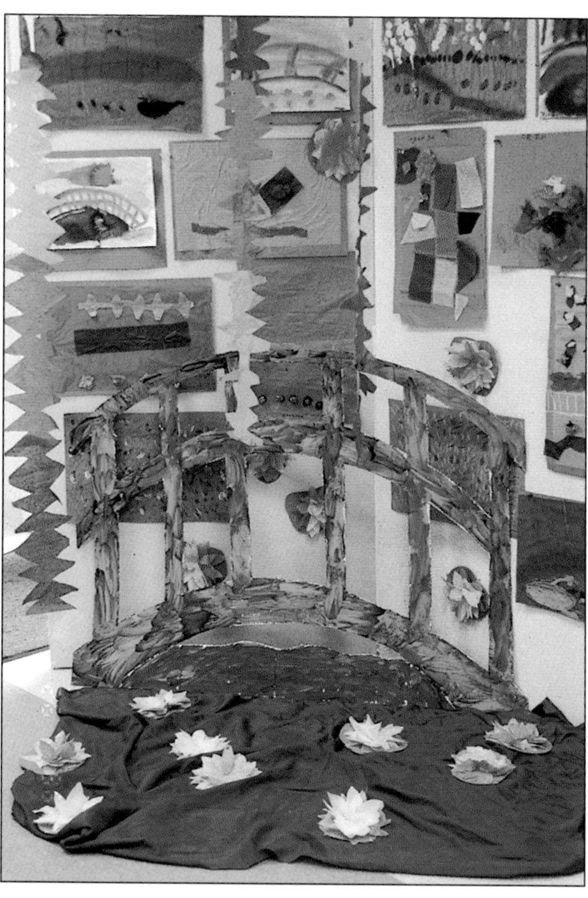

*Figure 3-19.* Display using Monet's ***Bridge at Giverny*** as a spark, Elizabeth McKinley, art teacher, Westmont Montessori School, Chester, New Jersey.

## Guiding Questions

A display validates students' work, supports the viewers' aesthetic experience, and documents children's understanding. When planning a display, the collaborating art specialist and classroom teacher work with the children to review the curriculum and aesthetic outcomes in light of the following considerations:

- What is the purpose of your display? Is this a culminating showcase or a works-in-progress display? What is the focus: a particular medium, image, or process?

- Where and how can you best present children's work? What type of setting, display criteria, and lighting will enhance it? How will the setting stimulate viewer response? Will it give insight into the children's thinking, feeling, or creative process? What documentation will viewers need to intelligently view the works?
- Which concepts about the integrated theme or project can be highlighted? How will the documentation make that connection? What values about learning are being communicated to other students, families, teachers? What artistic aspects of the art curriculum and standards are being reinforced?

## Explorations: Showcases for Learning



In *Art as a Way of Learning®*, collaboration between classroom teachers, the art specialist, and children reinforces the interactive nature of the learning process. To facilitate your collaboration in displaying and documenting children's work, it is helpful to see the process in three parts: defining the purpose of the display, creating the display, and documenting the process.

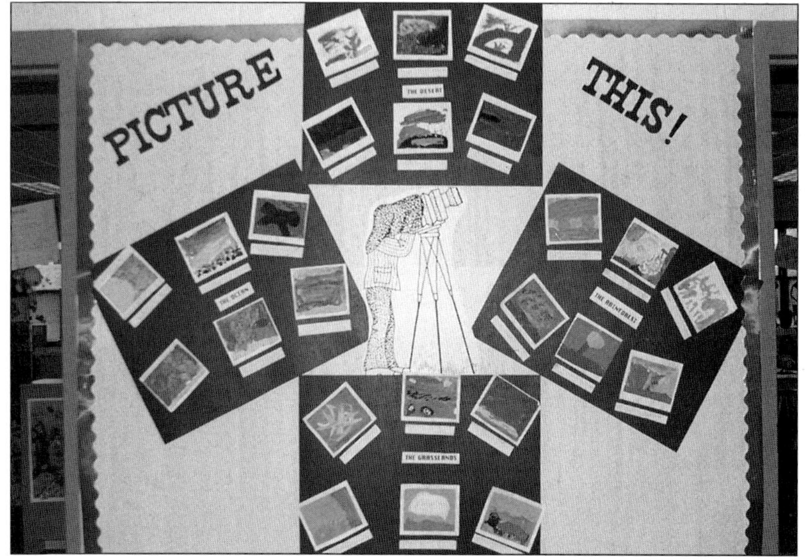


*Figure 3-20.* Second graders take a unique perspective on environments by creating picture postcards with a monoprinting technique, Resica Elementary School, East Stroudsburg, Pennsylvania.

### Define the Purpose

In collaboration with the children, reflect upon the purpose, define the selection criteria, and discuss the process and learning experience. Try different types of shows. Ask children to help select from their portfolio or from among a body of works on a theme or project after the purpose or theme has been decided. Decide together whether the purpose for the display will be to demonstrate performance understanding or to present a culminating exhibit, and whether it will be static or will change as more work is completed. Some children may be interested in doing an individual show. Another possibility is to do a show highlighting an artistic medium or process, such as crayon resist or mobiles.

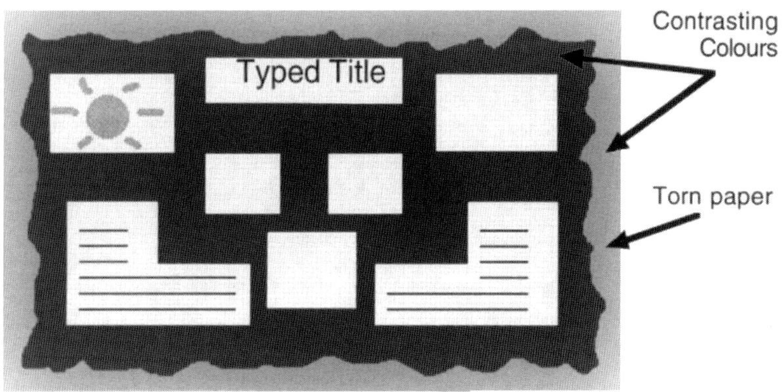


Symmetry

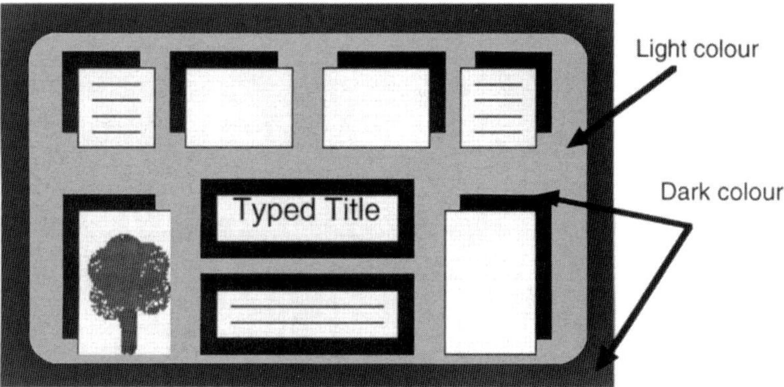


Mounted symmetry

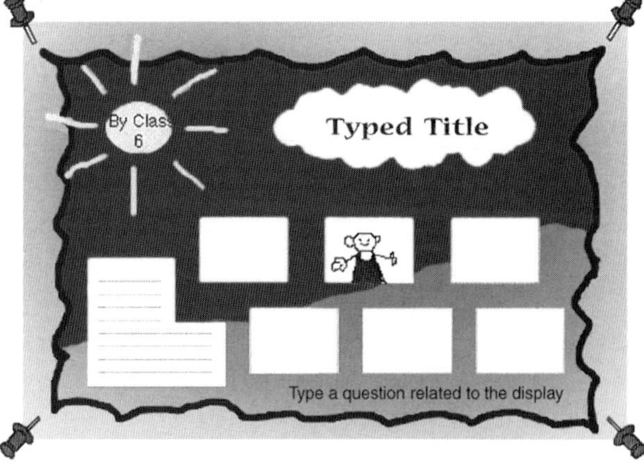


Free-form pictorial display

*Figure 3-21.* Encourage student artists' documentation and reflective writing. These are a few ways to create displays of their work. Designed by Netty Reddish, Leeds Metropolitan University, Leeds, England.

## Create the Display

Encourage children to design their own display as they explore an idea or topic through a series of visual work. Support children's creative and critical thinking as they pick a space and create their display. The design of the display can enhance visual thinking and stimulate the imagination of the viewer, while valuing children's learning in a creative way.

First, choose the location and then decide the best way to design the display for the space. Some exhibit areas may have restrictions about how works can be hung, so find out what the requirements are before you plan. Work with your arts partner to help children identify aspects of visual displays that appeal to them, and then work together to find ways to use these techniques in their display.

Compose the display arrangement in a way that will best address your purpose. Encourage children to design their display so it has a strong visual focus and makes concrete connections between their work and the display techniques. Brainstorm possible ways to emphasize and complement aesthetic elements that support learning. For example, you might hang symmetrical butterfly designs from a large tree branch, or view a group of landscapes through a trompe l'oeil (fake but realistic) window.

Your class may want to enlist the help of families, college students, older students, or community volunteers to mount and prepare children's work for display.

**Mounting.** For a finished look, mount and/or frame two-dimensional works. Use a sheet of colored construction paper at least one inch larger all around than the piece to be mounted, or use mat board or other kinds of paper. Use a glue stick or other adhesive to attach the work to its mounting. Choose a backing that will complement the work and coordinate with the display. A neutral color such as black, gray, or white is often used as the unifying background for all artwork in the display.

**Positioning.** To showcase works that are three-dimensional, consider platforms, pedestals, shelves, or ceiling hangers. Screens, boxes, corrugated paper, shelving, and tree branches can become flexible display components (Figure 3-21). Vary the height and positions of the displayed art works to add visual interest. Different backgrounds can also be used to bring out colors or textures in artwork.

**Hanging.** Organize a display team and prepare a list of things to do to hang or position work in a show. This list can be particularly helpful if your display team changes with each exhibit. Make sure you have all the tools you may need in your display tool box. Use sturdy ladders for climbing. Follow all the requirements for hanging, so that the facility will be happy to have your group exhibit again.

**Display Tool Box Contents**

**Use a sturdy container to hold:**

- hammer
- pliers
- scissors
- stapler
- staples
- staple remover
- T-pins
- masking tape
- double-sided tape
- adhesive tape
- twine
- fishing line
- paper clips
- retractable tape measure
- pencil
- screwdrivers (flat and Phillips heads)
- push pins
- sticky adhesive

## Document Learning

Documentation is an essential aspect of any display, and involves more than just adding a title and class name. Use documentation to communicate the value and meaning of the learning experience, the types of processes children used, or the kinds of thinking that occurred during their work.

Plan ahead. Large projects such as murals or group sculpture lend themselves well to preparing a display of work in progress. Be sure to record information and save artifacts that inspire the children. Regularly take photos to chronicle the project's development. Refer often to early drafts and references as children reflect on their visual thinking and the artistic process.

*Displays support children's creative and critical thinking.*

In every display, include children's descriptions, feelings, or thoughts. Engage children in reflective writing, recording their ideas either by hand or with a computer. Encourage student artists' documentation and reflective writing by asking them to:

- Describe the connection between the artistic purpose and curriculum content.
- Describe the technical or expressive aspects of the work, process, or medium.
- Explain the kinds of thinking and artistic problem solving in which they engaged.
- Identify personal and curriculum connections with cultural, social, or historical contexts.
- Connect to artistic heritage by discussing a culture, artist, period, or style, possibly including a reproduction or art references.
- Include their comments on the work or title for the piece.
- Challenge viewers to look carefully, reflect on how images relate to the theme, or describe how these particular artists communicate meaning through their work.
- Encourage viewers to add their own comments to the exhibit in a designated space, in a response book, or on sticky notes placed near the work.

*Figure 3-22.* Two third graders create a display to demonstrate two different ways to depict Venus. Resica Elementary School, East Stroudsburg, Pennsylvania.



Documentation may also capture children's learning in more permanent ways. Many groups like to make a book describing their process from start to finish. Their book might accompany the display and will certainly be a treasured object in the class library. Or create a class catalogue of all the shows throughout the year, with children's comments on the connections they made between the curriculum and art processes.

## Challenges

Use these challenges to enhance your visual thinking in relation to displays so you can better help students, who in turn will inform and enhance the learning of others.

### Visit Museums and Galleries

- Visit galleries, and art, natural history, and children's museums with your art partner to discover creative ideas on display and organization in action. Sketch ideas that work.

### Facilitate Learning

- Using displays as a learning tool is a wonderful way to validate the understandings in children's work and reinforce visual thinking. Encourage other teachers and students to view the display and talk about it.
- Ask students to act as docents, explaining themes, demonstrating techniques, or describing particular types of artistic problem solving.
- Engage in an artful conversation in front of a display (such as at a museum).

### Use Photos/Slides/Drawings

- Take photos or slides of children's displays throughout the year. Incorporate these into presentations for back-to-school nights, school board meetings, conferences, and portfolio evenings with families and children.

### Assessment

- With your students, develop a survey or interview form to evaluate displays. Questions may cover aesthetic qualities, design, and how well the display communicates understanding. A simple survey might ask the viewer to write a comment, a question, or a compliment about the display.
- Ask other classes, as well as the principal, art specialist, librarian, families, or other viewers, to fill out the survey. Children record and analyze results using their math skills.
- Use survey information in planning your next display.
- Encourage students to use concept mapping as a way to assess what they have learned.

## Reflections

Think about your class's most recent display and assess what its benefits were for students, children in the school, other teachers, families, and yourself.

- How did your display enhance the school environment?
- What types of feedback did you receive about it?
- Does the time and effort required to create the display balance the impact and results?
- How could you enhance perception and extend visual thinking? Make a list of ways to improve future displays.

## Bibliography

### Teacher Resources on the Visual Arts


Arnhiem, R. (1969). *Visual thinking.* Berkeley: University of California Press.

Arnhiem, R. (1974). *Art and visual perception.* Berkeley: University of California Press.

Arnhiem, R. (1986). *New essays on the psychology of art.* Berkeley: University of California Press.

Beggs, S. (1991). *The no-nonsense guide to teaching art.* Minneapolis: T.S. Denison.

Berk, L.D., & Winsler, A. (1995). *Scaffolding children's learning: Vygotsky and early childhood education.* Washington, DC: National Association for the Education of Young Children.

Bresler, L. (1993). Three orientations of arts in the primary grades: Implications for curriculum reform. *Arts Education Policy Review, 94*(6), 29-34.

Broudy, H. (1972). *Enlightened cherishings.* Urbana, IL: University of Illinois.

Carlson, L. (1993). *EcoArt! Earth-friendly art and craft experiences for 3- to 9-year-olds.* Charlotte, VT: Williamson.

Dean, J. (1972). *Room to learn: A place to paint.* New York: Citation Press.

Depree, H., & Mackinnon, L. (1993). *Art, books, and children: Art and literature in the classroom.* Bothell, WA: The Wright Group.

Edwards, B. (1989). *Drawing on the right side of the brain.* New York: Putnam's.

Ernst, K. (1994). *Picturing learning: Artists and writers in the classroom.* Portsmouth, NH: Heinemann.

Feeney, S., & Moravcik, E. (1987). A thing of beauty: Aesthetic development in young children. *Young Children, 46*(6), 6-15.

Gardner, H., & Perkins, D. (Eds.). (1989). *Art, mind & education.* Chicago: University of Illinois Press.

Getty Education Institute for the Arts, The. (1985). *Beyond creating: The place for art in America's schools.* Los Angeles: Author.

Gilliatt, M.T. (1983). Art appreciation: A guide for the classroom teacher. *Educational Horizons, 61*(2), 79-82.

Henri, R. (1923). *The art spirit.* New York: Harper & Row.

Jackson, M. (1993). *Creative display and environment.* Portsmouth, NH: Heinemann.

Kohl, M.A.F. (1985). *Science arts: Discovering science through art experiences.* Bellingham, WA: Bright Ring.

Kohl, M.A.F. (1985). *Scribble cookies and other independent creative art experiences for children.* Bellingham, WA: Bright Ring.

Kohl, M.A.F. (1989). *Mudworks: Creative clay, dough, and modeling experiences.* Bellingham, WA: Bright Ring.

Langer, E. (1997). *The power of mindful learning.* New York: Addison-Wesley.

Lasky, L., & Mukerji-Bergeson, R. (1980). *Art: Basic for young children.* Washington, DC: National Association for the Education of Young Children.

Linderman, E.W., & Linderman, M.M. (1984). *Arts and crafts for the classroom.* New York: Macmillan.

Marantz, S.S. (1992). *Picture books for looking and learning: Awakening visual perceptions through the art of children's books.* Phoenix: Oryx.

Milford, S. (1990). *Adventures in art: Art and craft experiences for 7- to 14-year-olds.* Charlotte, VT: Williamson.

Murray, P., & Murray, L. (1983). *Dictionary of art and artists.* New York: Penguin.

Music Educators National Conference (MENC). (1994). *The national standards for arts education.* Reston, VA: Author.

Olson, J.L. (1992). *Envisioning writing: Toward an integration of drawing and writing.* Portsmouth, NH: Heinemann.

Perkins, D.N. (1989). Art as understanding. In H. Gardner & D. Perkins (Eds.), *Art, mind & education* (pp. 111-131). Chicago: University of Illinois Press.

Ritter, D. (1991). *Literature-based art activities.* Cypress, CA: Creative Teaching Press.

Ritter, D. (1993). *Multicultural art activities from the cultures of Africa, Asia, and North America.* Cypress, CA: Creative Teaching Press.

Schuman, J.M. (*1981*). *Art from many hands: Multicultural art projects.* Worcester, MA: Davis Publications.

Smith, N.R. (1993). *Experience and art: Teaching children to paint* (2nd ed.). New York: Teachers College Press.

Szekely, G. (1991). *From play to art.* Portsmouth, NH: Heinemann.

Tuchman, G. (1993). *Great art ideas for kids K-3.* Mahwah, NJ: Troll.

## Resources for Art Centers and Integrated Curriculum Areas

### Children's Books

Aronsky, J. (1988). *Sketching outdoors in autumn.* New York: Lothrop, Lee & Shepard.

Banyai, I. (1995). *Re-zoom.* New York: Viking.

Berry, M. (1988). *Georgia O'Keeffe: American women of achievement.* New York: Chelsea House. (Other women are also included in this series)

Bjork, C. (1987). *Linnea in Monet's garden.* New York: R & S Books.

Brown, L.K., & Brown, M. (1990). *Visiting the art museum.* New York: Dutton.

Bunting, E. (1994). *Smoky night.* New York: Harcourt Brace. (excellent use of collage, suitable for older children)

Catalanotto, P. (1995). *The painter.* New York: Orchard.

Chermayeff, I., & Chermayeff, J.C. (1990). *First words.* New York: Abrams. (simple words in five languages represented by famous works of art)

Cohen, M. (1996). *No good in art.* New York: Bantam Doubleday Dell.

Cummings, R. (1979). *Just look.* New York: Scribner's.

Davidson, M.B. (1984). *History of art.* New York: Random House.

dePaola, T. (1989). *The art lesson.* Huntington Beach, CA: Putnam.

dePaola, T. (1991). *Bonjour, Mr. Satie.* Huntington Beach, CA: Putnam.

Epstein, V.S. (1987). *History of women artists for children.* Denver: VSE.

Giraudy, D. (1988). *An art play book: Picasso the minotaur.* New York: Abrams. (also available for other artists)

Glass, A. (1984). *Jackson makes his move.* New York: Random House.

Goffstein, M.B. (1981). *Lives of the artists.* New York: Garrar, Straus, Giroux. (poems about Rembrandt, Guardi, Van Gogh, Bonnard, Nevelson)

Jonas, A. (1989). *Color dance.* New York: Greenwillow.

Lamarche, H. (1985). *Picasso for children.* Montreal, Quebec, Canada: The Montreal Museum of Fine Arts.

Lepsky, I. (1984). *Leonardo daVinci.* Woodbury, NY: Barrons.

Lepsky, I. (1984). *Pablo Picasso.* Woodbury, NY: Barrons.

Locker, T. (1995). *Sky tree: Learning science through art.* New York: Puffin. (excellent source for teaching weather and seasons through paintings)

Lyons, M.E. (1993). *Starting home.* New York: Macmillan.

Micklethwait, L. (1992). *I spy—An alphabet book.* New York: Greenwillow.

Meyer, S.E. (1990). *First impressions.* New York: Abrams. (series includes several artists)

Moss, S. (1995). *Peter's painting.* New York: Mondo.

Myers, W.D. (1993). *Great migration, The: An American story.* New York: Harper Collins.

Peppin, A. (1980). *The Usborne story of painting.* Tulsa, OK: Hayes.

Perl, L. (1987). *Mummies, tombs, and treasure—Secrets of ancient Egypt.* Boston: Clarion.

Raboff, E. (1988). *Art for children.* New York: Doubleday. (series includes more than 15 artists)

Sills, L. (1989). *Inspirations—Stories about women artists.* Morton Grove, IL: Whitman.

Simmonds, P. (1989). *Lulu and the flying babies.* New York: Knopf.

Venezia, M. (1988). *Getting to know the world's greatest artists.* Chicago: Children's Press. (artists in series include Picasso, Cassatt, Van Gogh, Monet)

Voss, G. (1993). *Museum colors.* Boston: Boston Museum of Fine Art.

Whiteford, A.H., & Vernon, O. (1973). *A Golden guide—North American Indian arts.* New York: Golden.

Ziebel, P. (1989). *Look closer.* Boston: Clarion.

## Art Education Resources

*Web site addresses are constantly changing. If an address is not available, a search for the key words may help you locate the site.*

**Alarion Press**
P.O. Box 1882
Boulder, CO 80306
(303) 443-9039
Sound filmstrips and videos on art history, periods of art, and other topics

**CRIZMAC**
Box 65928
Tucson, AZ 85728
(800) 913-8555
Videotapes, materials, games, and activities for art history and culture

**Crystal Productions**
Box 2159
Glenview, IL 60025
(800) 255-8629
(847) 657-8144
crystal@interaccess.com
Contains videotapes, videodisks, prints, filmstrips, slides, and books for students on artists and techniques

**Metropolitan Museum of Art**
255 Gracie Station
New York, NY 10028-9998
(212) 570-3930
www.metmuseum.org
Catalog of reproductions, videos, and children's activities

**National Gallery of Art**
Publications Mail Order Department
2000B South Dr.
Landover, MD 20785
(301) 322-5900
fax (301) 322-1578
www.NGA.gov/shop/shop
Catalog of reproductions including postcards costing 35¢ each

**Roland Collection of Films on Art**
3120 Pawtucket Rd.
Northbrook, IL 60062
(847) 291-2230
www.roland-collection.com
Video tapes of various artists and periods of art

COMPONENT FOUR

# Teaching Strategies

MODULES

- Support: Respond to Children's Ideas
- Stimulate: Increase Knowledge and Understanding
- Stretch: Develop Imagination and Artistic Skills
- Spark! Discover Personal Meaning

Your *Art as a Way of Learning*® journey so far has been a fascinating exploration of opportunities that the arts open up for educators, the community, and children alike. You have read about teachers and art specialists who use art to pique children's creative and critical thinking and to integrate the curriculum—remember the inquiring children who built underground vehicles with Ms. Vista's and Mr. Angelo's guidance? In each scenario, we saw that children's explorations are personally meaningful, visually rich, and require thoughtful reflection. By now, you have most likely gained deeper understandings about

- how children's creative and critical thinking develops and how students construct meaning and learn new skills while using art as a visual language to lead their learning in all curriculum areas
- the exciting potential that collaboration brings for teachers and art specialists who plan and implement arts-integrated learning
- ways that educators and others in the community develop an aesthetic visual learning environment in which children's problem-solving abilities and artistry are cherished



## Art Is an Opportunity

Ms. Vista and Mr. Angelo, along with other teachers and art specialists like you, are continuing the quest to become more adept at designing integrated learning opportunities with *Art as a Way of Learning.* Art partners who combine their understandings about the cycle of children's creative and critical thinking (Figure 1-4) with the reflective teaching strategies described here are likely to realize that:

- As art partners collaboratively design an integrated curriculum and plan art explorations, the focus shifts from what is being taught to what children are learning. When educators cultivate children's creative and critical thinking, students construct understanding and meaning from their experiences.
- Interactions among adults and children become more reflective, creative, and joyous. Awareness of individual student strengths, styles, and cultures are honored as the group's enthusiasm for learning evolves.

- Student engagement in learning is deeper and more adventuresome. Children develop positive learning dispositions such as commitment, enthusiasm, and curiosity. They can transfer and apply their learning in different contexts and disciplines.

What teaching strategies activate children's artistic and learning dispositions and build skills that are essential for them to create and respond to art and other curriculum content? To guide the learning process, teachers and art specialists support, stimulate, stretch, and spark! children's learning and development (Figure 4-1). These four teaching strategies—called the four Ss of *Art as a Way of Learning*®—are elaborated upon in this component.

> **We "must invite students to experience the world's richness, empower them to ask their own questions and seek their own answers, and challenge them to understand the world's complexities."**
>
> **(Brooks & Brooks, 1993, p. 5)**

*Figure 4-1.*

**Four *Art as a Way of Learning*® teaching strategies**

**Support**

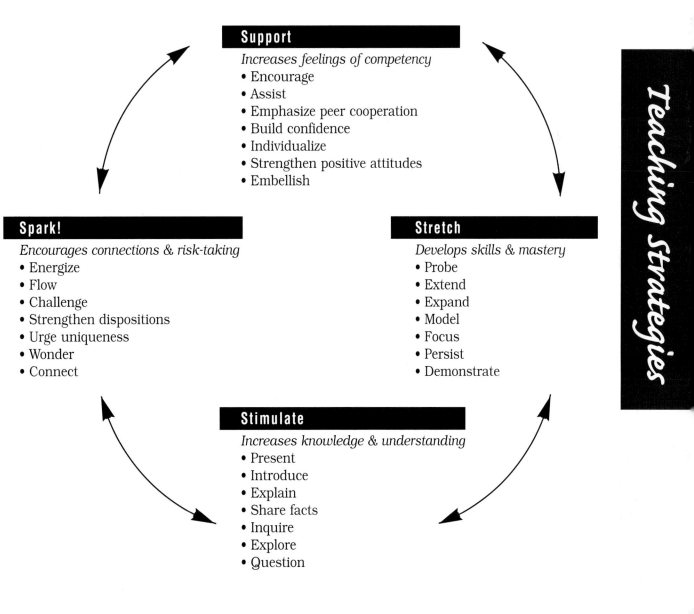

*Increases feelings of competency*
- Encourage
- Assist
- Emphasize peer cooperation
- Build confidence
- Individualize
- Strengthen positive attitudes
- Embellish

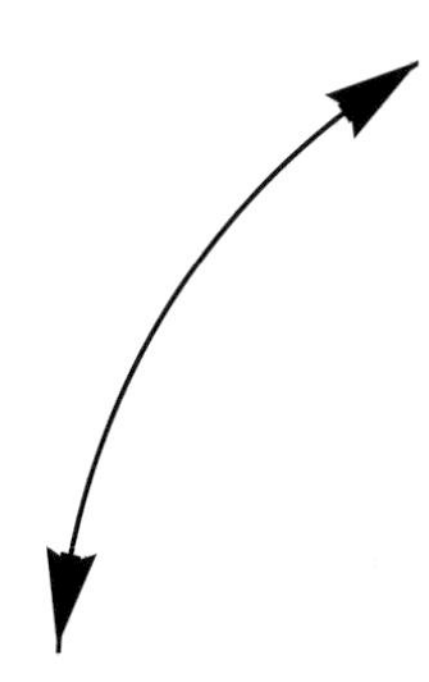

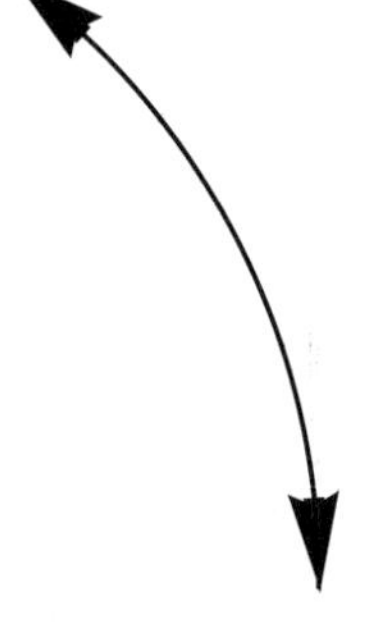

**Spark!**

*Encourages connections & risk-taking*
- Energize
- Flow
- Challenge
- Strengthen dispositions
- Urge uniqueness
- Wonder
- Connect

**Stretch**

*Develops skills & mastery*
- Probe
- Extend
- Expand
- Model
- Focus
- Persist
- Demonstrate

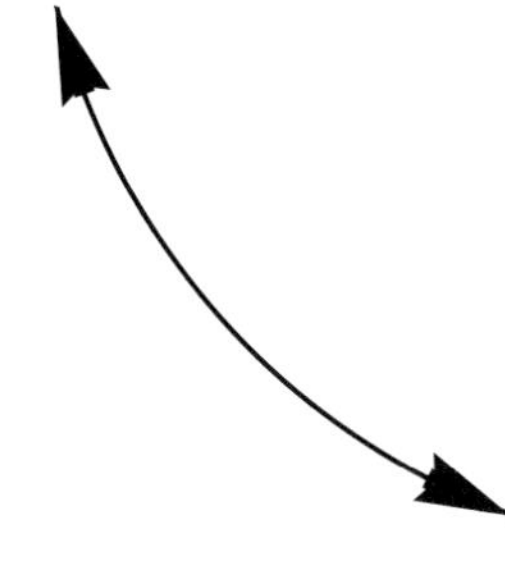

**Stimulate**

*Increases knowledge & understanding*
- Present
- Introduce
- Explain
- Share facts
- Inquire
- Explore
- Question

When you link these planning and teaching strategies with the Curriculum Planning Frames (Figure 2-11) and the ideas generated with the Integrated Arts Curriculum Planning Form (Figure 2-15), you are well on your way toward moving children's learning forward through a truly engaging arts-integrated curriculum.

**Support**—Teachers and art specialists who support children's learning provide opportunities for them to be personally engaged in the learning process. Strategies that tap into children's prior knowledge and individual perception of an event, story, topic, or work of art offer you better insight into a child's culture and experiences. Children who are nurtured as they learn are likely to experience increased feelings of competency, peer cooperation, and confidence.

**Stimulate**—When you stimulate children's thinking, you enable them to think intelligently about curriculum content, including works of art. There are many ways to look at and think reflectively about a topic. In this thinking process, children begin to grapple with the meaning of their experience, and increase their knowledge and understanding of languages such as art. When students talk with adults and each other about curriculum content—including art, artists, and the creative process—they are stimulated to discover, explain, share, and explore various artistic questions.

**Stretch**—Children whose thinking is stretched are able to construct their understanding in more elaborate and flexible ways. Teaching strategies that stretch will extend children's artistic thinking while enhancing many skills and techniques. When they are artistically engaged, students expand their repertoire of problem-solving skills. These skills, which are relevant to other disciplines, are gradually mastered and used as tools for learning. Children's interactions with each other and adults are enhanced through strategies such as demonstrations, modeling, joint problem-solving, and by conveying your own commitment and enthusiasm.

**Spark!**—Teachers can inspire unique opportunities for reflection by exploring a wide spectrum of cognitive reasoning possibilities. Imaginative ideas and a sense of wonder result. Strategies that Spark! encourage students to take different perspectives, pose new problems, seek novelty, and muse upon the world. Challenging questions energize students and teachers to find multiple connections among ideas. You discover cultural patterns, aesthetic insights, personal meanings, and a wide range of emotions.

Each of these four teaching strategies make it possible for you to tailor your interactions with children to ensure successful learning. As your teaching skills evolve, you will incorporate all four Ss in order to engage children to their full potential. As you become more comfortable with *Art as a Way of Learning*®, children will become increasingly independent thinkers who construct their own knowledge.

*Art is one of the most effective means we have to truly understand what children are learning.*

## Authentic Assessment

Some people see art only as fun, and thus do not believe children's art explorations should be evaluated in the same way as other subject areas (if at all). Others may think art is important to include in the curriculum, but may not see it as a real indicator of learning. These types of thinking about art and assessment keep art on the fringes of education. They erroneously consider art as a nonacademic frill, making it an easy target for budget slashes.

In contrast, *Art as a Way of Learning* focuses on children's learning and ways in which art can help us discern what children know and are able to do. Tools to assess program success and student development have been woven into the text. In this component, each module provides a range of assessment tools that enable you and your art partner, students, families, and others to value and reflect upon the quality of individual student art work and thinking.

Figure 4-2.

**National Visual Art Content Standards**

- Understand and apply media, techniques, and processes.
- Use knowledge of structures and functions.
- Choose and evaluate a range of subject matter, symbols, and ideas.
- Understand the visual arts in relation to history and culture.
- Reflect upon and assess the characteristics and merits of their work and the work of others.
- Make connections between visual arts and other disciplines. (MENC, 1994)

Keen observation and documentation of children's knowledge, skills, problem-solving, and their products is essential to authentically assess their learning. Authentic assessment strategies allow students to show what they have learned in the context of settings which closely match real life. Art is one of the most effective means we have to truly understand what children are learning.

Art partners jointly share curriculum goals, develop criteria for evaluation, and reflect on student learning. Criteria for success are established early and are tied closely to national (Figure 4-2) and state standards as well as your school district's or program's curriculum. Assessment begins in the perception phase of the Creative and Critical Thinking Cycle, taking note of prior knowledge and image vividness, and continues through instruction, reviewing drafts, and technical steps in the development of imaginative images and the product. Performance assessment requires students and adults to value and evaluate the final product and reflective process.

Abundant opportunities for you to transform and revitalize your teaching—and to spark student's development—await you. As you continue to explore each of these four strategies, you and your students will even more fully reap the benefits of using *Art as a Way of Learning*®. Enjoy the adventure as you construct new ways to think about teaching and learning!

# MODULE 1
# *SUPPORT:* RESPOND TO CHILDREN'S IDEAS

> Aaron and Zak (age 5) have built a beautiful reciprocal relationship for math. Aaron, more skillful in the concepts of math, shares his knowing with Zak, who is highly motivated to learn about math. Zak keeps Aaron on task, representing, playing, instructing him in math concepts. Aaron, who feels he already knows this and is therefore less motivated, internalizes math concepts at a deeper level as he and Zak work together. They both help each other learn math more fully.
>
> –Sandra Murgacz, teacher,
> Children's House Montessori,
> New Brunswick, New Jersey

Curriculum planning for *Art as a Way of Learning*®—and everything that children learn in school—is most effective when we begin with children's interests, experiences, and questions. We support learning by building upon and extending what children already know as a result of growing up within their culture, community, and family. Art partners, and all other successful educators, recognize the power of supportive responses to scaffold children's learning.

**The deadliest of sins is the mutilation of a child's spirit.**

**–Erik Erikson**

Adult-child interactions, such as those between teachers and children, can be likened to a "cognitive apprenticeship" (Rogoff, 1990) where two minds think together about the same thing, one an expert, the other an apprentice. More capable children often can play the role of expert as well, as Zak and Aaron's relationship demonstrates.

## The Dance of Learning

In order for adults to identify what children already know, we look at what children can do independently (retrospective). When we want to figure out what remains for them to learn, we note what they can do only with the help of an adult or more capable peer (prospective). The space between the two—the **Zone of Proximal Development (ZPD)**—is where learning and cognitive development occurs (Vygotsky, 1978).

Vygotsky (1896-1934) was a Russian psychologist who deeply believed in the dynamic relationship between learning and development and the role of others to move children's thinking and actions forward. Through interactions with adults and other children, children actively construct meaning and understanding, acquire knowledge and skills, and develop new cognitive abilities.

**The teacher's role in scaffolding learning**

- Encourage
- Assist
- Emphasize peer cooperation
- Build confidence
- Individualize
- Strengthen positive attitudes
- Embellish

One extremely effective technique for working with children in their Zone of Proximal Development is called *scaffolding.* In your interactions, the children lead, and you move in and out of the learning situation as needed—a dance of learning. Teachers who are warm and responsive to children, sensitive to their interests, ideas, experiences, questions, and personal feelings, make excellent learning partners with students. Children are quick to pick up on your attitude about them, about learning, and about the arts! Classroom climate instills confidence in children.

## Supportive responses to scaffold learning

- How did you achieve this (effect, process)? How would you describe what you're doing?
- What are you planning to accomplish today (do next)? Are you satisfied with your progress? Who else in the class might help you?
- You look puzzled (stuck, frustrated). What's up?
- Have you thought about … (another material, looking at something from another angle, using a different art process)? I'm wondering how …?
- Your impression is that … (repeat or paraphrase child's comments). (Pause to wait for child to elaborate. This is called active listening.)
- What else do you need to know (be able to do, in the way of materials) to continue?
- How did you use (elements of art, academic content) to get to this point?
- My impressions of your work so far are (constructive comments about process, art elements, other academic content).
- What do you think about (the process, product, progress)?
- You've really been concentrating on (some aspect of project).
- How are you expecting to incorporate (art elements, academic content, contributions of other students)?
- What an interesting use of (material, process, art element). Tell me more.
- Remember when you first started this project? Look how far you've come!
- Which of these colors (techniques) do you think was most effective to accomplish (effect)?
- Why did you choose (topic, materials, process)?
- That's a new idea! What could you do with it?
- Your smile tells me you're satisfied with what you're doing.
- Let me suggest (a book, Web site, artwork) that might give you some ideas.
- Tell me about the documentation in your portfolio.
- You know, I can tell this is something that you created, and not anyone else in the room, because (cite defining characteristics).
- Where (how) did you find your information? How do you know it is accurate?
- If you could start over, what would you do differently? The same? What did you enjoy most?
- You and (other child) seem to be a good match. Tell me how your partnership is working out.
- How do you think this would display best?
- What kind of people do you think might enjoy doing this kind of project? Seeing your work?

*Teachers who are warm and responsive to children make excellent learning partners.*

Children and teachers begin their adventures in learning at different places, but you work toward intersubjectivity, a coming together of shared understanding. You scaffold children's artistic capacities—much as you would in dancing—through conversation, shared meanings, and modeling. As a result, you build satisfying relationships with each other. Gradually, children begin to self-regulate their own cognitive activity regarding their skills, reasoning processes, or body of knowledge.

To support children's thinking and doing in the arts, teachers guide students' artistic explorations. You engage children in artistic activities that support, clarify, and stretch their thinking about all aspects of visual language (structural, functional, and aesthetic). At the same time, you are tuned to their needs, feelings, and developing competencies. When you and your students think together in this way, you support children's artistic efforts, a critical aspect in all learning and development.

## Guiding Questions

Use these questions to think about how you support and extend children's learning.

- How do you learn about your children's interests?
- How do you respond to children's questions? In what ways do you show warmth with children? How do you demonstrate responsiveness? How do you connect their questions to a standards-driven curriculum?
- Do children feel that you take their ideas seriously? How have you put their ideas into action?
- How are you making artistic explorations integral to the learning process?
- How do you pair children for successful, satisfying relationships?

# Explorations: Playful Nurturing

One excellent way for you and your art partner to design art explorations that encourage children's learning is to begin your planning with the Support Communication Frame (see Figure 2-11). Use it to get started on identifying children's ideas and interests upon which to build a curriculum that is responsive and emergent.

The *Art as a Way of Learning*® approach to art incorporates children's delightful spontaneity, the marvelous plasticity and unlimited potential of visual art media, and your deliberate yet flexible guidance. A playful, nurturing attitude is an essential ingredient in responsive teaching because it encourages children to more openly share their ideas, interests, and feelings. Let the children lead as you support, guide, honor, and extend the directions in which they are moving. Here are two powerful ways to help children get what's inside out.

## The Wonderful Web

A topic web is a "mapping of the key ideas and concepts that a topic comprises and some of the major subthemes related to it" (Katz & Chard, 1991, p. 88). Webs provide a picture of how ideas are related—a coherent web of learning possibilities. By looking at a web, you and the children can identify what they know, what they need or would love to learn, and what resources they need to help them learn.

*A playful, nurturing attitude is an essential ingredient in responsive teaching.*

You can generate a web individually or with your art partner. Remember the web that art partners Ms. Vista and Mr. Angelo created on the topic of the earth (Figures E-1 to 3)? Better yet, work with children to create one, using a topic that they are eager to pursue (see Figure 4-3). Children who are experienced web makers can create their own. Encourage the use of webs in the classroom, art room, or in combination. However your class creates a web, make sure you generate many more ideas than you need. Then you can select the ones that are most suitable for your group and that are better, more inherently aesthetic themes.

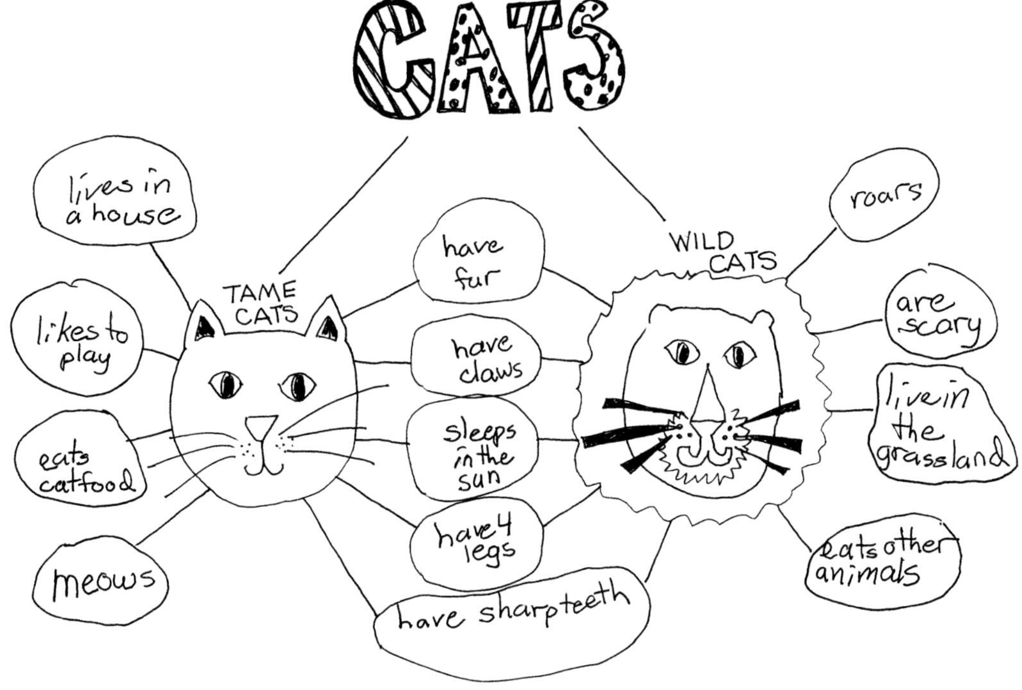


*Figure 4-3.* A topic web on cats developed by second-grade children at Resica Elementary School, East Stroudsburg, Pennsylvania, Sally Viney, teacher.



*Work with children to create a web, using a topic they are eager to pursue.*

## Creating a Topic Web With Children

**1.** Select an intriguing idea or topic. Create a word spill by listing every idea on a small slip of paper (you may need 100 for one web). Every idea is equally valued at this point.

**2.** Find how the concepts fit together by moving the individual ideas around on a table or the floor. Put ideas that fit together near each other.

**3.** Take slips of paper of different colors to create a heading or title for each group of ideas. Talk about the similarities and differences in ideas to get a read on the unique perspective each person brings to the topic.

**4.** Find the aesthetic concepts: ones which connote beauty, a set of qualities, a metaphor, or personal meaning in the web. This may become the title for your project. Be sure to include the art specialist at this point, if you have not done so already. Ask the children to discuss with the specialist their art curriculum ideas that support the theme (see Visual Literacy Module 3). Eventually, you and the children will become quite facile at recognizing the visual, artistic aspects of any topic.

**5.** Record the web on a large sheet of paper as a visual reminder about the work at hand. Add ideas and new information as they evolve. Use a different color to highlight development during the learning process. This web can be included as part of the project documentation or in a display. What a wonderful picture of learning that can be easily shared with families.

## A Playful Script

How do you and your art partner tap into what and how children know? Daily listening and observing children in the classroom, art room, playground, and within the community, as we have already seen, is extremely helpful. Remember, what children know, and are curious about, is embedded within the context of their culture. The more you learn about children's cultures, the better you will be able to support their learning.

If the two of you art partners and the children have selected a topic to pursue, be sure to engage in conversation, either as a group or individually. Make it a natural exchange, one in which people get to know each other, share their thoughts and feelings about a topic, work together, and then chat about how it went and what the children learned from the experience. Be sensitive to how culture shapes children's comfort and ways of communicating with adults and each other.

Record your conversations (notes, drawings, on tape) to document the discussion. In language arts, reading, and other traditional academic areas, K-W-L forms are common (Figures E-20 and 4-4). Create your own way to capture the reflective, collaborative process when planning an arts-integrated curriculum. Encourage children to show as well as tell about their ideas, thus using their visual thinking.

### K What do you know?

Ask children to describe their thoughts, feelings, and suppositions about a curriculum or art topic, or an integrated theme. Listen carefully to detect children's varying perspectives and insights. Some children may have rather sophisticated understandings, while the topic may be relatively unfamiliar to others, depending on their experiences. Pose questions in ways that will help you and your art partner better grasp each child's knowledge base, as well as gaining a sense of the group's general understanding. What are children's first-hand experiences with the topic? What have they heard or read about it? What art processes have they tried? With which elements and principles of visual language are they familiar?

### W What do you wonder about?

This question can be asked before the learning experiences begin, to take stock of what children know, but it should also continue to be asked as children proceed. Wondering often occurs in the context of action. Sometimes the better questions come during or after hands-on exploration. One question asked by an adult, or a supportive response such as those suggested earlier, may unleash more musings as children realize you expect them to verbalize their curiosity. "I wonder how an artist in (a different period) might have interpreted this idea?" "Did you ever think about why ...?" "What might happen if ...?"

### L What have you learned?

Encourage children to look again at their first thoughts and see how much more they understand. Help them validate their growth and make connections to what they know. Consider not only children's vocabulary, but research skills, art processes, expanded ideas, aesthetic appreciation, new ways of thinking and sharing what they know, friendships that developed, and other areas of individual and group growth in all areas—cognitive, social and emotional, and physical.

*Figure 4-4.* KWL chart related to art.

# *ARTISTIC KNOWLEDGE AND SKILLS – K W L Chart*

***NAME*** ***ART FORM – CONCEPTS***

| | WHAT DO I KNOW? | QUESTIONS I HAVE | WHAT I HAVE LEARNED |
|---|---|---|---|
| ART PRODUCTION<br>materials<br>techniques<br>planning<br>safety<br>manipulative skills | | | |
| ART CRITICISM<br>perception<br>visual skills<br>tactile skills<br>forms | | | |
| ART HISTORY<br>artists<br>cultures<br>background<br>works<br>styles | | | |
| AESTHETICS<br>art looking<br>judgments<br>connections<br>attitudes | | | |

## Challenges

If involving children in the planning process, such as with webbing, is a new way to begin a class, children may be distrustful or cautious at first. Your challenge is to make your artful conversations natural and useful. After children see its potential to contribute to the group and affirm what they are learning, most will become eager to continue to use these techniques. When you hear children saying to each other, "Well, what do you know about this already?" you will know they have incorporated the strategy into their repertoire!

**Comparing webs**—Individuals see things differently because they have varying experiences within their cultures and may perceive the same experiences differently. Pick a topic and do a web with a number of different groups or individuals. Ask children, the art specialist, a same-grade teacher, another group of children at a higher grade. Compare and contrast the similarities and differences.

Second graders sought feedback from other grades, their art teacher, and principal to compare their ideas with others on the theme of transportation.

Kindergarten ideas: "Number of wheels—2, 4, 18." "Scooters—there are no scooters on there."

Fourth grade ideas: "What about space travel?" "Under wheels include one—unicycle."

Principal: "Subways could fit under 'trains'. And in Chicago the subway is above the ground and it's called the L. What about animals?"

Art teacher: "One of my favorite artists is Anne Coe from Arizona. She often puts her pink Cadillac convertible in her prints. Remember the suit of armor we saw for a horse at the Metropolitan Museum? Did you think about pollution?"

**The sharing club**—Begin group time by asking children to share something they know, wonder about, or have learned so far in the project. Make sure you ask them how they know it.

Second grader: "I've learned that people from different parts of the country, like cities, use different transportation."

"Yes, and if you're older or lived long ago it was different, too."

"Today, transportation is good and bad—good for traveling, bad for the environment."

**The storyteller**—Provide opportunities for children to share the story, message, movement, or feeling expressed in their own artwork. Begin by saying "Who would like to tell us about their painting?" With ample opportunities, even reticent children will begin telling stories. Model appropriate responses, and then encourage children to ask questions, make comments, or give compliments to the artist/storyteller.

Armand's story: "My painting is called the 'Not-So-Magic Schoolbus' and it has all the funny or yucky things that go on in my bus. Hats get thrown out windows, a little kid threw up, kids laugh and throw spit balls. This didn't happen on the same day, but it has happened."

**"You did what?"**—Represent the webbing or playful scripting process in another form. Allow children to act it out, make a metaphoric connection to a story they read, create a poem about the process, or devise a recipe or flow chart of their creative thinking.

Teacher: "We took Armand's idea and embellished it. We divided the class into three groups: 1—The Great Ride School Bus, 2—The Magic School Bus, and 3—The Not-So-Magic School Bus. Each group acted out the scenarios, based on the stories and attended to safety and creative behaviors to show the drama on board the buses.

## Authentic Assessment

In order to support and extend children's learning we must help them see where they started, where they are now, and how they moved from point A to point B. A child who previously drew landscapes from a one-dimensional perspective might now be able to use line and color to create depth and illustrate soil conservation practices. Children who might have liked a painting or sculpture simply because it was of a dinosaur might now be able to describe how elements such as balance and harmony make it more pleasing to them. Here are a few suggestions for developing reflective thinking through formal assessments with children.

**Portfolios.** Portfolios, historically in the domain of the visual arts, are an excellent way to consider children's progress. Portfolios may include ideas, drafts, photographs, and finished products. These portfolios are particularly helpful in looking at each area of growth and unique styles. Children might use shoe boxes, folders, scrapbooks, or other containers to suit the project.

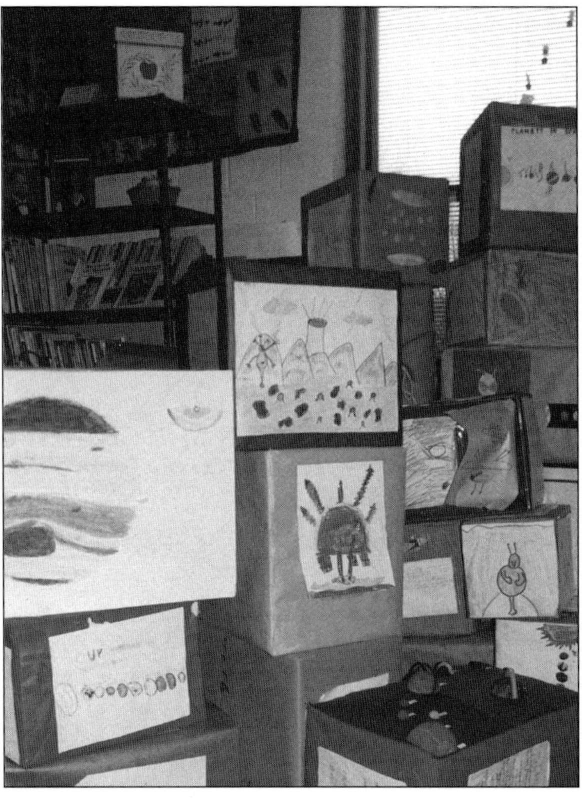

*Figure 4-5.* **Planet cubes.** A clever way of reporting on a research project, Resica Elementary School, East Stroudsburg, Pennsylvania. Photo by Jane Oplinger.

**Group critique session.** Critique sessions, as they are known in art school, are conducted in the classroom or art room in a supportive and nurturing manner. Children, teachers, art specialists, and even the principal can participate. Place work samples, or works in progress, out where all may see. Urge children to make a constructive comment, ask a question, or give a compliment using artistic language.

After children understand the positive nature and value of these critique sessions, you will begin to hear this type of conversation as they work: "Here, let me take a look at that. Hmmm." or "I need someone to give me some feedback on this."

**Individual conferencing.** Create a formal procedure to discuss a child's work, either with the child or family members. Set up conference times to review children's visual work, just as you would for writing. These one-to-one exchanges about children's visual processing and artistic skills are very productive and enable you to discern individual learning styles. Focus the conversation on the artistic-thematic information, skills, or connections that children have demonstrated. Support their visual thinking and artistic problem solving using the content and process of art.

**Portfolio Night.** Invite families and the entire community to come to the school for a Portfolio Night so that children may describe their work to interested adults and youth. Children show their portfolios, demonstrate techniques, share videos, or use other types of documentation (Figures 4-5 and 6) to describe the integrated project.

### Valuing and Cherishing

A trusting, positive climate must be established before responding to and evaluating student work and visual thinking. Use your knowledge, such as that gained in Visual Literacy (Component One) and through your collaborative relationship, to think together and assess student artwork. The following five areas give form to the discussion and questions, and can be used in any of the assessment formats. Children will begin to use your model of supportive language as they begin to naturally reflect on their work and that of their peers.

**Artistic organization—**Talk about the choices made related to the elements and principles of design. What is it that gives the work harmony or a feeling of completeness?

**Technical skills—**Identify the student's increased mastery and competency with media and tools. Give suggestions for further development.

**Expressive quality—**Discuss the feeling or mood evident in the work(s). How was this accomplished through choices of color, line, shapes, and subject matter?

**Creative imagination—**Discover the unusual connections, novel images, insightful problem-solving, or the unique way the student used media.

**Thinking process—**Discuss how the work was done, steps in the process, where images and ideas originated. What was the role of the media or others in the student's thinking? Talk about varied ways children and other artists solved the same artistic problems.

## Reflections

Your warmth and responsiveness with children make it possible to engage them in a reflective dialogue about their work. Think about your relationships with children in these reflections.

- How comfortable are you in responding to children's ideas and incorporating them into your planning?
- Share a scaffold experience with your art partner. Use it to highlight your strengths and look for ways to extend learning.
- What aspects of conversations are you more aware of as you talk with children? How has your conversation with children changed? Do children respond differently to you?

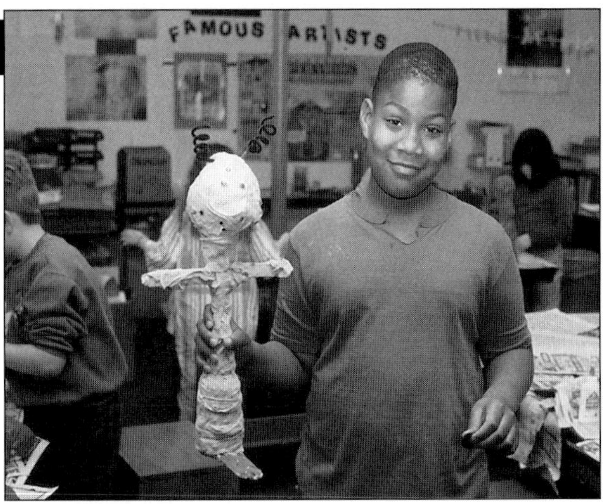


*Figure 4-6.* Sculpture designed from research and story on planet cube, Resica Elementary School, East Stroudsburg, Pennsylvania. Photo by Jane Oplinger.

MODULE 2

# *STIMULATE:* INCREASE KNOWLEDGE AND UNDERSTANDING

The arts are one of the main ways that humans define who they are. They often express a sense of community and ethnicity. Because the arts convey the spirit of the people who created them, they can help young people to acquire inter- and intra-cultural understanding. The arts are not just multicultural, they are transcultural; they invite cross-cultural communication. They teach openness toward those who are different than we are. The arts teach respect.

–Charles Fowler (1994, p. 8)

The visual arts, an artistic language, depict the story of the world's history and the universality and uniqueness of cultures. Both two- and three-dimensional art forms from different time periods and cultures present a vast artistic legacy. This rich heritage defines our humanness and chronicles our development. Artists have painted, sculpted, drawn, printed, and otherwise created through the arts about every conceivable idea and feeling. Artistic representations are built upon the structure of one's language(s), prior knowledge, feelings about experiences, and sociocultural traditions.

The Creative and Critical Thinking Cycle (Figure 1-4) is not only useful in making art, but also for "reading" works of art. This cycle deepens the structural and aesthetic knowledge of art and assists in the transfer of learning to other topics. Skills in responding to and evaluating works of art require astute observation and reflective thought. These visual thinking strategies can be applied to valuing the aesthetic aspect of an experience, examining works of art and cultural artifacts, or extending appreciation for the everyday world.

## Analyzing Art With Children

One goal in using *Art as a Way of Learning*® is to find and use art references that stimulate children's understanding, increase their perceptual awareness, and heighten artistic sensitivity. Learning the visual reasoning skills to look at, make judgments about, and connect to personal meaning is the focus of this module. This is achieved by jointly attending, thinking together, and scaffolding children's looking at art.

**The teacher's role in increasing children's knowledge and understanding of art**

- **Present**
- **Introduce**
- **Explain**
- **Share facts**
- **Inquire**
- **Explore**
- **Question**

*Teaching Strategies*

Research demonstrates that children can and do respond positively to the artistic and perceptual qualities in works of art. Even at a young age, children are able to engage in active thinking/feeling dialogues about art. Looking at art requires reflective thinking and it also provides an excellent opportunity for the development of better thinking (Perkins, 1994).

*The visual arts depict the universality and uniqueness of cultures.*

Looking dispositions that are intelligent are inherent in the Creative and Critical Thinking Cycle when we respond to art. These dispositions can be strengthened by thoughtfully attending to the structural aspects and surprises found in works of art. "So, better than most situations, looking at art can build some very basic thinking dispositions" (Perkins, 1994, p. 4).

Encourage a reflective looking attitude to discover the choices an artist made to provoke, inspire, and delight the viewer. To do this, Perkins (1994, p. 55) suggests four basic looking principles that enhance thinking:

1. **Give looking time.** Perception is more than look and see. The longer you spend looking at a work, the more you can literally see. Good thinking takes time, too. Revisit works that you have looked at before. Think about them again in different contexts, with different feelings.
2. **Make your looking broad and adventurous.** Do not be so quick to judge. Art is complex visually. Look for surprises. What was obvious? Artists want us to discover this first. What is more subtle?
3. **Make your looking clear and deep.** Work together to understand the meaning in a work of art. Find out what others said—art critics, the artist. Compare it to other works by the same artist or in the same time period. What else was going on socially, politically?
4. **Make your looking organized.** Looking that randomly moves over a surface may not see well. Use a systematic approach like the one detailed in the next section of this module to fully explore a work of art.

*Even at a young age, children are able to engage in active thinking/feeling dialogues about art.*

Thinking together enables you to model a structure for looking-at-art behavior. You scaffold children's visual thinking and their ability to put into words visual information, ideas, and feelings. This cognitive reasoning process engages children in a critical and creative dialogue that makes them better thinkers. Connections are made to what they already know, and then their experiences can be extended through art. Thus, a child seeing Renoir's *Girl With a Watering Can* might joyfully realize that "My grandparents have a watering can just like that one!"

*Thinking together enables you to model a structure for looking-at-art behavior.*

Your discussions will reveal individual perceptual sensitivities and preferences, and help you better understand children's cultural environments. Children may comment, "There's a sculpture at the library that is made out of brass, too!" or "Our exchange student from Thailand brought us some cloth with those same bright colors" (see Figure 4-7). These reflective looking dispositions and the organized strategies for looking at art can build a repertoire of thoughtful skills for everyday visual learning.

*Figure 4-7.* Sample of Thai fabric with traditional design.

## Guiding Questions

The art works you and your art partner select to share with children need to stimulate imagination and curiosity—yours and the children's. By jointly considering each piece, you both become partners in the learning process.

- How do you encourage children to find their own meaning in a work? What types of connections do the children make between the art references and their experiences?
- What new dimension or insight have you added to the curriculum theme by including these works?
- How well do they represent works from different cultures, time periods, and styles?
- Which artistic elements will you emphasize in discussions with children or explore through projects?
- How will you use art references to enhance your aesthetic environment?

## Explorations: Viewing and Responding to Art

When you guide children's looking and responding to art, their perceptual awareness and visual reasoning increases. Together, you perceive, comprehend, and think about works of art in an organized way. This model is consistent with Discipline-Based Art Education (DBAE) (Getty Education Institute for the Arts, 1992; 1993). The works you and your arts partner choose to discuss with children are found in many places and forms, such as:

- originals in a museum or other public areas
- reproductions
- slides
- on-line images and resources
- children's picture books
- an artist-in-residence's work
- family memorabilia
- artifacts from travels
- collections of art work in museum exhibit books
- natural objects such as leaves or animals
- photo albums
- children's own art

Look around and ask. Your everyday environment is rich with possibilities.

With experience, children will begin to use the four processes in this model—describe, analyze, interpret, judge—as part of their repertoire for viewing and responding to art.

*Figure 4-8.* Martha Posner, artist-in-residence, shares her collection of masks from around the world to stimulate children's imagination and artistic knowledge.

## Describe

Try to understand how a work is organized.

Challenge children to look carefully, to see everything. At first, or when introducing new concepts, you will need to model the use of visual language as it is used in looking behaviors. Always scaffold children's learning so that it hinges on what they already know.

You might say, for example, when describing a mobile, "I see five items hanging from golden wires. These wires are thinner than coat hangers. Look! The pieces are blowing in the wind. Sometimes they bounce off each other, so they must not be breakable. The wires are suspended from a flat object, about the size of a dinner plate. The most interesting object in this mobile to me is the one that is red with white speckles...." Your enthusiasm for art will spill over into the children's responses.

As children describe what they see, you will gain a sense of their visual comprehension skills, which will improve with your guidance and as they use them. Together you can discover new details or impressions about the work. Engage children verbally and visually in an aesthetic dialogue, using strategies such as these.

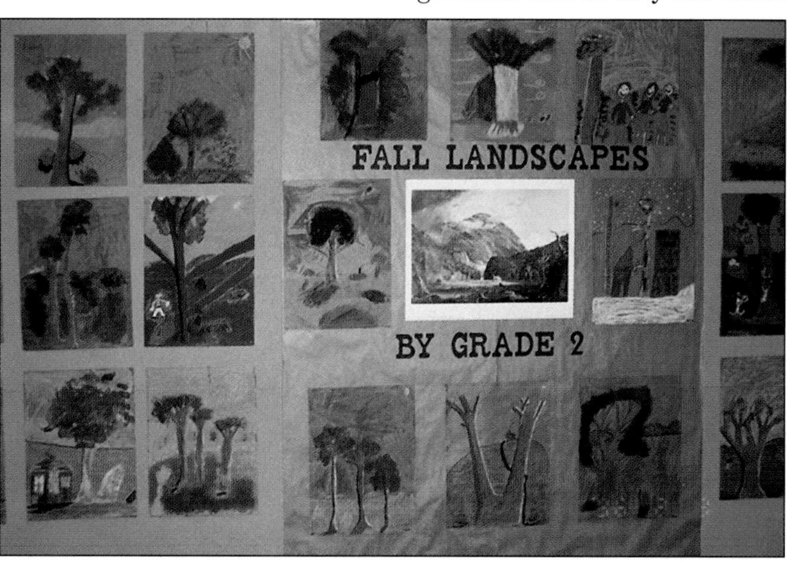

*Figure 4-9.* Challenge children to look carefully, to see everything. Fall Landscapes, grade 2, Resica Elementary School, East Stroudsburg, Pennsylvania.

- Make a list of what is visible in the work of art. Concentrate on what is depicted, size, media, or other aspects. The illustrations in Donald Crews' books, such as *Freight Train*, are a great place to begin.
- Start the discussion by making a word spill or language experience chart.
- Take advantage of your surroundings to find parallels. Ansel Adams'-type photographs of clouds, trees, bridges, and other everyday objects can be found in nearly all neighborhoods.
- Work in pairs to describe the art. One person looks away from the work, the other describes it in rich detail.
- Play games such as "I spy" or "Look and draw"—look for a minute, then sketch what you remember.
- Take the words from a word spill or chart and make a drawing.

## Analyze

Children are nearly always curious about how things are made. Focus children on how an art work was made by exploring the artistic elements (line, shape, form, color, texture) and principles of visual organization (balance; emphasis; proportion; movement; repetition, rhythm, and pattern; variety; and unity) in the work.

At first, use lots of examples to illustrate these elements and principles so that children have a broad concept about them, rather than limited, static ideas. First relate each visual idea to children's surroundings, then extend the concept to the artwork at hand. For proportion, as an example, you might have children look for evidence of it in the school library or what they're wearing. Then consider how proportion is evidenced in a photograph of the Grand Canyon, a divided ceramic dish, an abstract painting, an ancient Greek or Roman building, and some sterling silver Hopi earrings. After children have accumulated several experiences with the idea, they are ready to create an artwork that demonstrates their understanding of the concept.

When you analyze art with children, emphasize relationships among the objects or qualities in the work. Try to understand how a work is organized, what media were used, and how they were combined. You might ask closed questions to focus attention, such as "What kinds of shapes did the artist use in this collage?" Here are some other ways to pursue the analysis of artwork.

- Follow a line in the painting or recreate the movement with your body.
- Consider how effects were achieved. The collages of water color prints and lace doilies in Leo Lionni's *Swimmy* are delightful visual puzzles.
- Draw the shapes, cut them out, and rearrange them differently. Paul Klee's *Protected Children*, for example, would work well for this type of activity.
- Use the same colors in an exploration to get the visual feel of the work.
- Compare elements or principles in two or more works.
- Provide sound effects or select different types of music to accompany the work.
- Represent the visual aspects of a work by representing it in another medium.

*Children delight in finding their own personal meaning in each work.*

- Compare and contrast the action in Maurice Prendergast's *Going to School* with contemporary morning street scenes in your neighborhood.

## Interpret

Discover the mood, ideas, or feelings conveyed in a work by considering why it might have been made. Use the descriptive information gathered about the work to elicit children's personal responses and feelings. Ask open-ended questions to encourage children to express their interpretations: "How would you describe what you think the artist felt when he drew these ballet dancers?" or "What do you think the designs on this Klickitat basket might represent?" "How would you feel if you could wear this silk fabric?"

Figure 4-10. When you guide children's looking and responding to art, their perceptual awareness and visual reasoning increases. ***Moon City,*** interpretation of Van Gogh's *Starry Night*, Jason Benny, age 7, crayons, marker, colored paper, and slick paint. Courtesy Crayola® Dream-Makers® Program.

Extend the meaning of the work—for baskets, children might investigate basket materials and their origins, steps involved in weaving, different kinds of weaving, parts of the world where baskets are made, how difficult it is to weave evenly, the pride of accomplishment that basket weavers feel, how much baskets cost. The possibilities, of which these are a few, are endless!

- Choose works with a range of feelings and let children write or select music to elaborate.
- Compare and contrast feelings in works of art by writing a story about each one.
- Take an imagination journey inside a painting. Talk to the people or animals. Wander about asking questions out loud about that place and time. Pieter Brueghel's *Children's Games* has great potential in this regard.
- Use an interpretation that grabs children's interest as a jumping off point for a project.
- Represent the mood or feeling in different art forms, (poetry, drama, music). Recreate the pleasant scene depicted in Renoir's *Luncheon of the Boating Party.*

- Set up an imaginary dialogue with an artist by writing a letter or interviewing a teacher or classmate who plays the role of the artist.

## Judge

Children delight in finding their own personal meaning in each work. Encourage them to express these meanings through their descriptions, analysis, and interpretations. Help children to make judgments that connect to and extend from their own experiences. Responses will vary, so be sure to commend their uniqueness. Also, these "ah-ha" moments of meaning may not happen with every child, so provide options.

Here are some possible homework or project choices. Share the results whenever children complete their work.

*Children delight in finding their own personal meaning in each work.*

- ***Approximate!*** Use a piece to think and work like the artist did—paint in the artist's shoes. Approximate or imitate the style, movement, and technique to help students explore a particular style as well as develop unique insight into the moving mind of that artist. Discuss children's different interpretations. Monet's *Sailboats at Argenteuil* and Renoir's *The Seine at Argenteuil*, both painted at the same time from the same place, perfectly illustrate how artists depict scenes differently.

- ***Transform!*** Encourage children to use their artistic knowledge, art technique, or ideas by changing some aspect (color, shapes, emphasis) of a work. Ask: How would you change this work and make it your own?

- ***Transfer!*** Children can pick up on an image, idea, or feeling and transfer it to and through another art form or media to create a new work. Compare and contrast their work and the artist's original.

Part of our art curriculum is to introduce famous artists. I introduced Georgia O'Keeffe using the art card game to expose students to a variety of her paintings. Students then used garden books and catalogs to choose one flower to draw using pastels. We discussed using warm colors for highlights and cool colors for shadows. A follow-up lesson was used to discuss the various styles of art work covered. Students looked at, discussed, and chose a preference among DaVinci, O'Keeffe, and a Rousseau painting. They had to select their preference and explain why. Here are some of the responses:

I like the O'Keeffe *Yellow Calla* because the textures of the background helps [sic] the flower stand out more. Also, I like the way the petals of the flower overlap each other. The shapes are not very complex but the lines make the flower look complex. When I look at this painting I feel excited because of the bright colors.

–Andrew Faust, fifth grade

I like this painting by Henri Rousseau because of all the different green. I like how the leaves look 3-D. I like how the picture looks like a cool climate with a little bit of warmth from the flowers. I like how the painting takes me out of the world and puts me into the painting.

–Derek Stone, fifth grade

I chose the *Mona Lisa* because of the great distance and of the shadows and the beautiful colors. When I look at a picture of the *Mona Lisa* it makes me feel like I'm in the picture with her. This picture makes me feel peaceful. *Mona Lisa* looks like a real person. I wish I was (sic) an artist so I could of drew [sic] the *Mona Lisa.*

–Carlina Castro, fifth grade

The painting I like the most was the *Mona Lisa* by Leonardo DaVinci. I like the picture because of the background and the shadows. The way it makes me feel is that the war just ended because the painting is so dark and so are her clothes. If I was [sic] in a dim room her eyes are sort of bright, but if I look at it I would probably think it was a ghost.

–Fallon Rauch, fifth grade

I like *Pansy* by Georgia O'Keeffe because of the shadows around the flower. The shadow of white and blue seems to bring out the black flower. The colors blend together like water. The shapes are good. They're not ordinary that's what makes them great. The texture looks good. It makes me feel good when I look at it because I like flowers and the color black so I like the black flower even if there aren't [sic] such a thing as a black flower.

–Kathy Weaver, fifth grade

–Sylvia Radvansky, art teacher,
Clearview Elementary School,
Bethlehem, Pennsylvania

## Challenges

Encourage children to be curious about works of art and use them as a reference for further explorations.

- Use a variety of art references when you teach or demonstrate concepts or ideas. Include works, both two- and three-dimensional, artifacts, artists representing different cultures, styles, types, or periods in history, and local artists. Make these references part of your art learning center (see Aesthetic Environment).
- Make learning materials for art history and appreciation at a fraction of the cost of buying ready-made games. Prepare matching games, concentration activities, bingo-like games, or board games using brochures from art exhibits, museum guides, and postcard reproductions. Wolf (1984) describes an interesting and rewarding way to include art history using art postcards. Her various levels of matching create opportunities for peer and teacher-led dialogue about artist's styles and children's personal preferences.

Most of the materials I have made for the children are visual bulletin board displays designed as learning centers or games. Two bulletin board games I use are:

**# 1**—Put up 20 or more reproductions of famous paintings. Ask students to categorize them into landscapes, still life, or portraits. Divide the class into teams and keep score. Extra points are awarded when students know the name of the artist or the title of the paining. I then teach a follow-up lesson where students dip colored chalk into tempera paint and draw their choice of landscape, still life, or portrait. The texture of these paintings very often has the look of an oil painting.

**# 2**—Put up reproductions of abstract artists such as Klee or Kandinsky. Have the students categorize pictures as to the amount of realism or abstractness. We then discuss the elements of design and where they occur in each painting. A good follow-up lesson is to teach collage where each student has the choice of going totally abstract or attempting realism. We then critique students' artwork, looking for and discussing elements of design.

–Sylvia Radvansky, art teacher,
Clearview Elementary School,
Bethlehem, Pennsylvania

## Artful Conversations

Whenever you talk with children about art, their own or someone else's, make sure you engage in joyful conversations in which all pay close attention while using visual language. Small groups make it possible for children to exchange their ideas. Vary the types of questions you ask, sometimes focusing on specific visual elements, sometimes prompting new discoveries.

Find your own personal meaning along with the children. Keep a catalogue or notebook of the art references you use and a record of children's use of visual reasoning. Older students can take charge of this inventory.

*Figure 4-11.* Encourage children to be curious about works of art and use them as a reference for further explorations. ***City Scene,*** Gregory Dreyfuss, age 8-1/2, markers, crayons, and watercolors. Courtesy Crayola® Dream-Makers® Program.

**The Detective—Wonder!** Use a work of art to begin children's wondering about process, to pose questions, to make a list of what they already know, what they want to find out. Tap into their knowledge and experiences through the art reference.

**The Plumber or Architect—Connect!** Use the works of art to connect to the curriculum theme, or others' feelings or ideas. What did the artist know about this topic or theme when he or she worked? What was important for the artist to know? What do you know about the topic or theme that they did not?

**The Announcer—Think aloud!** Begin by asking children to talk while they work, describing their thoughts and feelings. Thinking aloud reinforces artistic processes and the notion that art is cognitive. Try it yourself.

**The Scientist—How do you know that?** By asking this simple question, you often can see the logic in children's thought processes or their underlying understandings or feelings. Remember this is their logic and beliefs, not yours. Continue to ask questions for clarification. Then plan activities accordingly to expand children's thinking.

## Authentic Assessment

After you have stimulated children's ability to know and describe the structural aspects of a work as well as analyze, interpret, and judge its functional and aesthetic aspects, you will want to capture children's information, knowledge, and ability to be thoughtful about art. Here are some ways to value children's learning as you gather information and evaluate their knowledge.

- Informal tests on vocabulary, artists' names, periods, or other points of discussion.
- Games, tailored to the context, through which children can demonstrate mastery of information and knowledge, such as "Jeopardy," crossword puzzles, word searches.
- Research projects on an artist, work, or other topic, organized and presented in clever ways. Resources might include the library, interviews with local artists, or the Internet (see the list of online resources in Component Two).
- Interpretive questions where children back up their feelings and insights from personal experiences using the structure of visual language.
- Interview and audio/video tape a class's or individual children's thinking and responding process.

## Reflections

Think about your own ability to attend to the perceptual, artistic, and aesthetic qualities in a work of art.

- How are you making this experience meaningful to children? What are you doing to stimulate their curiosity?
- How have children's visual reasoning experiences engendered respect for others?
- In what ways do you introduce new cultures, styles, or media?
- What surprises you about children's visual reasoning? How have you adjusted your curriculum accordingly?

MODULE 3

# *STRETCH:* DEVELOP IMAGINATION AND ARTISTIC SKILLS

[Children's] problem-solving seems to improve most when their partner is an "expert."

–L.E. Berk & A. Winsler (1995, p. 20)

Every child is capable of engaging in imaginative, skillful artistic explorations. Even toddlers have first-draft knowledge of artistic and cognitive strategies for solving visual problems. You and your art partner's "can do" attitudes make it possible to schedule sufficient time to stretch each child's imagination, add to a repertoire of imagery strategies, improve artistic problem-solving abilities, and develop mastery of technical skills.

## Learning the Language Together

The ability to identify and imaginatively solve problems with any language is a skill, a benchmark of competent use. Problem-solving strategies are somewhat similar in mathematical, verbal/written, musical, and dramatic/gestural symbol systems, but the physical and social medium with which the problem solving occurs is different. A student might work a problem backwards in math to check an answer; in art children must be able to visually think backwards to do crayon resist.

Artistic problem posing and solving always begin with children's knowledge, not the teacher's suppositions. If you are interested in children's experiences, you are in a better position to scaffold their learning, to stretch and prompt them to elaborate upon their artistic work.

*Through collaboration, all of us stretch our knowledge and skills.*

Children see us, their teachers, as experts. They are rightly disappointed if we are unable to help them move their learning forward. Yet art is often one of the areas in which classroom teachers feel less competent. This is where one of the strengths of *Art as a Way of Learning*®—Creative Collaboration (Component Two)—comes into play. No classroom teacher is without resources to assist children in finding and solving artistic problems. Through collaboration with the art specialist, the principal, and artists in the community, all of us stretch and elaborate our own knowledge and skills. Children, too, can apprentice themselves to an expert, even if that expert is someone who knows just a little bit more than they do.

## The teacher's role in developing children's artistic imagination and skills

- Probe
- Extend
- Model
- Focus
- Persist
- Demonstrate

When anyone, child or adult, masters the skills of a language, we are better at using it imaginatively to solve problems. In the visual arts, problem-solving strategies demand visual literacy, analytical thinking, technical skills, visual reasoning, and imagery ability. How delightful it is to work with our colleagues and children to jointly solve visual dilemmas using our imaginations! In doing so, we model a flexible, interactive thinking system while developing skills and mastery in the visual arts.

*When we master a language, we are better at using it imaginatively.*

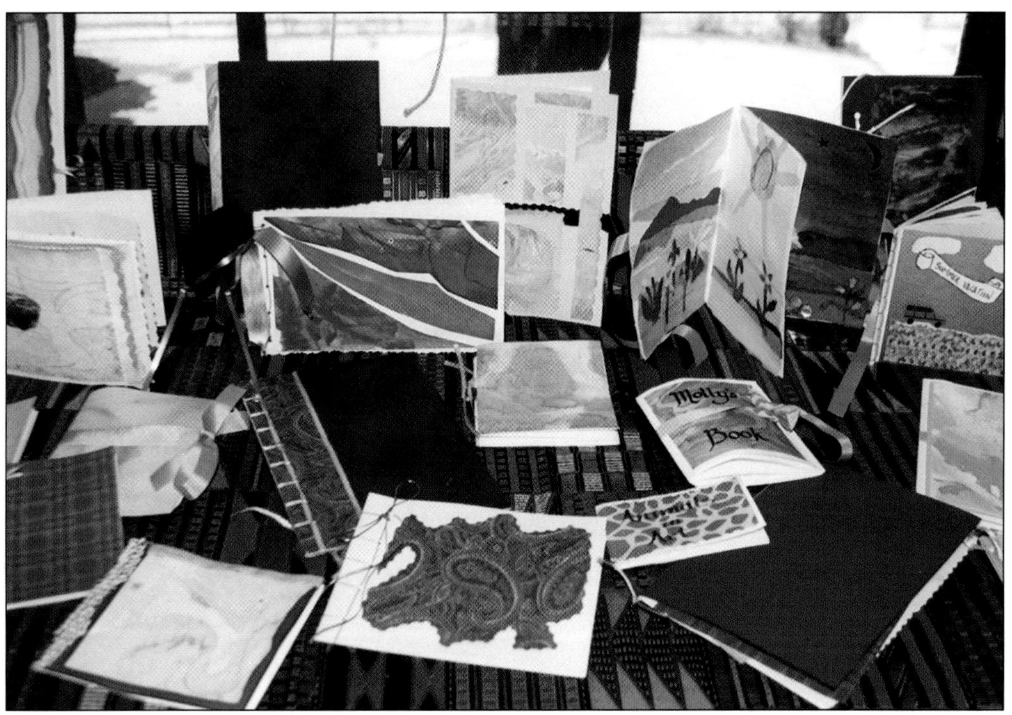


*Figure 4-12.* Every child is capable of engaging in imaginative, skillful artistic explorations. Handmade books with handmade textured papers. Art as a Way of Learning® professional development, Cincinnati, Ohio.

*Figure 4-13.* Artistic thinking begins with children's knowledge. Zak's bicycle drawing, second grade.

It's bicycle safety month and Zak, a second grader, is sent home with the assignment to "Draw a picture of your bicycle." This says something important to Zak, for he knows how to draw from observation—it means look at your bike!! He sets himself up in front of his bicycle, then returns 30 minutes later with a problem. "I don't have enough room for the wheels. Should I just make them really little to fit them in?"

His mother, seeing a wonderful observational drawing in the making, stretches his thinking by responding, "You know how some artists leave part of the picture up to your imagination? You could do that with the wheels." He knew just what to do (Figure 4-13).

–Zak's mother

## Guiding Questions

These guiding questions will help you examine your level of artistic expertise and consider how perceptual challenges are part of your teaching.

- Which visual thinking strategies and imagery abilities do you use regularly? When?
- What strategies are similar to the ones your art partner uses?
- How do children function as experts for each other?
- What can you do to stretch your current level of visual literacy?

# Explorations: Strategies for Artistic Learning

The arts are the only language in which media are used for resolving questions, so it stands to reason that children who continue to improve their artistic skills are far better visual problem solvers, just as children who learn more math skills are better at solving number problems. There is always something new to learn in every language and in every culture.

*Figure 4-14.* Children who continue to improve their artistic skills are far better visual problem solvers. Elephant, Laura Nelson, age 12, construction paper and oil pastels. Courtesy Crayola® Dream-Makers® Program.

## Imagery Strategies for Problem Solving

When you and your art partner are ready to design a curriculum that values the artistic disciplines, stretches children's artistic strategies, and develops their imaginations, we suggest you begin with the Curriculum Planning Frame (Figure 2-11). This frame is also a good way to take concrete steps as partners, by using what you are learning about art in the classroom. The Integrated Arts Curriculum Planning Form (Figure 2-15) will help you assure that the concept you wish to teach applies to many areas of study.

*Assure that the concept you wish to teach applies to many areas of study.*

Artists often choose one or more of these six imagery strategies to solve visual challenges (Table 4-1). They might also use unconscious strategies that they discover as they reflect on the process of creating a particular piece of art. Add these strategies for visual problem solving to your repertoire of skills useful in any discipline. Use them to explore ideas from different perspectives and to design more mindful, imaginative curriculum.

*Table 4-1.*

**Imagery strategies for imaginative problem solving**

| Strategy | Art explorations that strengthen the strategy as it is used |
|---|---|
| **Use a model** | Draw from observation<br>Sculpt an animal while looking at toy animals<br>Create a mobile to show how things balance and hang together |
| **Use a picture** | Engage in visual brainstorming<br>Explore architecture through line and shape<br>Take a guided imagination journey<br>Try cartography: make and read maps |
| **Account for all possibilities** | Mix a variety of different colors<br>Draw radial designs<br>Try computer graphics<br>Design different calligraphic alphabets |
| **Work backwards** | Use watercolors<br>Try batik<br>Engage in scratch art<br>Try linoleum printmaking |
| **Guess and check** | Do crayon resist<br>Try positive/negative space drawing<br>Sculpture armatures<br>Create clay pots blindfolded |
| **Simplify the problem** | Do contour line drawing<br>Try animation—create a flip book<br>Paint with sand<br>Print with everyday objects |

*Figures 4-15, 16, and 17.* This is prime time for art partners to observe and guide children's constructive learning. Shape pictures, kindergarten, marker and watercolor, Sue Czahor, teacher, Resica Elementary School, East Stroudsburg, Pennsylvania.

## Creative Imaginations at Work!

You and your art partner set the stage to stretch children's artistic imaginations and skills. The two of you usually will show children the technique or material and most certainly leave plenty of time for children to experiment and construct their ideas. Children work at their best when the atmosphere is relaxed, their senses are tuned in to their own observations, and they can concentrate.

*Quiet is not the sound of learning.*

Guide perception, construction, and performance by scaffolding and modeling artistic skills and visual thinking. Some classroom teachers prefer to have their art partners come to their rooms for this, or if your partner is the art specialist, she or he may want to introduce a new skill in the art room. Depending on your focus, and whether any new tools or media are being introduced, you may want to demonstrate first, or do a process one step at a time until children are more comfortable with the strategy at hand.

Be sure to pay attention not only to the visual strategy you want the children to use as they explore, but to the structural aspects of each type of media as well (see Visual Literacy). This is prime time to consider all the possibilities, and for you as collaborators to observe and guide children's constructive learning. Then use this strategy often as a tool for communication.



Children are usually eager to plunge right in to technical thinking in the artistic language—they are always delighted with opportunities to try out the materials and use their imaginations. They will want to play with their ideas, and see what the materials will do. A sense of wonder pervades the room.

*Art explorations are playful, yet serious and important work!*

Through artful conversations, you guide children's imagery, helping them recall vivid details to heighten their awareness. You ask questions to encourage children to extend and elaborate. This process is truly joint problem solving. Quiet is not the sound of learning. Instead, children need to move about, to talk softly with each other, to stand or sit or work on the floor, whatever is comfortable for them. Sometimes music can add another dimension to the creative process.

As children manipulate their materials and ideas, they transform them, perhaps several times, before settling on a direction for the final product. They may shift or rotate, expand or contract what they do with the media. They may reverse or invert their actions. Children are rehearsing, much as they practice a musical instrument or a sport. Eventually, through experimentation, children see how they can harness artistic media and processes to accomplish their goals.

As children move toward completion of their work, the art experts—partners or other children—discuss the connections between children's experiences and their new learning through art. Sometimes knowledge is synthesized, sometimes it is an overlay on what has come before. Children may personify what they know. Ideas may be simplified to their essence, or expanded. As with spoken and written language, the language of art lends itself well to metaphor and analogy, but children may need a bit of gentle nudging to use it in this way.

Messes are almost inevitable, and are usually indications that children are deeply involved in what they are doing. Have clean-up materials available so children can leave the room in order when they are finished for the day. Art explorations are playful, yet serious and important work!

The fourth grade team of teachers and the art teacher thought the ideas of tessellations would be a challenging way to explore shapes and stretch children's mathematical problem solving and visual thinking. Together we created a number of mathematical and artistic problems related to tessellations and the art of M.C. Escher. We then designed a Tessellation Studio on Wheels, which could be rolled from class to class and down to the art room. We even used it as a learning center in the hall between two rooms. The joint problem solving was nonstop among students, the art room, and the teachers (Figures 4-18 and 4-19). We extended the tessellation project to three weeks the next year because of all the great ideas that surfaced and the incredible amount of learning and visual thinking. We wish Mr. Escher could see what he started!

–Tessellation project, New Jersey

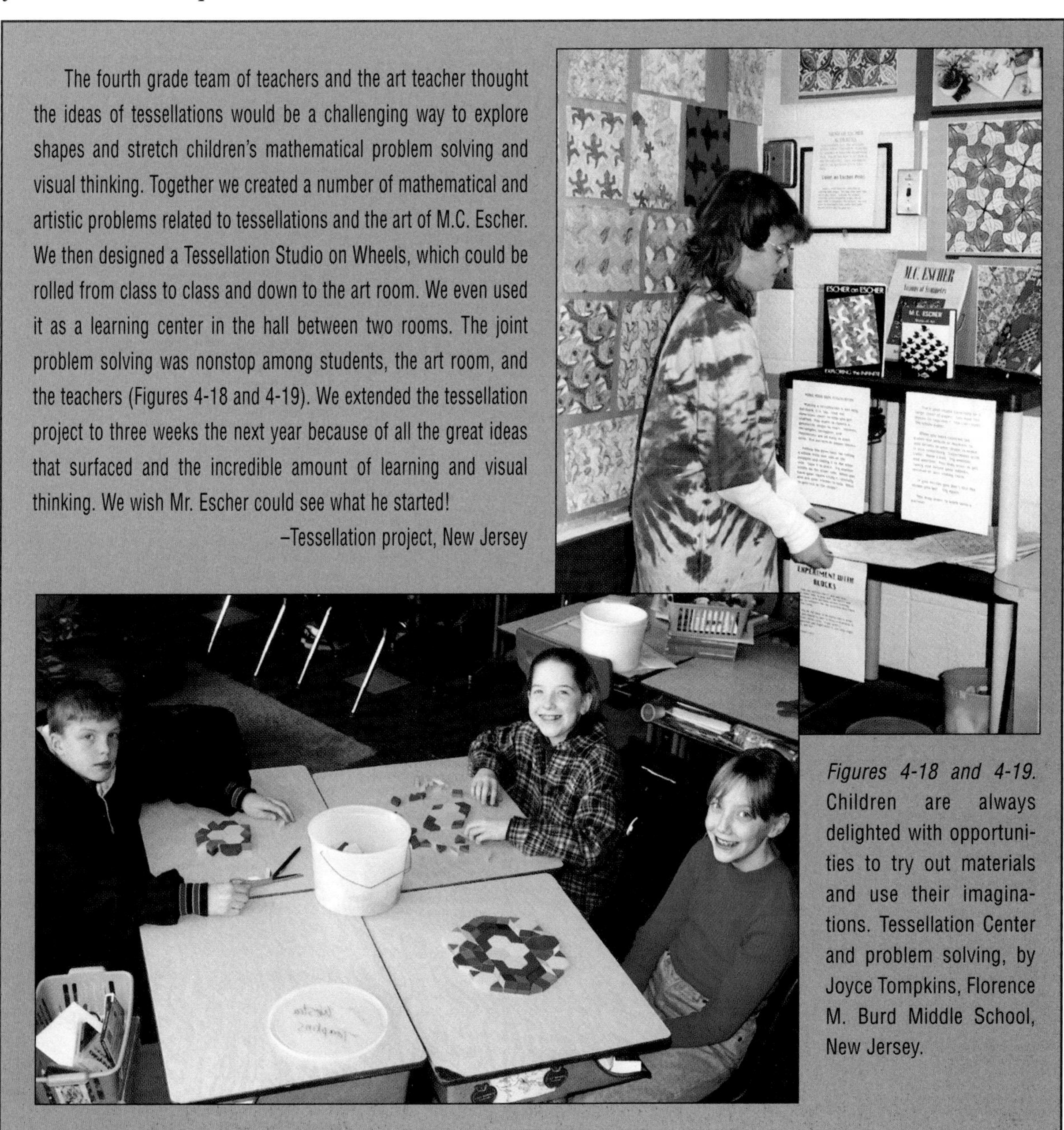


*Figures 4-18 and 4-19.* Children are always delighted with opportunities to try out materials and use their imaginations. Tessellation Center and problem solving, by Joyce Tompkins, Florence M. Burd Middle School, New Jersey.

## Authentic Assessment

Imaginative visual problem-solving activities are great for integrated curriculum projects because they can be assessed on many levels: from a curriculum standpoint, an artistic perspective, and a problem-solving mode. The National Assessment Governing Board (1994) has prepared a set of rubrics for art education that will get you started on developing specific criteria for arts assessment.

Some assessment tools are especially good for tracking how well children are stretching their problem-solving and learning. Checklists, rating scales, and rubrics are excellent for recording children's visual language achievement levels, curriculum knowledge, and related skills. Children can assist in developing the assessment tools and setting the criteria. You will find they often set fairly high expectations for themselves. Make sure children realize that you and your art partner will use the same tool for assessment. Older students can begin to use these tools to evaluate their own work.

**Checklist—**A checklist usually lists tasks to be completed, skills to be demonstrated, and knowledge used (see Table 4-2). There is no indication of which items are of greatest value, nor does a checklist make is possible to evaluate any of the items. Children are usually eager to volunteer to keep a checklist. Make sure it validates all areas of the curriculum included on your Integrated Arts Curriculum Planning Form (Figure 2-15).

**Rating scale—**A rating scale format allows the teacher and student to get a broader picture of the child's abilities. One typical way to do a rating scale is to list performance criteria with ratings such as always, sometimes, or never. Teachers usually use these scales with younger groups; older students might be encouraged to rate themselves.

**Demonstrations—**Student presentations may be done for class members, children in other grades, as part of a display (see Aesthetic Environment), or captured on video. The student or group of students are expected to prepare an artistic demonstration, talk about the techniques using correct art

*Table 4-2.* Weaving checklist for recording children's skills.

**Weaving Checklist**

**Child's name** ______________________ **Date** __________

___ Knows the sequence from sheep/flax to woven fabric.
___ Can manipulate weaving tools: needles, shuttle, beater, heddle.
___ Consistently applies over/under concepts.
___ Varies over/under to create patterns.
___ Weaves evenly and with consistency.
___ Demonstrates an awareness of color and design in weavings.
___ Incorporates texture through use of various knots or selection of fibers.
___ Identifies Native American weaving patterns.
___ Can recreate on graph paper or computer Hopi, Navajo, and Zapotec weaving designs.
___ Demonstrates originality and personal artistic choices in weavings.
___ Knows weaving terms.
___ Uses weaving terms.
___ Expresses preferences in technique, style, or design.
___ Is familiar with contemporary artists/weavers.
___ Uses weaving resources for ideas and technical assistance.
___ Understands relation between the functional and artistic merits of weavings.
___ Can discuss the weavings of a particular country: kilims, kente cloth.
___ Knows and understands the impact of weaving inventions on society.
___ Demonstrates cooperative behaviors.
___ Completes all weaving projects.

language, and explain the reasoning processes used in the exploration. A demonstration such as this could become part of a video portfolio if your school is technologically prepared.

**Rubric—**Criteria related to creating and responding with art knowledge and skills are outlined in basic, proficient, and advanced performance levels in the drawing rubric shown in Table 4-3. This rubric parallels the National Standards for Arts Education (MENC, 1994) and NAEP project (National Assessment of Educational Progress Arts Education Consensus Project Team, 1994). A form on which you can design your own rubric is also provided (Table 4-4).

Table 4-3.

# Drawing and Color Series — Assessment Rubric

| Visual Art Processes | Basic Level | Proficient Level | Advanced Level |
|---|---|---|---|
| **Creating** | Develops one or two ideas/approaches to a problem, with little originality in content or form, reflecting no awareness of the relationship between the art/design work and the context. | Develops several ideas/approaches to a problem, some of which are original in their content and form, and reflect some awareness of the relationship between the art/design work and the context. | Develops many ideas/approaches to a problem, most of which are original in content and form, and reflects awareness and understanding of the relationship between the art/design work and the context. |
| | Visually and in written form demonstrates a limited understanding of the relationship between principles of visual organization and the construction of meaning or function. | Visually and in written form demonstrates a general understanding of the relationship between principles of visual organization and the construction of meaning or function. | Visually and in written form demonstrates a high level of understanding of the relationship between principles of visual organization and the construction of meaning or function. |
| | Explores ideas, media, and tools in a limited way. | Explores a variety of ideas, media, and tools. | Experiments creatively with a variety of ideas, media, and tools. |
| | Seeks the most obvious answer to a question about process or content rather than integrating information from a variety of sources. | Integrates information from a variety of sources, takes an idea and expands upon it, and finds answers to questions about process and content. | Integrates information from a variety of sources, takes an idea and expands upon it, and is inventive in finding answers to questions about process or content. |
| | Demonstrates a limited ability to recognize personal strengths and weaknesses in own work; cannot select and discuss own work. | Recognizes personal strengths and weaknesses and can select and discuss own work. | Recognizes personal strengths and weaknesses; can select, discuss, and give specific examples from own work; identifies works of varying quality while reflecting on personal artistic processes. |
| **Responding** | Demonstrates a limited ability to use vocabulary that describes visual experiences and/or phenomena. | Can express response to works of art/design using a general vocabulary that describes visual experiences and/or phenomena. | Can articulately express response to works of art/design using a specialized vocabulary that describes visual experiences and/or phenomena and supports assertions. |

*Table 4-4.* Rubric for assessment of visual arts processes.

## Visual Arts Assessment

- **Basic** denotes partial mastery of the content but performance that is only fundamental for adequate work at the grade level.
- **Proficient** represents solid academic achievement and competency in challenging subject matter such as suggested in the National Standards for Arts Education (MENC, 1994).
- **Advanced** performance on this assessment represents achievement that is equal to that expected of the most proficient students.

| Visual Art Processes | Basic Level | Proficient Level | Advanced Level |
| --- | --- | --- | --- |
| Creating | | | |
| Responding | | | |

## Artful Conversations

Children's learning styles and cultures vary, so as you engage children in conversations about art, be sure to select strategies that are a good match for each child. Here are just a few ideas to prompt children's reflective thinking about what they are learning and to assess what they have done.

**The Writer—Write it down!** Ask simple questions for children to answer, perhaps about their portfolio, either by dictating to an adult (a great chance to involve volunteers!) or writing on the computer or in a journal. Stretch their visual thinking so they must call upon their artistic knowledge and skills. Possible questions: What do you like best about this work? What would you change? How could you embellish this work? What would you take away to simplify it? How would you do this in a different medium?

**The Actor—Show us!** Making art is very physical for children. Have them recreate the work by showing how they moved to make it. You might begin by saying, "Could you show us what you did to make this collage? Show us, don't tell us, the sequence of events, movements, steps." Tape demonstrations like these to show during a portfolio evening with families.

**The Apprentice—How do you do that?** Have children take the role either of the master or the apprentice and work with another student to exchange knowledge and skills. If you have been using effective scaffolding language, children will follow your model. Encourage mentors to step back as the apprentice shows promise.

## Reflections

Try to establish a realistic picture of your own visual and artistic abilities by answering these questions.

- Have you designed an integrated project assessment tool in collaboration with your art partner and the children?
- How do you share your visual and artistic abilities with children?
- How has your ability to problem solve changed?
- In what ways can you continue to enhance your visual thinking?

# MODULE 4
# *SPARK!* DISCOVER PERSONAL MEANING

Artists develop within themselves a deep perceptual sensitivity to their environments. Their ability to see the world anew allows them to always search for another possibility, to represent ideas, experiences, and feelings in a different way. New places, dramatic events, and daily rituals all are vital parts of the artist's palette. Without a wide realm of personal experiences from which to draw, artists would have no emotions to express, no interpretations to make, no enlightening insights to share.

**The greatest of all human potentials is the ability to take an attitude toward the possible.**

**–Kurt Goldstein**

Like all artists, children construct knowledge and make meaning out of their experiences. They, too, have inquiring minds. Children may be intrigued by the concentric ripples caused by dropping an object in a tub of water, or wonder how red shoes could be made from pieces of leather, or stand in awe before a powerful statue in the park. Your task is to heighten perception and ask challenging, thought-provoking questions to spark discovery.

*New places, dramatic events, and daily rituals are vital parts of the artist's palette.*

Science and geometry, language and art, all are interwoven in an integrated curriculum, but the connections may not yet be clear to students. When children have abundant guided opportunities to represent their ideas in different media, they construct knowledge and think in symbol systems, artistic and otherwise. As their teachers, we continue to be confident that they will learn and see the relationships that surround them. We are delighted by the sparks that occur when children eagerly improve their artistic skills and thinking (Figure 4-20).

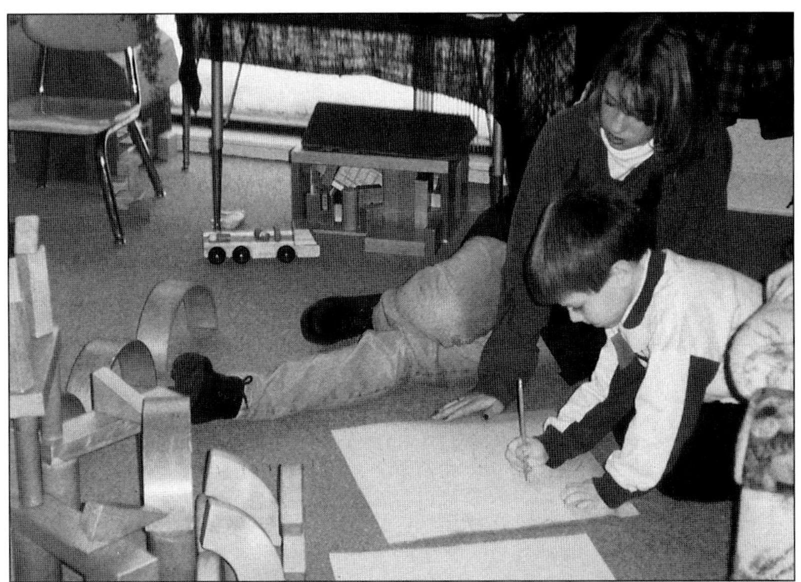

*Figure 4-20.* We are delighted by the sparks that occur when children eagerly improve their artistic skills and thinking. Child Development Center, Northampton Community College.

## Scaffolding Artistic Thinking

> Anna is 2-1/2 and she is looking at two reproductions by Mary Cassatt: *Children on the Beach* and *Girl With a Straw Hat*. Looking intently at them, she wonders out loud, "Are these the same pictures?" Obviously they were not, but Anna's question was posing an interesting problem: I know these are similar, but why? What is it about them?
>
> Anna's mom, sensing her visual insight, explained, "They are not the same picture, but they were painted by the same artist. Would you like to see more of her work?" What ensued was joint attention to the qualities found in Mary Cassatt's work—a mother and child discovering Cassatt's paintings of mothers and children.
>
> –Anna's mother

Artists enjoy solving visual problems while they work with media and with people, but more importantly they relish the opportunity to find problems to solve. One of the biggest professional challenges is for you and your art partner to create a collaborative teaching environment in which artistic thinking is scaffolded in such a way that children can seek out visual problems. In an arts-integrated curriculum, children search for questions that intrigue them, and then embark on a quest for their own unique solutions. In the process, they become increasingly responsible for their learning.

**The Four Ss Educators Use to Scaffold Children's Learning With Art as a Way of Learning®**

- **Support—** responding to children's ideas
- **Stimulate—** inspiring visual reasoning
- **Stretch—** developing children's artistic imagination and skills
- **Spark—** discover meaning

Imagine, for example, the learning possibilities, and even potential for humor, in discovering how red shoes are made and then designing colorful footwear. Where does leather come from? How is it made? What makes the red color (whoever saw a red cow)? From where do the dyes come? How many pieces are needed to make a shoe? What are their shapes? Could the shoe be made with other shapes? How are the pieces held together? How could you design shoes to make your feet look shorter, or longer? Think of all the learning opportunities—artistic and otherwise—that await children who wonder about something as simple as what they are wearing on their feet!

By now, most of you will have found that *Art as a Way of Learning*® makes it easier to recognize the cognitive skills and processes that children acquire and improve through guided art explorations such as this. You have probably noticed that problem solving occurs—not only on the artistic level but in the social, cognitive, and physical domains as well—when children use artistic thinking. Their interactions and conversations during art making are rich with new-found relationships and respect for different perspectives among their peers. They become engrossed in what they are doing, whether they are constructing a model city located along a river, enjoying slippery fingerpaint on a tabletop, or forming a candle by carefully dipping it again and again into different colors of hot wax.

*Figure 4-21.* Problem solving occurs not only on the artistic level but in the social, cognitive, and physical domains. Students in this photo are engaged in an integrated curriculum in science and art with art specialist Jane Oplinger, Resica Elementary School, East Stroudsburg, Pennsylvania.

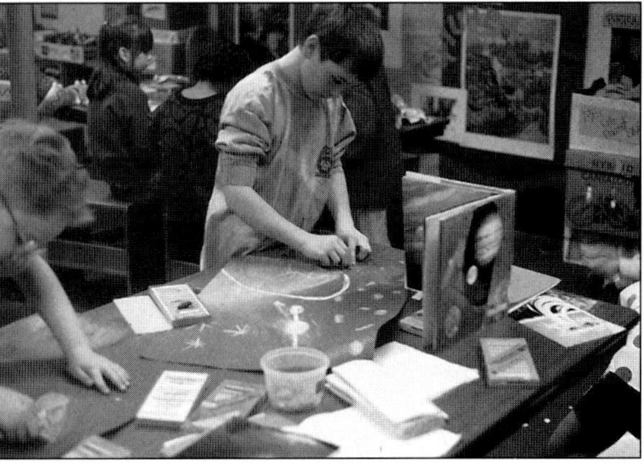

*Figure 4-22.* Notice the science texts being used in art class.

You and your art partner are undoubtedly building trust in the creative learning process as you see children become more knowledgeable while they identify visual questions, make original connections to their experiences, use their imaginations, and take artistic risks. You are becoming skilled at scaffolding children's artistic thinking and working by wondering together.

**The teacher's role in scaffolding artistic thinking**

- Energize
- Facilitate flow
- Challenge
- Strengthen dispositions
- Urge uniqueness
- Wonder together
- Connect

*Artists relish the opportunity to find problems to solve.*

As you listen to children's comments and questions while they work and play, you hear ample evidence that they are curious. Children who are learning have a sense of wonder. Their thinking is not always linear, like it usually is in scientific problem solving, nor does it occur in a bolt of lightning. Rather, when you scaffold children's experiences, you are sure to be delighted every time you see little flashes of insight or sparks and smiles of satisfaction.

*Figure 4-23.* In an arts-integrated curriculum, children search for questions that intrigue them, and then embark on a quest for their own unique solutions. Vessels in Model Magic®.

Artistic learning is physical. It can be very messy. It also holds surprises. The random, intuitive, kinetic connections children make during problem-posing and artistic experimentation move them deeper and deeper into developing meaning and understanding in a variety of realms. Create a classroom culture of possibilities by letting curiosity reign. Encourage original connections and applaud the sparks.

## Guiding Questions

These questions may help you recognize the ways to spark connections in children's thinking and wondering. The path for creating sparks is not clear, and cannot be found in any traditional lesson plan. But artistic wondering and imagining can be one of the most rewarding learning experiences.

- How do you encourage children to find their own problems to solve with visual thinking?
- What do you do to assure that children make choices and connect materials in original combinations?
- What are the creative possibilities inherent in an integrated arts curriculum for you and your art partner?
- How have other artists, scientists, poets, or explorers found and considered similar possibilities?

## Explorations: Wondering and Imagining

Finding something about which you are curious is not as clear cut as solving problems, because finding a problem is inherently more personal, non-linear, and intuitive. If you are responsive to children's interests, curiosity, and abilities, you will help them make connections. Celebrate the leap and find out how the seemingly random connections happen. You will better understand each child's inherent logic and aesthetic insight.

### Just Imagine!

Within any curriculum, children's wondering will lead to projects that enrich their learning through integrated artistic explorations. The following suggestions are intended to get children's problem-finding juices flowing. Watch and listen, and you'll soon have more material than you can possibly incorporate. Then comes the challenge: How could these ideas or qualities be represented visually?

*Children's wondering leads to enriched learning through integrated artistic explorations.*

**Let it flow!** Take water, or any harmless liquid, and let it flow, drip, run, splash. Try to make it flow as many ways as possible. Set up barriers. Make it soar.

**Be a clown!** Think about a place—a bank, a castle, a car, an island—and make a list, or dictate one, describing the funniest things that could happen there. No one gets hurt. Just clown around. Generate laughter.

**What can it do?** Take a block or a ball or a balloon, any little thing will do and as a group list everything the object can do, can be, can become.

**Why is the sky blue?** Experiment with color, runny, thick, melting color. Add every color to blue, one at a time, and give each a name. How light can a color get before it is white? How dark before black? Keep a color sketchbook. Paint outside, in the dark, with sunglasses.

**Dream on...** Ask students to help you design guided imagination journeys for every area of the curriculum: be trapped in a trapezoid, a soccer ball, or a stone in the Great Wall of China. Let students explore their inner landscape to discover the wealth of ideas and images they hold. Look for resource ideas in the bibliographies at the end of each component of *Art as a Way of Learning®*.

The children were studying about ponds in science, which included studying the nature of the water, plant life, and animal life. In the art room, I initially approached the subject matter with pure play. Children were encouraged to soak paper with water-filled sponges and drop or brush on some paint. I then asked them to think of colors that might be found in pond water. The kids discovered that if they restricted their palette to these colors the free-form paintings began to look like sheets of water.

Our next challenge was to somehow shape these paintings into the forms of a pond or how pond water appears on the surface. I asked them to think of what happens when you drop a pebble into water. We even tried it in class. What shape did that ripple make? Could we control the shape of our water pictures? When we answered those questions we also discovered that if each child made a controlled ripple painting and one was placed to overlap another and this was repeated over and over for each child in the class we had a living, rippling, colorful, life-size pond. Inviting enough to jump in?

–Denise Mastroieni, Lake Drive School
Mountain Lakes, New Jersey

## Challenges

The ultimate challenge in artistic thinking is to make the invisible visible. If your classroom is rich in aesthetic language and artful conversations, you will sense and treasure those moments when children discover an intriguing question to solve. Try some of these opportunities for exploring the possible with children.

**The Critique—Interpret This!** Begin a conversation by asking how children would title a work (a child's or someone else's). Encourage children to wonder about the mood or feeling the work conveys to them. Explain that they are interpreting the meaning for themselves and that other people are likely to have different interpretations. Create a new piece of work with the same mood, feeling, or technique. Don't forget to share your ideas, too!

**The Poet!** Create poems, make metaphors, discover similes for everyday classroom activities, children's work, the school, or art resources. Keep a metaphor log to document the best ones and use them in your displays. You will be amazed at the lunch conversations you hear after doing this.

*Figure 4-24.* ***The Characters in Mrs. Witmer' s Class.*** Children's art reflects how they use their imagination to convey personal meaning. Mixed media. Mrs. Witmer's third-grade class, Bragg School, Chester, New Jersey.

## Authentic Assessment

We all need time for reflection. It is an important part of the problem-posing process as we seek answers or create a product. Questions which may lead children to reflect on their visual thinking and make aesthetic judgments are suggested here.

- What kind of a mood or feeling did you create with your colors? How did you do that?
- Tell me about the problems you had to think about before you started this project. What new questions did you discover while working?
- Describe what you think is the most successful part of your creation and explain why.
- What do you most hope a viewer will think/feel when looking at your artwork?
- Which of these do you feel is your best work? Why? If you did these again, what would you change? Give your work a title and explain why you chose it.

## Reflections

*Art as a Way of Learning*® is just the beginning! What challenges are you creating for yourself to solve in your teaching and art making?

- How do you keep track of children's discoveries? How do you validate the learning process?
- How does your environment spark wonder and imagination—yours and the students'?
- What topics or themes spark your curiosity as a teacher or artist?

## Bibliography

Armstrong, C.L. (1994). *Designing assessment in art.* Reston, VA: The National Art Education Association.

Armstrong, T. (1994). *Multiple intelligences in the classroom.* Alexandria, VA: Association for Supervision and Curriculum Development.

Berk, L.D., & Winsler, A. (1995). *Scaffolding children's learning.* Washington, DC: National Association for the Education of Young Children.

Bresler, L. (1992). Visual art in primary grades: A portrait and analysis. *Early Childhood Research Quarterly, 7,* 397-414.

Bresler, L. (1993). Three orientations of arts in the primary grades: Implications for curriculum reform. *Arts Education Policy Review, 94*(6), 29-34.

Brooks, J.G., & Brooks, M.G. (1993). *The case for constructivist classrooms.* Alexandria, VA: Association for Supervision and Curriculum Development.

Fowler, C. (1994). Strong arts, strong schools. *Educational Leadership, 2*(5), 4-9.

Gallas, K. (1991). Arts as epistemology: Enabling children to know what they know. *Harvard Educational Review, 61*(1), 40-50.

Getty Education Institute for the Arts, The. (1992). *The DBAE handbook: An overview of discipline-based art education.* Los Angeles, CA: Author.

Getty Education Institute for the Arts, The. (1993). *Discipline-based art education and cultural diversity.* Los Angeles, CA: Author.

Hyerle, D. (1996). *Visual tools for constructing knowledge.* Alexandria, VA; Association for Supervision and Curriculum Development.

Katz, L., & Chard, S. (1989). *Engaging children's minds: The project approach.* Norwood, NJ: Ablex.

Mitchell, R. (Ed.). (1994). *Measuring up to the challenge: What standards and assessment can do for art education.* New York: American Council for the Arts.

Music Educators National Conference. (1994). *National standards for arts education.* Reston, VA: Author.

National Assessment of Educational Progress (NAEP) Arts Education Consensus Project Team. (1994). *Arts education assessment framework.* Washington, DC: National Assessment Governing Board.

Perkins, D.N. (1994). *The intelligent eye: Learning to think by looking at art.* Los Angeles, CA: The Getty Education Institute for the Arts.

Perrone, V. (Ed.). (1991). *Expanding student assessment.* Alexandria, VA: Association for Supervision and Curriculum Development.

Rogoff, B. (1990). *Apprenticeships in thinking: Cognitive development in social context.* Oxford: Oxford University Press.

Smith, N.R. (1993). *Experience & art: Teaching children to paint.* New York: Teachers College Press.

Vygotsky, L.S. (1978). *Mind in society: The development of higher psychological processes.* Cambridge, MA: Harvard University Press.

Wolf, Aline D. (1984). *Mommy it's a Renoir: Art postcards for art appreciation: A parent and teacher handbook.* Altoona, PA: Parent Child Press.

# Appendices

**APPENDIX I**

Art as a Way of Learning®: Five Guiding Principles

**APPENDIX II**

Key Words

# APPENDIX I. ART AS A WAY OF LEARNING®: FIVE GUIDING PRINCIPLES

## Belief statement

We believe the arts, as a language, empower children to construct, communicate, and express understanding and meaning.

### 1. Art is a language

The arts are symbol systems organized by elements and principles of visual organization which provide a medium for communicating information, posing and solving artistic problems, and expressing feelings.

**1.1** Verbal language and visual language have parallel structures and uses

**1.2** The structure of visual language is built from elements and principles of visual organization and visual reasoning

**1.3** The primary uses of visual language are
Functional: Used to communicate, describe, think creatively and critically, and solve problems
Aesthetic: Used for artistic ends governed by cultural norms for beauty and personal meaning

### 2. Children use art

The arts are a natural language which must be nurtured and developed so children remain creative and literate in multiple symbol systems.

**2.1** Children must know the structure of visual language so they can competently use it for visual thinking and aesthetic appreciation

**2.2** The visual arts provide another symbol system for children to use for representing and constructing

**2.3** Children naturally use the visual arts to communicate what they see (perceptions), know (representations), and feel (emotions)

### 3. Art leads learning

The arts provide a medium for creative and critical thinking.

**3.1** The visual arts provide children opportunities to create and transform images generated from ideas based on their perceptions and experiences

**3.2** The visual arts allow children to use visualization and imagination to hypothesize

**3.3** The visual arts provide children with a concrete way to represent their ideas and receive immediate visual and kinesthetic feedback

**3.4** The visual arts provide children with opportunities to reflect on and evaluate process and product

### 4. Teachers guide learning

The arts provide a central thread to guide and integrate learning across all curricular domains.

**4.1** Adults enrich learning by guiding children's interactions with aesthetic environments

**4.2** Adults and children use the visual arts to engage in collaborative learning

**4.3** Adults stimulate and stretch critical and creative thinking

**4.4** Adults spark connections between students and across curricular domains

**4.5** Adults support and respond to the individual learner's interests, learning style, knowledge, and skills

## 5. Adults are learners and advocates

The arts, when central to a school, create a dynamic collaborative environment for teaching and learning.

**5.1** Teachers, art specialists, and administrators examine their beliefs about the role of the visual arts to improve teaching and learning

**5.2** Collaboration becomes the context for adults to exchange and expand views, knowledge, and skills

**5.3** Classroom teachers increase their personal visual literacy and art specialists increase their knowledge of classroom curriculum

**5.4** Reflection and assessment become integral to teaching and learning

**5.5** Advocacy and collaboration extend into the community

# APPENDIX II. KEY WORDS

**Aesthetic environments—**Settings, such as a school, that highlight the interconnected relationship between people's visual perceptions and thinking.

**Art criticism—**Describing and evaluating the media, processes, and meanings of works of visual art, and making comparative judgments. Art criticism is an individual response to a work of art, taking into account techniques, subject, elements, and principles of visual language.

**Artistic/visual literacy—**Fluency in an artistic language such as the visual arts.

**Artistic/visual problems—**Interesting questions, perceptual challenges, or visual dilemmas that can be identified, explored, and resolved in an original way through artistic media.

**Art partner—**A collaborator, usually a classroom teacher, administrator, artist-in-residence, or art specialist, with whom one can explore *Art as a Way of Learning*®.

**Art Studio Space—**An area set aside in the school or classroom that highlights art content. The space is designed to stretch students' artistic knowledge and skills that run parallel to learning in another discipline. The Art Studio Space and the Integrated Curriculum Area engage students in visual imagery, creative problem solving, and critical thinking. The Art Studio Space usually is directly linked with the four Curriculum Planning Frames—Skill, Response, Knowledge, and Concept.

**Balance—**Distribution of visual weights in a work of art which arrives at an equilibrium of the art elements. Balance can be formal (symmetric, radial), with identical forms/images/colors placed equidistant from a central axis; or informal (asymmetric), having dissimilar, unequal parts that balance in the eyes of the beholder.

**Construction—**One of three components of critical and creative thinking. Constructive processes facilitate the manipulation, development, and playful elaboration of ideas, images, and feelings using the structural content of the visual art language.

**Creative and critical thinking—***Art as a Way of Learning®* uses the terms *creative and critical thinking* to refer to the active process of generating, gathering, representing, analyzing, evaluating, and understanding new information in relation to prior knowledge. This thinking process involves imagination, creativity, genesis, analysis, reflection, synthesis, evaluation, and reasoning.

Creative and critical thinking is not hierarchical but rather divergent, global, synergistic, intuitive, and interactive, all of which are necessary to use a language aesthetically. Three dynamic and interconnected aspects—perception, construction, and performance—form a cycle which delineates critical and creative thinking in any symbol system. This process is sometimes called *higher-order thinking, analytical thinking, or complex thinking.* The concept of creative and critical thinking should not be confused with the judgmental role of an art critic, nor is it a process aimed at making adverse comments about or finding fault with the work or ideas of others.

**Curriculum Planning Frames—**Four frameworks—Skill, Response, Knowledge, and Concept (Figure 2-11)—that enable teachers to think about a theme and how to teach about it from different perspectives. Children's cultures, experiences and ideas, big concepts and important questions, and curriculum standards and guidelines are all taken into account in planning.

**Elements of visual language—**Line, shape, color, texture, and form.

**Emphasis—**Use of an artistic device to draw attention or give importance to one or more focal points. Subject matter, increased detail, light, contrast, visual pointers, and converging lines are commonly used to emphasize portions of a work of art.

**Guided explorations—**Engaging children in purposeful, meaningful, artful conversations and experiences in which they gain knowledge and skills and communicate with art as a language to solve visual problems.

**Integrated Curriculum Area**—A designated area in the school that links art with curriculum topics, skills, and knowledge. It combines various aspects of art (history, production, and criticism) with another discipline (such as science, social studies) in one integrated learning center. This, and the Art Studio Space, engage students in visual imagery, creative problem solving, and critical thinking.

**Metacognition**—Thinking about thought, awareness of mental activity. One can engage in metacognition about self, tasks, or others.

**Movement**—An effect or representation of motion. Movement can be perceived (e.g., an illusion created by patterns) or real (e.g., a mobile) in a work of art.

**Perception**—Visual thinking. One of three components of critical and creative thinking. The process involves a heightened sense of visual awareness, attention to details, ability to recall vivid sensory images, and sensitivity to the affective content of images.

**Performance**—One of three components of creative and critical thinking. Performance processes develop the ability to rethink, analyze, monitor, and ultimately evaluate, own, and transfer understanding through artistic endeavors.

**Principles of visual organization**—Unity; variety; balance; repetition, rhythm, and pattern; emphasis; proportion; and movement.

**Problem posing**—An essential aspect of critical and creative thinking. The ability to identify visual challenges requires access to prior knowledge and imagery strategies which facilitate the original and meaningful use of a symbol system.

**Proportion**—The relationship of one part to another and of each part to the whole in terms of size, mass or volume, weight, linear dimension, and color. Proportion may be realistic, exaggerated, or distorted.

**Rhythm, repetition, pattern**—Arrangement or grouping of the elements of works of art so the parts appear to have an ordered or planned relationship. The effect can be regular or irregular.

**Scaffolding—**Matching children's acquisition of new information and skills with content and supportive teaching strategies in ways that build upon and integrate children's cultures, knowledge, experiences, capacities, self-esteem, and learning styles.

**Spark!—**Children's connections among themselves and their ability to see relationships among various knowledge disciplines are furthered. Children discover personal meaning. Spark! is *Art as a Way of Learning's*® fourth S (see Figure 4-1).

**Stimulate—**The second S of *Art as a Way of Learning*, in which children's knowledge and understanding are increased, visual reasoning is inspired (see Figure 4-1). Artistic skills are developed through visual and aesthetic references.

**Stretch—**The third *Art as a Way of Learning* S, in which children's abilities to reflect, respond, and create grow through teaching practices that nurture their development (see Figure 4-1). Children's imagination and artistic skills expand as they understand the historical, cultural, scientific, and other contexts of knowledge.

**Support—**The first of the four S's of *Art as a Way of Learning*. Teachers respond to children's ideas, feelings, interests, and creative and critical thinking with strategies that encourage learning (see Figure 4-1).

**Unity—**Harmony among artistic elements such that the viewer of a work of art senses its completeness. Techniques to achieve harmony include clustering, overlapping, opposing (see variety), and interlocking shapes.

**Variety—**Varying art elements in a composition to create interest. For example, a composition featuring large and small triangles exhibits variety of size (or scale). A composition featuring rough and slick textures exhibits variety of texture.

# INDEX


## -A-

Aaron, 189
Abeles, H., 129
Administrators
  as art partners, 92-93
  role in supporting collaboration, 100-107
  vision, 100, 124
Advocacy for the arts, 26-30, 101-106, 123-134
  how to generate support, 125-127, 128-133
  resources, 125-139
Andrew, 76
Angelo, Mr., 6-8, 71, 184, 193
Anna, 228
Architecture, 54
Armstrong, T., 25, 26
Arnhiem, R., 144, 147
Art
  advocacy, 26-30, 101-106, 123-134
  center, 145
  criticism, 114
  curriculum design, 78-86
  elements, 46-61
  explorations, 48-49, 51-52, 55, 57-58, 60, 67, 170-177
  materials center, 152-159
  orientations toward, 23
  partner, 26, 37, 47, 63, 75, 78-86, 92-99, 110, 122, 156, 176, 184, 188
  research, 1, 2, 22-23, 24, 36, 70, 128-129
  Scan, 82-83, 86, 115, 163
  viewing and responding, 205-210
  ways children use, 11-26
*Art as a Way of Learning*®
  classroom characteristics, 20
  Four Ss, 21, 162, 228
  Guiding Principles, 10-31
  origins, 1
  Program Components, 28
Art Materials Center
  location & design, 154
  materials selection, 155-158
  safety, 157-158
  survey, 169
Art Scan, 82-83, 86, 115, 163
Art specialist, 92-93, 149
Art Studio Space, 161-164
Artist-in-residence programs, 80, 92, 102, 104-105
Artistry, children's, 67-77
Arts agencies/councils, 92, 123
*Arts Education Research Agenda for the Future*, 107
Assessment, authentic, 4, 25, 26, 64, 80, 84-85, 120, 177, 187-188, 199-201, 213, 222-226, 233
  analyzing art, 202-204
  checklist, 222
  conference, individual, 200
  criteria, 85, 120, 121
  demonstrations, 84, 222
  formative, 84
  group critique, 200
  methods, 84-85, 120, 121
  performance-based, 84
  performances, 84
  planning, 84-85
  portfolios, 84, 85, 200
  prescriptive, 84
  projects, 84
  rating scale, 222
  rubrics, 222-225
  summative, 84
  tests, 85
Auditory images, 49

## -B-

Balance, 46, 62
Beaty, D.K., 84
Benfante, J., 153
Benny, J., 208

Berk, L.D., 12, 18, 39, 146, 214
Bigus, D., 167
Binney & Smith Inc., 1, 2
Blocks, 55
Bounard, P., 59
Bragg School, 233
Brain development research, 129
Bray, J., 24, 106
Bredekamp, S., 36, 79
Bresler, L., 22
Brittain, W.L., 70
Brooks, J.G., 20, 26, 185
Brooks, M.G., 20, 26, 185
Brown, A., 19
Budget process, 104
Burton, J., 129

## -C-

Caine, G., 129
Caine, R.N., 129
Calvin, B., 34
Capra, C., 166
Casagrande, E., 44
Castro, C., 210
Cattaffo, M., 19
Center for Arts in the Basic Curriculum, 126
Challenges, 42, 63, 74, 86, 98, 106-107, 118, 120-122, 133-134, 149-151, 159, 167, 176-177, 198, 211, 232-233
Chang, E., 62
Chard, S., 17, 20, 193
Children's art, characteristics of, 70-74
  artistic learning, 71-72
  development & knowing, 70-71
  perception & style, 72-73
  understanding & personal meaning, 74
Children's books, 179-180
Children's House Montessori School, 153, 189
Cin, S., 113
Clearview Elementary School, 116, 118, 210, 211
Close, C., 59
Cognitive development, 4
Collaboration, 4, 5, 6, 8, 12, 18, 19, 26, 37, 46, 91-139, 173
  creative, 109
  stages of, 94-97
Collage
  color, 58
  line, 48
  supplies, 158
  texture, 60
Collograph, 60
Color, 46, 55-58
  complementary, 56
  intermediate, 56
  monochromatic, 58
  perception, 55
  primary, 56, 57
  secondary, 56
  shades, 57
  subtractive, 56
  temperature, 58
  tints, 57
  value, 57
  wheel, 56
Communication, see Language
Computer drawing, 51
Conklin, J., 113
Construction
  processes, 36, 38, 40-42, 144
  supplies, 158
Conversations, artful, 212, 220, 226
Cooperative learning, 156
Cornett, C.E., 129
Cosgrove, L., 26, 96-97, 108
Council of Chief State School Officers, 84, 125
Crawford, T., 48
Crayola® Dream-Makers® program, 11, 34, 49, 50, 52, 54, 56, 57, 61, 62, 73, 118, 208, 212
Crayon rubbing, 60
Creativity, see Thinking
  Cycle of creative and critical thinking, 35-42, 184, 202-203
Culture, influence on art, 18, 34, 40, 47, 49, 53, 57, 58, 67, 72, 165
Curriculum design, arts-integrated, 4, 7, 24, 34, 37, 50-51, 78-86, 103, 108-122, 164-165
  backwards planning, 81-83
  connections, 160-169
  enduring understanding, 83, 120, 121
  key knowledge & skills, 81-83, 120, 121
  links, 103
  planning resources, 79-84
  Planning Form, 109-111, 117, 119-121, 186, 217
  Planning Frames, 109-116, 186, 217
  planning time, 103
  steps in design, 81-84

Index

visual arts content, 81-83, 187
Curriculum Planning Form, 109, 117, 119, 120, 121, 217
Curriculum Planning Frames, 109-119, 217
communication, 111, 112, 114
curriculum, 111, 112, 115-116
inquiry, 111, 112, 114-115
self-discovery, 111, 112, 116
Cute activities, 85
Cycle of creative and critical thinking, 35-42, 184, 202-203
construction, 35, 36, 144
perception, 35, 36, 143-144, 188
performance, 35, 36, 144-145

## -D-

Decorations, 148
Describing children's art, 64
Development, children's artistic, 67-77
adolescence, 69
early childhood, 68
middle childhood, 68-69
Displays of children's art, 75, 150, 170-177
creating, 174-176
interactive, 171
purpose, 173
tool box contents, 175
Documentation of learning, 170-177
Donaldson, M., 9
Donkur, M., 105
Dorn, C.M., 128
Dorothy, 160
Drawing supplies, 158
Dreyfuss, G., 212
Dubbs, D., 22, 122, 156

## -E-

Einstein, A., 34
Eisner, E., 9
Elements of art, 46-61
Emphasis, 46, 62
Engle, B.S., 63-64
Environments
aesthetic, 4-5, 85-86, 141-181
forms, 147
functions, 146
Art Materials Center, 152-159
arts-friendly, 101-102, 105-106, 141-181
connections, 147-149
Imaginative Art Spaces, 160-169
learning, 4-5, 121, 141-181
scan, 169
visual, 142-151
Erikson, E., 189
Esquibel, B., 169
Exhibits, 75, 150, 170-177
creating, 174-176
purpose, 173

## -F-

Families
as advocates, 123-134, 149
interact with, 75, 92
Faust, A., 210
Feeney, S., 142
Fein, S., 70
Finger painting, 49
Fink, L., 60
Fishman, B., 43
Florence M. Burd Middle School, 221
Fogel, N., 82
Form, 46, 53-55
abstract/realistic/nonrepresentational, 53
additive/subtracting, 53
construction, 53
context, 54
contour, 54
gravity/movement, 54
interior space, 54
modeling, 53
scale, 54
selection, 53
surface, 54
volume, 54
Four Ss of AWL, 21, 162, 228
Fowler, C. 10, 128, 202
Fritz, K., 73

## -G-

Gallas, K., 11
Galleries, 176
Gardner, H., 2, 9, 10, 15, 20, 34, 36, 68, 70, 73, 128
first-draft knowledge of arts, 15, 68
progression of artistry development, 68
theory of multiple intelligences, 73, 128
Getty Center for Education in the Arts, 129

Giacometti, A., 53
*Goals 2000 Arts Education Partnership, The*, 1, 6, 125
Goldstein, K., 227
Golomb, C., 70
Gorton, R., 1
Graff, R., 35
Grants, 132-133
Greene, A., 128, 132
Gregson, E., 11
Guardino, D., 14
Guided exploration, 34, 85-86
Guiding Questions, 28-29, 37, 47, 69, 80, 93, 100, 110, 124, 143, 153, 166, 172, 192, 204, 216, 231
Gurin, R., 2

## -H-

Hamilton, R., 118
Hanging art work, 175
Harris, D., 147
Harrison, B., 57
Henri, R., 46, 143
Herbholz, B., 61
Herbholz, D., 61
Hereford Elementary School, 43
Hertzell., J., 102
Hiram Dodd Elementary School, 20, 27
Hockney, D., 48
Horowitz, R., 129
Humanities and Arts Education Partnership,
129
Hyatt, T., 52

## -I-

Idol, L., 92
Imagery strategies, 217-219
Imagination, teacher's role in developing, 214-215, 220-221, 231-232
Imaginative Art Spaces, 160-169
  Art Studio Space, 161-164
  finding, 160
  transforming, 161-167
Impression tiles, 60
Integrated Arts Curriculum Planning Form, 109-111, 117, 119-121,
Integrated curriculum, 4, 7, 24, 25, 34, 37, 78-86, 108-122, 161, 164-165, 189-233
Integrated Curriculum Area, 161, 164-165
  art content, 164, 187
  curriculum content, 164, 187
International Reading Association, 112

## -J-

Jensen, E., 129
Jesse, 25
Journals, visual, 43-45, 85
Justin, 170

## -K-

Kandinsky, W., 78
Katz, L., 17, 20, 71, 193
Kellogg, R., 70
Kindler, A., 46, 47, 128
Klein, K., 18, 52, 59, 61
Knowledge & skills, art, 81-83, 120, 121, 195
Kollwitz, K., 73
Koval, E., 54
Kuck, R., 52
Kuprewicz, S., 118
K-W-L chart, 30, 195-197

## -L-

Lake Drive School for Deaf and Hard of Hearing Children, 12-14, 232
Langer, E., 34, 147
Langer, S., 37
Language
  aesthetic, 9-12
  art as a visual language, 3, 7, 9-12, 19,
    46-66, 67, 77-78
  learning, 214-215
  structural aspects of visual language, 9
  systems, 9
  visual, 3, 7, 9-12, 19, 46-66
Lauren, 152
Lewin, L., 128
Librarian, 93, 149
Lichtenstein, R., 36
Lillard, J., 50
Line, 46, 48-50
  connected, 48
  static/dynamic, 48
Literacy
  visual, 5, 19, 33-90
Lizzie, 76-77
Local Resource Team, 2
Lowenfeld, V., 70

Index

-M-
Mabry, L., 22
MacDonald, S., 14
Martinez, A., 60
Mastroieni, D., 12, 232
Materials, art center, 152-159
Matisse, H., 58
Matthews, D., 118
McFarland, S., 43
McKinley, E., 150, 172
McNider, C., 61
McTighue, J., 79, 83, 128
Meaning, see also Thinking, 9-10, 34, 39, 47, 74, 227-233
Metacognition, 39-41
Mission statement, 124
Mitchell, M., 41
Modeling, 21-22, 215, 220
Monet, C., 39, 172
Monoprints, 49
Moravcik, E., 142
Motherwell, R., 50
Mounting art work, 175
Movement, 46, 62
Murgzcz, S., 189
Murphy, M., 21
Museums, 92, 176
Music, 49
Music Educators National Conference, 112, 125, 142, 166, 223

-N-
National Academy of Sciences, 112
National Art Education Association, 132
National Assessment Governing Board, 80, 222
National Assessment of Educational Progress, 223
National Council for the Social Studies, 112
National Council for the Teachers of English, 112
National Council of Teachers of Mathematics, 112
National Endowment for the Arts, 129, 131-132
Naudascher, G., 26, 100-107, 159
Nevin, A., 92
Nicole, 15-16
Northampton Community College, 1, 2
  Child Development Center, 18, 44, 45, 50, 52, 59, 61, 73, 82, 148, 170, 227

-O-
Observation
  by children, 51
  of children, 25, 31, 37, 74, 175, 187
O'Keeffe, G., 51, 210
Oplinger, J., 38, 99, 102, 122, 229

-P-
Painting supplies, 158
Pak, J.H. 13
Pancoast, B., 28
Paolucci-Whitcomb, P., 92
Paper, 155, 158
Partnerships, 26, 37, 47, 63, 75, 78-86, 92-99, 105
  community, 105, 131-132
  stages of, 94-97
Pasos, J., 113
Pattern, rhythm, & repetition, 46, 62
Perception processes, 36, 38, 39-42, 143-144, 188
Perceptual
  abilities, 4-5
  challenges, 144
Performance
  -based assessment, 84
  processes, 36, 38-42
Perkins, D.N., 34, 36, 146, 203
Perrone, V., 26
Piazza, C.L., 129
Picasso, P., 49, 51, 67, 74
Pinciotti, P., 1, 24, 106
Pinciotti, R., 51
Planning Form, Integrated Arts Curriculum, 109-111, 117, 119-121, 186, 217
Planning Frames, Curriculum, 109-119, 186, 217
Playful nurturing, 193-197
Pollock, J., 65
Portfolios, 84, 85
Posner, M., 18, 60, 205
President's Council on the Arts, 129
Principles of visual organization, 46-47, 61-64
Problem solving, imagery strategies for, 217-218
Processes
  assessment, 225
  construction, 36, 38-39, 144
  internal, 36, 39-41
  external, 36, 38-41
  perception, 36, 38-40, 143-144

performance, 36, 38-39, 41, 144-145
Professional development, 3-4
AWL components, 3
dimensions of, 24
encouraging, 102
Proportion, 46, 62
Proposal, grant, 132-133

-Q-

-R-

Radvansky, S., 116, 210, 211
Rauch, F., 210
Rauscher, F.H., 1129
Reddish, N. 174
Reflections, 29-31, 45, 66, 75, 86, 99, 107, 122, 134, 151, 159, 169, 177, 201, 213, 226, 233
Reform, education, 1, 36
Repetition, rhythm, & pattern, 46, 62
Research, 1, 2, 22-23, 24, 36, 70, 108, 128-129
brain development, 129
conducting, 107
learning, 128
literacy, 128-129
model programs, 129
tools, 25
Resica Elementary School, 35, 38, 40, 57, 99, 100, 101, 102, 103, 105, 106, 112, 122, 127, 147, 153, 159, 168, 176, 194, 201, 206, 219, 229
Resources
art center, 179-180
art education, 181
budget, 104
community, 124
on-line, 136-138
organizations, 135-136
planning, 79-84
Responding
to art, 205-210
to children's ideas, 189-201
Rhythm, repetition, & pattern, 46, 62
Richards, M., 94, 96-97, 145
Roberti, K., 50, 170
Robinson, G., 44
Rogoff, B., 189
Rorty, R., 9
Rosenberg, H.S., 36, 39
Rosegrant, T., 36, 79
Rubens, P.P., 72

-S-

Safety, of art materials, 157-158
Santrock, N.W., 34
Scaffolding learning, 21, 63, 67, 85, 92, 146, 228-230
teacher's role, 190-192, 203, 220, 230
Scherer, M.M., 129
Sculpture, 53-55, 119
Sham, C., 118
Shape, 46, 50-52
area, 50
irregular, 51
silhouette, 50
symmetric/asymmetric, 50
Shearer, M., 52
Shoemaker, B.J., 128
Simons, H., 108
Snyder, J., 56
Snyder, K., 56
Social skills, 5
Spark!
self-discovery, 111, 116
personal meaning, 185-186, 227-233
Stake, R., 22
Standards for Arts Education
national, 2, 4, 10, 79, 112, 122, 125, 142, 166, 187, 223
state, 79, 112, 125
school district, 79
Steigerwalt, J., 38, 112
Stella, F., 53
Stern, I., 142
Stimulate
inquiry, 111, 114-115
knowledge and understanding, 185-186, 202-213
Stone, D., 210
Strategies for artistic learning, 217-219
Stretch
curriculum, 111, 115
imagination and artistic skills, 185-186, 214-226
Support
communication, 111, 114
respond to children's ideas, 185-186, 189-201
Survey, how to conduct, 130-131
Sylwester, R., 129
Symbol systems, 9, 11
Szekely, G., 153

-T-

Tait, Z., 49

Task Force on Children's Learning and the Arts, 128
Taunton, M., 70
Teaching
  Four Ss, 21, 162
  responsively, 21
  strategies, 4-5, 6-32, 183-234
Tesselation, 221
Texture, 46, 59-60
  tactile, 59
  visual, 59
Thinking
  analytic, 4, 20
  cycle, 35-42, 188
  creative and critical, 2, 9-11, 17, 20-25, 34-45, 188, 202-203
  metacognition, 39
  visual, 35
Thompson, C.M., 44
Three-dimensional art, 53-55, 158
Tilley, K., 12
Tompkins, J., 221
Travis, 161
Truman Elementary School, 94, 96-97, 108, 145

## -U-

Unity, 46, 62
U.S. Department of Labor, 129, 132

## -V-

Van Rijn, K., 19
Variety, 46, 62
Viewing and responding to art, 205-210
  analyze, 207-208
  describe, 206
  interpret, 208-209
  judge, 209
Vista, Ms., 6-8, 34, 71, 184, 193
Visual
  displays, 170-177
  journals, 43-45
  language, 3, 7, 9-12, 19, 46-66, 78-79, 168
  literacy, 33-90
  organization, principles of, 46-47, 61-64
  problems, 39
  thinking, 144, 168
Vygotsky, L.S., 12, 189-190

## -W-

Walsh, D., 15
Ward, D., 49
Warty, R., 13
Weaver, K., 210
Weaving
  checklist, 223
  Studio, 163
Web, curriculum/topic (mind map), 8, 193-194, 198
Web sites, 136-138
Weinberger, N.M., 129
Welch, N., 128, 132
Westmont Montessori School, 150, 172
Whitecoate Primary School, 7
Wiggins, G., 79, 83, 128
Wildwood School, 19
Williams, H., 123
Winsler, A., 12, 18, 146, 214
Wolf, A.D., 211

## -X-

## -Y-

## -Z-

Zak, 76, 189, 216
Zimmerman, E., 128
Zone of Proximal Development, 189-190
Zurmuehlen, C. M., 46